AF556342

Karunanidhi

The Definitive Biography

Vaasanthi

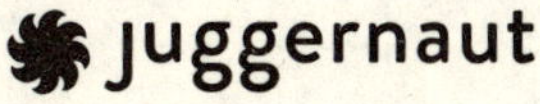

JUGGERNAUT BOOKS
C-I-128, First Floor, Sangam Vihar, Near Holi Chowk,
New Delhi 110080, India

First published by Juggernaut Books 2020

10 9 8 7 6 5 4 3 2 1

P-ISBN: 9789353451042
E-ISBN: 9789353451059

Typeset in Adobe Caslon Pro by R. Ajith Kumar, Noida

Printed at Thomson Press India Ltd

Contents

Timeline ix
Introduction xix

1. Born to Rebel 1
2. Love, Marriage and the Lure of Politics 10
3. Periyar vs Annadurai 22
4. The Rising Sun 33
5. The Anti-Hindi Conflagration 42
6. Inheriting Annadurai's Mantle 54
7. MGR vs Karunanidhi 70
8. The Emergency and the Rise of MGR 80
9. The Long Shadow of Sri Lanka 95
10. A Woman Scorned 110
11. The Vaiko Affair 120
12. The Prima Donna 126
13. Administrator Par Excellence 135
14. Strange Bedfellows 145

15. The Wounded Tigress Fights Back 160
16. Family Matters 180
17. The 'Mother of All Scams' 198
18. Player on the National Stage 207
19. Autumn of the Patriarch 228
20. End of an Epoch 243

Notes 249
Acknowledgements 257
Index 259

Timeline

1916: The Justice Party is formed. The first major institutional manifestation of the Dravidian movement, it was composed of members of the regional elite – merchants, landlords and professionals. They came together under a non-Brahmin banner in opposition to what they regarded as Brahmin dominance in public life.

1924: Karunanidhi is born in a backward caste community on 3 June in Thirukkuvalai village, Thanjavur district. Experiences caste-based discrimination from his childhood.

1925: The Self-Respect Association is launched by social reformist E.V. Ramasamy Naicker, known as Periyar, to work together with the Justice Party for the social and cultural advancement of all Dravidians.

1938: At the age of fourteen, Karunanidhi leads an anti-Hindi agitation in Thirukkuvalai. Comes under the spell of Periyar.

1939: Karunanidhi starts a fortnightly handwritten magazine for students called *Manava Nesan*.

1944: Merger of the Justice Party and the Self-Respect Association into the Dravida Kazhagam (DK). Lured by its opposition to Brahminism and the caste system, Karunanidhi joins the DK.

Karunanidhi is married to Padmavathi from Chidambaram.

1945: Karunanidhi writes plays to make a living. Gets acquainted with Periyar and C.N. Annadurai (Anna), a brilliant speaker and member of the DK. Periyar invites Karunanidhi to work for his paper *Kudiyarasu* for a monthly salary of Rs 40. Karunanidhi works there for a year and thereafter joins Jupiter Films, a famous production house, to write film scripts.

1947: India attains freedom.

1948: M.K. Gandhi is shot dead in January.

Karunanidhi's wife, Padmavathi, dies after giving birth to a boy, Muthu.

Karunanidhi's second marriage to Dayalu Ammal takes place in September.

1949: Differences arise between Periyar and younger members of the DK. The DK splits and Annadurai forms the Dravida Munnetra Kazhagam (DMK).

Karunanidhi joins the DMK, becomes close to Anna and emerges as a very active member and organizer.

1967: The DMK defeats the Congress in Assembly elections and comes to power, winning a majority of seats. Annadurai is sworn in as the chief minister. Karunanidhi becomes the public works department (PWD) minister.

1968: Karunanidhi's relationship with Rajathi, a theatre artist, comes to light when a girl is born in a Chennai nursing home and the father is named as M. Karunanidhi. He admits in the Assembly that 'Rajathi is the mother of my daughter, Kanimozhi.' From then on, Rajathi was publicly acknowledged as his partner and Dayalu Ammal as his wife.

1969: Annadurai dies. Karunanidhi becomes the chief minister at the age of forty-five.

The Tamil Nadu Agricultural Fair Wages Act is passed to enforce payment of fair wages to agricultural labourers in the Kaveri delta region and penalize landowners who exploited them.

1970: The Tamil Nadu Land Reforms Act is passed, reducing the land ceiling limit from 30 standard acres to 15 standard acres.

The Rajamannar Committee is set up to suggest measures to secure autonomy for the state in the executive, legislative and judicial branches. Its recommendations laid out a comprehensive roadmap for a more federal Constitution.

Sattanathan Commission is constituted to give recommendations on improving the welfare of backward classes. On the basis of the report the government increased the reservation quota of the backward classes in educational institutions and government employment from 25 per cent to 31 per cent and for the scheduled castes from 16 per cent to 18 per cent.

1972: Crisis in the DMK. The party treasurer, Assembly member and matinee idol M.G. Ramachandran (MGR) publicly accuses members of his party of corruption. He is expelled from the DMK.

MGR forms the Anna Dravida Munnetra Kazhagam (ADMK) on 18 October, later renamed as All India Anna Dravida Munnetra Kazhagam (AIADMK). This would change the political landscape of Tamil Nadu.

1975: Indira Gandhi declares Emergency. The DMK, under Chief Minister Karunanidhi, which was at the time in alliance with Indira's Congress, is one of the most strident voices condemning the Emergency.

1976: Indira Gandhi dismisses the DMK government, citing corruption allegations on the basis of MGR's letters to the President of India. Karunanidhi's son M.K. Stalin and several DMK members are arrested under the Maintenance of Internal Security Act (MISA) and put behind bars.

1977: Indira Gandhi forms an alliance with MGR's ADMK. The DMK joins the Janata Party headed by Morarji Desai.

Morarji Desai becomes prime minister but Karunanidhi loses in the state Assembly elections. MGR wins and becomes the chief minister until his death in 1987. Karunanidhi remains in Opposition until 1989.

1987: MGR dies on 25 December. The AIADMK splits into two groups: one under his wife, Janaki, and the other under J. Jayalalithaa, his erstwhile co-star in films and later his political protégé. Janaki is propped up as the new chief minister but her government is dismissed for want of numbers. Jayalalithaa is more popular and the two groups merge, making her the undisputed leader of the AIADMK.

1989: The DMK wins the Assembly elections and Karunanidhi returns as chief minister after thirteen years out of power.

The Hindu Succession (Tamil Nadu Amendment) Act addressing gender inequality is passed, providing equal succession rights to women.

1991: The DMK government is dismissed on 30 January on the grounds that it allowed the Sri Lankan terrorist organization Liberation Tigers of Tamil Eelam (LTTE) to operate freely and carry out terrorist activities in Tamil Nadu.

Rajiv Gandhi is assassinated on 21 May by an LTTE suicide bomber near Chennai, shortly before the state and parliamentary elections.

The AIADMK–Congress alliance wins a decisive victory in the state Assembly elections and Jayalalithaa comes to power as chief minister.

1993: V. Gopalasamy, better known as Vaiko, who was emerging as a forceful leader in the DMK, is expelled from the party in November. Though it was officially said that he indulged in anti-party activities with the help of the LTTE, according to many insiders he was expelled because he was becoming a threat to Stalin, who was being groomed to succeed his father, Karunanidhi.

1994: Vaiko forms a new party called Marumalarchi Dravida Munnetra Kazhagam (MDMK).

1996: The Tamil Nadu Congress under G.K. Mooppanar revolts in March against the Centre's decision to align with Jayalalithaa whose regime had become unpopular due to alleged corruption.

Mooppanar quits the Congress and forms a new party called Tamil Manila Congress (TMC).

In the Assembly elections held in May the AIADMK crashes to a humiliating defeat. Jayalalithaa is defeated in her own constituency. The DMK, with its strong alliance partners, including the TMC, wins with a comfortable majority. Karunanidhi is back as chief minister.

Jayalalithaa is arrested on 6 December on charges of corruption in the colour TV scam.

1997: The Dr Ambedkar Law University is set up in Chennai, and Periyar University in Salem.

The Jain Commission indicts the DMK in the Rajiv Gandhi assassination case. The DMK is a partner in the United Front government under Prime Minister I.K. Gujral at the Centre. The Congress demands the DMK's dismissal, withdraws support to the Gujral government and the United Front government falls.

1998: Jayalalithaa joins hands with the Bharatiya Janata Party (BJP), which comes to power at the Centre under Prime Minister Atal Bihari Vajpayee, but she soon withdraws support, bringing the Vajpayee government down.

1999: The DMK's Golden Jubilee year. Karunanidhi makes a momentous policy decision to join hands with the BJP, going against the party's cherished secular ideology.

2001: The AIADMK comes back with a big majority in the Assembly elections, though Jayalalithaa is debarred from contesting, having been convicted for two years in a case. The DMK is routed.

Karunanidhi is arrested on 30 June on charges of corruption. He is released later when there is widespread criticism of his arrest.

2004: Karunanidhi forms a strong alliance with smaller parties in Tamil Nadu and the Congress for the Lok Sabha elections. This alliance sweeps all the forty Lok Sabha seats from the state, including Pondicherry.

2006: The DMK and its alliance partners are victorious in the Assembly elections. The DMK does not get a majority but forms the government with alliance partners, including the Congress, supporting it from outside. Karunanidhi becomes the chief minister once again.

An ordinance is passed to enable the appointment of priests from all castes. On 29 July 2018, a few days after Karunanidhi's hospitalization, the first non-Brahmin government-trained priest is appointed to a Madurai temple by the Department of Hindu Religious and Charitable Endowments.

2007: All is not well in Karunanidhi's family. On 9 May supporters of M.K. Alagiri, Karunanidhi's elder son, burn down the office of the daily *Dinakaran*, run by Karunanidhi's grand-nephew Dayanidhi Maran, because of a poll survey that showed Alagiri in poor light. Three people are killed. The DMK suspends Dayanidhi for his 'anti-party' act while Alagiri is not held responsible for the violence. Dayanidhi, who is Central minister for information and technology, resigns. But within a year all differences in the family are settled and Dayanidhi is back in the party and the family fold.

Kanimozhi becomes a member of the Rajya Sabha. She is

nominated again for a second term in 2013. She is elected to the Lok Sabha in 2019.

2009: Continuing with the United Progressive Alliance (UPA) at the Centre, the DMK wins eighteen seats in the Lok Sabha elections and the Congress comes to power at the Centre. Karunanidhi bargains with the Congress to get a Cabinet post for Dayanidhi Maran and A. Raja, who was in the previous UPA government. Karunanidhi surprises partymen by also getting a Cabinet post in the Central government for Alagiri even though he speaks neither English nor Hindi.

2G spectrum scam explodes in October. The report of the Comptroller and Auditor General (CAG) tabled in Parliament implies that A. Raja, minister for information technology, deprived the government of a staggering Rs 1,76,000 crore in 2G spectrum allocation. Raja resigns. He is later arrested, stays in jail for over a year.

2010: Anna Centenary Library built in Chennai on 8 acres of land, a state-of-the-art nine-floor structure housing 1.2 million books. This was one of Karunanidhi's most prized projects.

Another pet project of Karunanidhi, the new secretariat-cum-assembly building, is inaugurated. When Jayalalithaa comes back to power in 2011 she converts it into a multi-speciality children's hospital.

2011: Kanimozhi, a director of Kalaignar TV, is arrested on 21 May and sent to Tihar Jail because of the channel being linked to the 2G scam. She stays in jail for 190 days.

Jayalalithaa comes back to power in Tamil Nadu with an absolute majority in the Assembly elections held in May.

2014: After a souring of relations with the Congress over the 2G scandal, Karunanidhi decides to contest the parliamentary elections aligning with neither the Congress nor the BJP. The DMK loses power in the state as well as the Centre. The Modi wave sweeps the country and the BJP comes to power at the Centre.

Jayalalithaa is convicted on 27 September in the disproportionate assets case and awarded a four-year jail term and a Rs 100 crore fine by the Karnataka special court. O. Panneerselvam of the AIADMK takes charge as chief minister.

2015: The Karnataka High Court acquits Jayalalithaa and her associates of all charges on 11 May. Jayalalithaa is released from jail. She wins handsomely from R.K. Nagar and within six months takes charge as chief minister.

2016: Karunanidhi tries his best to form a grand alliance against Jayalalithaa in the May Assembly elections, but fails. The DMK loses by 1 per cent votes to the incumbent AIADMK regime. Jayalalithaa is back in power.

Jayalalithaa is admitted to Apollo Hospital on 23 September. She stays there for seventy-five days and dies on 5 December. Karunanidhi is in Kauvery Hospital at this time. He loses his ability to speak and Stalin takes charge of the party.

2017: After seven long years of hearings on the 2G spectrum case, the CBI court in Delhi acquits all the accused on 21 December.

2018: Karunanidhi, ninety-four, is hospitalized due to age-related problems. A week later, on 7 August, he passes away.

Introduction

I have been a Tamil writer for long but had never lived in Tamil Nadu till I moved to Chennai at the beginning of 1993 to take up the job of editor of the Tamil edition of *India Today*. The nine years I worked there were the most exciting years of my writing career. I was born into a Tamil-speaking family in Bangalore, and though I studied in an English-medium school, Tamil was the language I loved and chose to write in. Until my assignment with *India Today*, however, I had no knowledge of the colourful nature of Tamil politics.

I was, I admit, a little nervous about my challenging new assignment and certainly not prepared for the cultural shocks that awaited me in Chennai. The very first one was staggering. It came directly from M. Karunanidhi, leader of the Dravida Munnetra Kazhagam (DMK). He was the leader of the Opposition in the Tamil Nadu Assembly, then headed by the All India Anna Dravida Munnetra Kazhagam (AIADMK) and its young leader Jayalalithaa, perhaps the most fascinating that Tamil Nadu had yet seen.

In those days the Tamil edition of *India Today* published

translations of nearly 75 per cent of the articles from the same week's English edition.

That week the Tamil edition carried a piece on Karunanidhi's family, titled 'Karunanidhi's women'. Though I found the story to be in rather poor taste, I did not anticipate the reaction it triggered. The Tamil edition was on the stands on Saturday. The DMK party's journal *Murasoli* appeared on Sunday with a supplement devoted entirely to me – a big picture of me on its cover, an abusive heading, which put within brackets two letters in my name so that it read not as Vaasanthi but as Vaanthi, meaning vomit in Tamil. Every word, every page tore me to pieces and questioned my integrity. I was bewildered. After all, I was not the author of the *India Today* article, and surely they knew that? The write-ups against me in *Murasoli* did not have a byline. Was this the DMK's way of warning the new editor? Were the DMK and its supremo telling me what would happen if I carried articles that were critical of them?

I pulled myself together and decided to ignore it. I would not succumb to such pressures. But I also felt Karunanidhi was justified in being angry with my magazine.

The very next month the English edition of *India Today* wanted an interview with him, and my colleague Nirupama Subramanian, who worked for the English edition and was also based in Chennai, told me that Karunanidhi was not willing to give *India Today* an interview. I called Karunanidhi's personal assistant Shanmuganathan and requested an appointment with the thalaivar (leader). Shanmuganathan sounded surprised at my audacity, and slammed the phone down with an emphatic no. Nirupama looked worried. We knew our Delhi office would not take no for an answer from its correspondents.

And so I decided to gatecrash. The next morning Nirupama

and I stood at the huge iron gates of the *Murasoli* office building, sweating under the burning sun. I knew Karunanidhi came there at ten every morning. As his car approached, it slowed down near us; Nirupama hid behind me as Karunanidhi lowered the window and asked, '*Enna venum?*' What do you want?

I said, 'We want an interview with you.'

He said, 'Come to Gopalapuram [his residence] at nine-thirty in the morning.' He rolled the window up and the car sped into the compound.

We were pleasantly surprised at his quick and positive reply.

The next morning we were at Gopalapuram well before nine-thirty. I tried to prepare a convincing rejoinder, as I expected him to admonish us over the *India Today* article. I was sure he was still angry. He entered the room in his starched white veshti, full-sleeved shirt, with his trademark yellow shawl over his shoulder, and sat down facing us. As I readied myself for an angry barrage, he looked at me and said, 'Those articles in *Murasoli* got published without being sent to me to read. There is a man called Chinna Kuththoosi . . .'

I was taken aback. He was apologizing! Nothing could be printed in *Murasoli* without his knowledge, of course. Yet he wanted to express his regret and pacify me. He had charmed and disarmed me.

I met him several times after that day to interview him and always enjoyed those sessions, peppered with his quick wit, sharp arguments and clear reasoning – never once did he fumble for words even when I asked difficult questions. Off the record, he would even share with me his worries and fears. I became convinced he was a genuinely down-to-earth, intelligent politician with no airs, who had a vision for the state, but also the weaknesses of an ordinary mortal. He was always easily accessible – whether he was chief minister or not. You called his residence, and after being told who was at the other end, he would pick up the phone.

He regularly read the weekly column I wrote, in which I often censured him as well as Jayalalithaa. As soon as he had read it, I would get a call early in the morning. If he liked what I had written – he relished my criticism of Jayalalithaa – he would express generous appreciation. If he didn't, especially if it was critical of him, he would protest and present his side of the issue.

Once, at a big DMK party conference in Salem, he spoke vehemently against *The Hindu* which had carried an editorial severely criticizing him. He said the Brahmin paper was always critical of him because he was a 'Sudra'. I thought it was demeaning for a person, the chief minister of the state at that, to speak thus. I wrote a column that week strongly objecting to his claim that he was attacked because he belonged to a backward class. It was regrettable, I said, for a person of his erudition and intelligence to bring in the caste factor as the reason for a paper's criticism of him. The paper's right to freedom of expression was at stake if he showed no tolerance towards dissent – as he should surely be aware, since he himself had begun his career as a journalist. And the most disturbing question, my column went on to say, was why he suffered from such an inferiority complex after having risen to the most powerful position in the state. Shouldn't it be a matter of pride that he had done so despite the hurdles he must have faced as a person born in a backward community? I said all his reading and writing had not helped him overcome 'caste feelings'.

As expected, Karunanidhi called me the day the magazine was out. He asked me straight away, '*Ennammaa appadi ezudhitteenga*?' Why did you write such a column?

I reiterated that what he had said at the Salem conference was unbecoming. He tried to justify his argument and insisted *The Hindu* was 'a Brahmin paper' that always criticized him, and its prejudice against him 'ran deep in its veins'.

I said, 'You too suffer from a prejudice. Even if what you say is true, which I think it is not, you are the chief minister. Most importantly, you are a writer, a poet, a scholar. It does not behove a person of your stature to speak as you did.'

He listened to me patiently and then said with a chuckle, 'You must be a different kind of Brahmin.'

Looking back, I am surprised I was able to express myself so frankly and plainly and that he did not get angry. I could never have spoken that way to Jayalalithaa and survived as a journalist in Tamil Nadu. Jayalalithaa kept journalists at a distance, never read the press except what was brought to her attention and certainly never deigned to come on the line if a journalist telephoned her. Karunanidhi, on the other hand, read the press closely and always had time for journalists; yet, ironically, he was the chief minister most criticized by the press.

To understand M. Karunanidhi, five-time chief minister of Tamil Nadu, president of the DMK for sixty years and a man who never lost a single election he fought, you have to understand the Dravidian movement. Karunanidhi's life story, which began in June 1924 and ended in August 2018, is as much the story of the most tumultuous and fascinating period in the annals of modern Tamil Nadu. It is also a remarkable success story in terms of the welfare and progress of its 72.1 million people (2011 census) over seventy years, much of it under the rule of Dravidian parties, compared to the other states of India during that period. Tamil Nadu has raced ahead of most states on the parameters of growth, social justice and good governance.

Karunanidhi has been part of this success story to a great extent. He was at the forefront of important social justice movements and welfare schemes, a champion of state autonomy and protector and promoter of Tamil identity. From an early age, he was driven by the movement for a distinct Dravidian identity, language and culture that resisted domination by the 'Aryan' Brahmin-dominated culture of north India. And this movement has, from its very beginning, deeply affected and shaped politics in Tamil Nadu.

~

Under the British Raj, the Madras Presidency comprised the present-day states of Tamil Nadu, Andhra Pradesh, Telangana and a part of Kerala.

When E.V. Ramasamy Naicker, who later came to be known as Periyar or The Elder, entered active public life in his thirties, in the early twentieth century (he was born in 1879), the political air was vibrant with new movements and campaigns. It was the time when Annie Besant called for home rule in India. This period saw, too, the formation of the South Indian Liberation Front, commonly known as the Justice Party. The Justice Party was composed of members of a regional non-Brahmin elite – mostly educated, English-speaking landlords, merchants and professionals. They united under the 'non-Brahmin' banner and were opposed to what they regarded as Brahmin dominance in public life: though Brahmins were less than 3 per cent of the population, they dominated government administration and higher education and perceived the non-Brahmin elite as low-caste Sudras.

Since Brahmins were also members of the Congress and active in the Home Rule movement, the Justicites branded the Congress and the Home Rule movement as sectarian and casteist.

A silent storm had been brewing for a long time, and when it broke, it consumed the whole state and altered the course of Tamil history. The Justicites were not social reformers, but in a sense they echoed the feelings of the ordinary non-Brahmin against oppressive Brahmin domination.

~

There was another wind, 'Dravidianism', sweeping across the Madras Presidency. The European colonial scholars who came to the south and studied Tamil romanticized the idea of Dravidianism, sensing its political potential. When the Reverend Robert Caldwell developed the theory that Sanskrit was brought down to the south by Aryan Brahmin colonists, the underlying message was that the caste system and idol worship came along with it. Caldwell proposed that the term Sudra be dropped and, instead, the name Dravidian be used for native Tamils. Nothing was more welcome to the non-Brahmin elite, as this revelation vindicated their belief that caste hierarchies were introduced by outsiders.

Dravidianism was fuelled by a renewed interest in Tamil history and culture, an emerging 'classicism' in terms of a re-evaluation of the ancient Tamil literary and religious tradition. A linguistic chauvinism took birth which assigned to Tamil a status of pristine purity, the unique Dravidian language that was unrelated to Sanskrit, the language of classical Hinduism.[1]

Discoveries in language were linked to the theory of the 'superior Dravidian race' having been subdued and conquered by the invading Aryans. Tamil Brahmins, who represented classical Hinduism, and whose dialect was marked by a profusion of Sanskrit words, were seen as descendants of the Aryan race, different from the Dravidians.

Later, C.N. Annadurai (Anna), Periyar's disciple, would regale audiences thus: 'How could the Dravidian Tamils, once the conquerors of the world, great navigators and traders who traded pearls and spices with the Greeks and the Romans, how could the Tamils who had a literary tradition 5000 years old, that saw the birth of five epics when the rest of the world was in mute darkness, a people who could produce a gem like Sangam poetry that has no parallel in the literature of the world, how could they allow themselves to be conquered and subdued by a race inferior?'

The educated non-Brahmin Tamils were thrilled to hear the British official Grant Duff say at a gathering, 'You are of pure Dravidian race and I should like to see the pre-Sanskrit element amongst you asserting itself rather more.'

It suited the British to divide and rule, a strategy to contain the growing strength of Indian freedom fighters.

And when Periyar jumped on to the anti-Brahmin bandwagon, the movement gained momentum and a certain legitimacy. There were already sporadic expressions of protest against caste and class discrimination and Periyar was quick to cash in on that. The Brahmins did not realize what was in store. Nor did the short-sighted Congress party, which failed to notice the radical churning taking place among Tamils. Caste-based prejudices and the obscurantism of the party leadership, fuelled by Gandhi's remarks on varnashrama dharma during a visit to Chennai (known as Madras until 1996), seen as a justification of the caste system, were directly responsible for alienating the Congress from growing Tamil popular opinion. It was the beginning of the Congress's decline in Tamil Nadu.

The Congress had, however, become wary of the rise of the Justice Party, which it termed as 'selfish, unpatriotic and communal'. It was then that Periyar was persuaded to join the Congress by C. Rajagopalachari, a Congress leader. Rajaji, as he was popularly known, saw in Periyar a wealthy and popular landowner from Erode who had demonstrated amazing organizing ability, the potential to contain the influence of the Justice Party. The objectives of the Congress – of attaining national freedom, removal of untouchability and introducing prohibition – lured Periyar into it. Once he joined the Congress in 1919, Periyar, as was his nature, put his heart and soul into it.

However, he was not destined to remain in the Congress for long, and the final break came in the wake of the gurukulam controversy. V.V.S. Iyer, a well-known nationalist, was running a gurukulam on Gandhian principles at Sermadevi, a town near Tinnevelli, a stronghold of Brahmin orthodoxy. Periyar received complaints that there were separate dining areas for Brahmin and non-Brahmin students at the gurukulam and that the quality of the food served to the two sections was different. The influential non-Brahmin parents of the wards were outraged that such discrimination should be practised in a school run on donations from non-Brahmins, and by a man who was expected to be liberal-minded.

The matter was taken to Gandhi, but his response was ambiguous and somewhat dismissive. The argument in favour of Iyer was that inter-dining was not practised in society or even in institutions run by the government, so a change in the tradition would hurt the feelings of the highly religious Brahmins.

Periyar then broke with the Congress and soon after founded Suyamariyathai Iyakkam, the Self-Respect Movement, in 1925. He symbolized his cause by wearing a black shirt. He campaigned in a black shirt for nearly fifty years, till his death in 1973. Travelling at times by bullock cart, a hurricane lantern in hand, he railed against Brahminism, caste, the Congress, the Hindu religion and discrimination against women. He established the idea of 'self-respect marriages' for non-Brahmins – marriages conducted without Brahmin priests or religious vows. He offered a vision of a bright future without the need for God. Or Brahmins.

Periyar followed the line of the Justicites in supporting the continuance of British rule. But his rough style lacked polish and sophistication. A decade earlier the Justicites had attacked the caste system and Brahmin supremacy, but they radically differed from the Self-Respecters on the question of religion. They were deeply religious and were shocked at Periyar's atheistic speeches. They were also worried about the impact this would have on their support groups, mainly the affluent business communities. However, Periyar was careful not to impose his atheism on others. He asked people not to follow him blindly but think first and decide for themselves.

Periyar's Self-Respect Movement was another manifestation of the national freedom movement. The difference was in the poser, 'Who is to be feared? The white man or the Brahmin? If India got its freedom, who will benefit, the Aryan Brahmin or the subaltern Dravidian?'

Periyar later gathered a bunch of brilliant speakers to spread his message, like C.N. Annadurai and Karunanidhi, who created a new language of rhetoric, with catchy alliteration, rhymes and lilting rhythms, invoking the Dravidian glories of the past and the beauty of the Tamil language, pointing to Brahmin dominance as the reason for its decline.

In a society loaded with superstition and obscurantism, caste divisions and privilege, Periyar's revolt against Brahminical Hinduism and the inequities of the caste system, while it may have diverted people's consciousness from national issues, attracted an impressively broad base.

It was during this momentous period that Karunanidhi was born, in a backward caste community. A rebel at heart from childhood, keenly sensitive to caste-based discrimination, the young boy was swept away by the Dravidian movement. Periyar's words stirred in him a passion that propelled him towards a long and extraordinary political journey that began when he was just fourteen years old.

~

There is no dearth of material to document Karunanidhi's story. His own writings – six volumes of his autobiography *Nenjukku Needhi* (Justice for the Heart), his public speeches, the millions of words that went in the form of letters to the DMK cadres that he wrote every day in *Murasoli* – are enough to overwhelm a researcher. His followers have added a million more, regularly compiling and releasing special issues celebrating his speeches in the Assembly as well as speeches on non-political subjects, his witticisms and chronicles of his life. And then there are his literary works – his annotations, paraphrasings and interpretations of the epics, Sangam poetry and the *Thirukkural*; his historical novels and film scripts; and his script for the TV serial on the eleventh-century saint Ramanuja. His literary output alone would win Karunanidhi, or

Kalaignar (artist) as he was most popularly known, an exalted place in Tamil Nadu's cultural life.

Karunanidhi wrote every day. Writing was like yoga for him, says N. Ram, former chief editor, *The Hindu*. 'I do not know any other politician who dominated the scene like Kalaignar Karunanidhi in a cultural sense, in literature and poetry,' says Ram. 'And he was a great reader also. His literary output places him in a different category than most other Indian politicians.'[2]

But there was also Karunanidhi the consummate politician. As N. Ram observes, 'You could say many things about Karunanidhi. An able administrator, he was known to take very quick decisions; he was the first to get into alliances with the centre, with national parties [as a coalition partner]. I do not know if any other regional politician of his time could do that, so much so that no national party could aspire to lead the state ever since the Dravidian parties came to rule in 1967.'[3]

Karunanidhi indeed had a multifaceted personality. He was a visionary and a reformist pushing for social justice, the builder of modern Tamil Nadu. But he was also a man with human weaknesses and shortcomings. He failed to admonish those close to him when they did wrong, be they party workers or his own family. He trusted people perhaps too easily and then was shocked when they betrayed him. A series of such betrayals perhaps pushed him to put his family before able and loyal party members.

And then there were his failures of judgement. When it came to handling the Sri Lankan Tamil issue, his judgement was clouded by his emotional attachment to supporting the cause of his fellow Tamils across the Palk Strait, at the cost of law and order in his own state. When he allowed the infiltration of Muslim fundamentalists at Kottaimedu, his judgement was coloured by his desire to demonstrate secular brotherhood with Tamil Nadu's Muslims. He didn't do enough to stop corruption among DMK members. His detractors say he himself was corrupt, though none of the charges against him were ever proved in a court of law.

He was the Tamil Nadu leader most abused by the media, but that is because he gave them space to do so. I have in several columns and articles been very critical of him. But I never feared reprisal. Once when I was seated next to him at a function I told him, 'I write very critically about you. But I must tell you that I have great respect and regard for you.'

He looked at me and said, smiling, 'Don't I know that?'

This book looks at his life and work – the good and the bad – unsparingly, as a biography should. I am sure he would have understood and appreciated that I have tried in this biography to be true to my subject and also to myself and my ethics as a journalist.

1

Born to Rebel

The boy loved to hear his father play the nadaswaram, the traditional musical instrument played at occasions auspicious and sacred. Appa (father) was playing raga Sankarabharanam, which he especially loved. Appa seemed to be in another world, eyes closed, oblivious to his surroundings. The boy too closed his eyes, taking in the beauty of the melody, shaking his head in appreciation when the music reached moments of special nuance and delicacy.

Lost in the music, both father and son were jolted out of their reverie by a sharp knock on the front door.

The man standing in the doorway said, 'Pannaiyar [landowner] wants you to come and see him.'

The man did not step inside the house, nor did Appa invite him in. He gently put the instrument back in its cover, threw a thundu (towel used to cover the upper body) across his bare chest and followed the man, who walked ten steps ahead of him. Appa walked barefoot. The boy too ran barefoot alongside him. He was used to walking without shoes.

They arrived at a large house. In the front porch hung a swing made of solid, polished teak with silver cups fastening its heavy chains to the ceiling. The man sitting on it was chewing betel leaves, and there was a silver box with betel leaves beside him.

The boy watched his father's demeanour change as he approached the landowner. He removed his thundu and tied it around his waist like a belt, leaving his chest bare. With his torso bent, he covered his mouth with his palm and said, 'Vanakkam, Sami!' Respects to you, sir.

'Sami' opened his paan-stained mouth and said something that the boy did not hear. Appa's body shrank, as if in deference and submission.

As they walked back home he found that the thundu was back on his father's chest. Appa was humming a tune. Fighting his tears, the boy asked, 'Why did you remove your thundu before the Pannaiyar?'

Appa looked at him, surprised. He did not expect the little fellow to ask him such a question.

'They belong to the upper caste. We belong to the low. We have no right to wear the thundu in front of them,' he replied simply.

'But why?'

Appa did not answer.

The boy was angry. He was proud of his father. He was a good farmer. A learned man, who could read and write Sanskrit and Tamil. He could recite the Ramayana and Mahabharata better than the pandits. He was a poet. He wrote funny poems that made people laugh and clap. One of Appa's poems was about god and a temple and a woman who slipped into the bushes with other men while her hapless husband was silent like the god in the temple. It looked like Appa sided with the woman. He would write satirical poems even about the pannaiyar and regale his friends. But the bravado ended there. Before the pannaiyar he was a nobody. He could not even cover his chest. He had to stand at a distance. He was just a nadaswaram player, a 'nayanakkaran', and nothing more. No respect even for the divine music he played.

Muthuvelar wanted his son to learn the nadaswaram, as was the tradition in the family. But the boy refused.

'I will not play the instrument,' he said firmly.

'Why?' asked the father.

'I will not be able to cover my chest with the thundu before upper-caste people. I will have to tie it around my waist. I will not be allowed to wear slippers. However gifted a musician you are, they will dismiss you as a mere nadaswaram player! No, Appa, I will not become a nadaswaram player.'

Muthuvelar could only sigh and say, 'All right, then you must go to school and study.'

The boy smiled. That was his first revolt. And his first victory. Karunanidhi was not yet ten years old. The flame of rage and humiliation that was lit in his heart the day he went with his father to the pannaiyar's house continued to smoulder throughout his life.

~

Muthuvelar and Anjugam were simple folk, god-fearing and devout, who belonged to the small Isai Vellalar community of peasant stock, which traditionally played musical instruments, especially the nadaswaram, at temple festivals and at the homes of other castes during functions. After two daughters, the much-awaited son, for whom the couple had observed fasts and offered special prayers to the gods, was born on 3 June 1924, in the sleepy village of Thirukkuvalai, near the famous temple town of Thiruvarur.

He was a gift from the gods and became the darling of everyone in the family. His parents could not have imagined that this gift from the gods would turn against the gods, become an atheist and a fighter for social justice who would declare, 'Man is born free but is in caste chains everywhere.'

With his much-cherished only son stubbornly refusing to follow the family tradition of learning the nadaswaram, Muthuvelar was determined that the boy got the best schooling he could give him. He was enrolled in the village school in Thirukkuvalai and his father even engaged a private tutor for him.

Karunanidhi discovered early his love for words. During school holidays he would script plays, staging them in the cowshed in the backyard, with the village children as his fellow actors and his audience. He would don the role of Krishna himself, dusting his whole body with blue powder.

At the age of twelve, after he had completed class 5, in Thirukkuvalai, his father took him to Thiruvarur High School to seek admission in form two. But the headmaster rejected his application, saying he could not even be admitted to class 5 which was for much younger children. Karunanidhi was devastated. He had bragged to his friends that he was going to the high school in Thiruvarur for further studies. How would he face them now? Ignoring the protests of the peon who sat outside the headmaster Kasturi Iyengar's room, he went straight inside. Iyengar was surprised at the temerity of this child who had stormed into his office.

'What is it, who are you?' he asked, irritated.

'Please admit me in your school, sir,' said the boy.

'But you have to write the test, dear fellow!'

'I did write for forms one and two. My master had trained me for form two and said I would surely be admitted. But now they say I am not even good for class five!'

'What can I do, son?'

'If I go back to Thirukkuvalai people will make fun of me. Please take me at least in class five,' Karunanidhi said with tears rolling down his cheeks.

Iyengar shook his head. 'Once the decision is taken, it cannot be changed. I am sorry.'

'In that case I will jump into the pond in front of your eyes and die!'

Iyengar was taken aback by the child's outburst but also impressed by his determination. The pond, Kamalalayam, was slippery with scum and a few children had earlier drowned in it. Patting Karunanidhi's back, he told him he would be admitted in class five.

An overjoyed Karunanidhi came out and hugged his father.

He stood first in class that year.

At Thiruvarur High School, Karunanidhi became deeply interested in history and in biographies. As part of the syllabus there was a small biography of fifty pages titled *Panagal Arasar* that captured his imagination. He writes in *Nenjukku Needhi* that this book laid the foundation for his political beliefs.

~

Panagal Arasar (he died in 1928) was one of the founders of the Justice Party, which is regarded as the precursor to the DMK, the party which Karunanidhi led from 1969 till his death in 2018.

The Justice Party, as mentioned earlier, projected the concept of Dravidian identity distinct from that of the Aryans of north

India. It stressed that culturally and historically the Tamils were different from others in the country. They spoke a language that was different from the languages spoken in other parts including the south, which had roots in Sanskrit, a language the Dravidianists referred to as vadamozhi (language of the north).

After Periyar resigned from the Congress party in protest against its upper-caste members who discriminated between Brahmin and non-Brahmin students in a gurukulam run by them, and joined the Justice Party, he became an important voice for social justice for the Dravidians. To recap what has been said in the Introduction, the Self-Respect Movement Periyar started battled Brahmin domination and caste-based discrimination and oppression. He propagated atheism, arguing that the Hindu religion was at the root of the caste system that encouraged institutionalizing the abhorrent practice of caste-based discrimination. He established the idea of Self-Respect marriages for non-Brahmins, conducted without Brahmin priests or religious vows in Sanskrit, a language that no one understood. He called for a scientific temperament and equal rights for women. His clarion call for self-respect and social justice appeared most radical at that time.

In keeping with the Justice Party's stand, Periyar supported the continuance of British rule, though he had other differences with Justice Party members. Leading Justicites and the Self-Respecters came from non-Brahmin Hindu communities. A decade earlier they had attacked the caste system and Brahmin supremacy, their resentment fuelled by the fact that they were educated and affluent and felt they were in no way inferior to the Brahmins. But the British, for administrative convenience, put them in the non-Brahmin caste bracket along with all the other castes that were far below them in the caste hierarchy. They found their status in their villages diminished because of this categorization and it hurt their pride. But they also felt that Periyar was talking beyond his brief. They were deeply religious and baulked at Periyar's atheistic views.

R.M. Veerappan, better known as RMV, producer of several films starring MGR (M.G. Ramachandran) and, later, Rajinikanth, was very young when he joined a drama company and fell under the spell of Periyar, whose blunt, earthy language struck a powerful chord with the masses.

RMV recalls how Periyar mesmerized his often-illiterate audiences, whom he addressed as 'Fools!'

'Periyar would say, "Show that you have nothing but hatred for the Brahmins. Banish them for they are foreigners. Listen, how did the Brahmin become so influential? It is because of religion. So you must destroy religion. But you people cling to this barbaric religion because of your stupid faith in a piece of stone which you have been fooled to think is God by the paappaan [derogatory word for Brahmin]. How will you destroy the paappaan? By destroying his God."

'And then he would break clay images of Ganesha in the middle of the street, in full view of the public! He would say, "Look, I am breaking this image. Nothing has happened to me." He thought that was the only way he could convince people. But many of us were embarrassed.'[1]

It was indeed shocking behaviour in a land where even calendar pictures of gods are venerated.

But students across the state were captivated by the ideology of the Self-Respect Movement. One such was C.N. Annadurai, drawing notice at Pachaiyappa's College in Chennai as a firebrand orator, putting forth the ideology of the movement in an appealing language, studded with catchy rhymes and puns. He formed the Self-Respect youth body in the college in 1930.

In Thiruvarur Karunanidhi was devouring the book on Panagal Arasar, when the Justice Party, which had won all Legislative Council elections since 1920, lost the first Madras Legislative Assembly election held in 1937 and a Congress government was elected in Chennai. C. Rajagopalachari became the chief minister and, as if to provoke the Self-Respect sloganeers, made learning Hindi compulsory in schools. The resentment against this imposition of Hindi flared up into a conflagration among the Tamils that would eventually change the course of history in Tamil Nadu.

While for Periyar self-respect was 'personal liberation from ideas of caste', the language agitation that began as early as the 1930s was an expression of Tamil nationalism. The move to make Hindi, spoken in north India, a compulsory subject in the provincial schools was seen as an example of Brahmin/Sanskritic cultural dominance and led to a wave of protests that spread like wildfire all over Tamil-speaking areas in the Madras Presidency. Periyar and his followers were loud in their denunciation of the government for forcing an alien language on the Dravidian populace. Periyar's detractors said he had no love for the Tamil language (he spoke Kannada at home) and his opposition stemmed from his enmity towards the Congress. But he always drew huge crowds. The streets swarmed with young men and women taking part in protest marches and distributing pamphlets urging the people to rise in revolt. Many were arrested and two died in prison.

The young Karunanidhi was swept away by the charged atmosphere. On 3 June 1938, his fourteenth birthday, the first anti-Hindi protest was held at Saidapet, Chennai. Pattukkottai

Azhagiri Samy of the Self-Respect Movement led a march all over the state, protesting against the imposition of Hindi. A fiery speaker, Azhagiri Samy was called 'Sooravali' or whirlwind speaker. Indeed, his words blasted you like a whirlwind. Karunanidhi was fascinated by the passion Azhagiri exuded. He writes in his autobiography: 'The compelling arguments of Periyar's speeches, the bravery and courage in Azhagiri's sentences, Anna's beautiful Tamil – these mesmerized me.'

Karunanidhi managed to gather a group of boys and they roamed the streets of Thiruvarur with the Tamil Tai (Tamil Mother, a symbol of the Tamil language) flag perched on a pole atop a cycle rickshaw. A picture of Rajaji stabbing the Tamil Thai with the dagger of compulsory Hindi was added to it. They wrote on the walls of Thiruvarur, 'Down with Hindi, long live Tamil'. Karunanidhi composed catchy slogans that the gang chanted as they went along. Karunanidhi even dared to hand a pamphlet to his Hindi teacher and shouted, 'Down with Hindi! Long live Tamil!'

He received a hard slap from the Hindi teacher the next day when he could not read the Hindi words on the blackboard.

Thirty years later, the same teacher invited Karunanidhi to preside over a conference. He waited at the entrance to receive the student he had slapped all those years ago. He was no longer a Hindi teacher. He had become a homoeopathic doctor.

2

Love, Marriage and the Lure of Politics

One day, a bespectacled man arrived in search of 'someone called Karunanidhi who is running a handwritten newsletter called *Manava Nesan* (friend of students)'. It was a time when the Communist Party was trying to penetrate various parts of the country. The man, who did not expect to see a precocious youngster of hardly fourteen, exclaimed in amazement, 'You are the same Karunanidhi who writes the newsletter?' Assured that he was indeed the one, the man went on to reveal his plan. 'We have to mobilize all the students to raise their voices for freedom, conciliation and equality. We have started a camp for a convention of students. You must be in charge of enrolling students from your school for the camp.' He added, 'You must also begin a weekly tabloid.'

Though the man was wearing a khadi shirt Karunanidhi knew he was not a Congress worker. But he was not aware that the man was a communist. He found his words – freedom, equality and conciliation – inspiring. Karunanidhi was thrilled that his *Manava Nesan* newsletter had reached an older person who looked highly literate. *Manava Nesan* manuscripts were handwritten – fifty copies made by hand and distributed by Karunanidhi and his friends. Following the man's advice, he started a weekly handwritten leaflet called *Murasoli*.

Highly motivated, Karunanidhi brought two hundred students to the convention, who were inducted as members. Karunanidhi was elected as the secretary of the student group while his friend S.P. Chidambaram became the treasurer. But Karunanidhi felt uneasy as the convention proceeded. It was dominated by the Congress. When a member proposed 'Thamizh vaazga! Valarga Hindi' (Long live Tamil, Hindi be nurtured) as their slogan, students who supported the communists nodded in agreement. Karunanidhi was taken by surprise and objected. He felt he had been taken for a ride. After a sleepless night he decided to dissolve the association and not have any truck with either the communists or the Congress. He had collected a fee of Rs 100 from the students to join the association. The next morning he tried to return the money, but most students refused to take it back. With the Rs 75 that was left Karunanidhi started the Tamil Students Association in 1941.

He knew for certain which path he would follow – that of Periyar and Anna.

Karunanidhi had by now developed great love for the language he spoke. He was gifted with a rare felicity with words. They came to him easily and he realized this flair for the Tamil language was his strength. He could use it to propagate his ideals. The love for Tamil would in course of time lead him to devour the classics, from Sangam poetry, the *Thirukkural* and the epics, to Russian literature translated into Tamil. He also voraciously read Tamil dailies and magazines as well as the English daily *The Hindu*. Writing became a regular everyday habit from those turbulent days in the 1940s and continued till his hand was no longer able to hold a pen during his last years, around 2016.

But as a fifteen-year-old his main assets were his command over Tamil and a passionate involvement in the political ideals that fired his imagination. His parents were bitterly disappointed when he did poorly in the board exams, failing repeatedly for three years. Karunanidhi writes in his autobiography that he ran away from home out of shame after the third time, but his loving family brought him back and showered him with 'more love' that he 'did not deserve'.

In 1939 Rajaji's government resigned in protest against India's involvement in the Second World War. The interim government that followed, reading the public mood, withdrew the compulsory Hindi legislation. Young Karunanidhi was jubilant. He viewed it as his own big victory.

~

Whereas Karunanidhi's family wanted him to continue his studies, his burning ambition was to see his writing in print.

In 1942, Annadurai, who lived in Kanchipuram, started a magazine called *Dravida Nadu*. Karunanidhi thought that his writing would reach a wide audience if it was published in the magazine. He did not know the magazine's address, but wrote a piece and sent it addressed simply to 'Dravida Nadu, Kanchipuram'. He was overjoyed when his article titled 'Ilamaibali' (Sacrifice of Youth) appeared in the magazine the very next week. He roamed the streets of Thiruvarur for a week with a copy in hand, placing it casually in front of people and not budging till they read his article and praised it.

Two weeks later Annadurai visited Thiruvarur for a function. 'Who is Karunanidhi in this town?' Anna asked. 'Please bring him over, I want to meet him.'

An elated Karunanidhi, who was then eighteen, presented himself before Annadurai, expecting some praise and a request for more articles perhaps. He writes that Annadurai was surprised to see a short and puny youngster in front of him. 'Are you studying?' he asked Karunanidhi. In a trembling voice the boy said, 'Yes, I am.' Annadurai looked at him and said sharply, 'Do not send me any articles hereafter. Concentrate on your studies.'

Karunanidhi was devastated. He did not expect such a rude rejection from the man he so admired. But he was in no mood to follow the advice. He could not contain his urge to write. He began to write plays, his first love, and stage them in Thiruvarur. These plays were a vehicle to propagate the ideology of the Dravidian movement. To collect funds for his student association he staged a play titled *Palaniappan* in Thiruvarur. The collection was a meagre Rs 80 while he had incurred a cost of Rs 200 for staging the play. He did not know how to repay the debt he owed to people who now harassed him for it.

Desperate to try his luck elsewhere, he left with his friend Thennavan for Nagapattinam. There he met Gopal, a leader in the DK. Gopal heard the lad's story with sympathy but hesitated to lend him the money. Instead he bought the play for Rs 100.

It was a revelation to Karunanidhi that one could earn by writing plays. Back in Thiruvarur he began churning them out. His parents were worried that their only son was becoming a good-for-nothing vagabond. They urged him to get a job that would guarantee at least Rs 50 a month. Writing plays was a worthless use of his time and energy.

Even as he struggled to earn a rupee, Karunanidhi fell in love. The girl too was enamoured of him, he was sure.

When his family approached the girl's parents, they insisted that if there was to be a wedding it had to be done in the presence of Brahmin priests with Vedic chants. Karunanidhi refused, as this was against the Self-Respect ideology he so fervently believed in. The love story ended as quickly as it had blossomed, leaving Karunanidhi despondent. His sisters then decided to select a bride for him and found a suitable girl in Chidambaram – Padma, sister of the well-known singer Chidambaram Jayaraman. They summoned Karunanidhi to Chidambaram.

He was assured that the girl's family had agreed to a suyamaruyaathai wedding without the Vedic rituals.

Karunanidhi went to Chidambaram with Thennavan and was enchanted. He writes that when he first saw Padma, leaning against a pillar, he thought he was looking at a beautiful painting. He seems to have fallen in love with her instantly. Their married life was blissful. It is evident from his writing that they had a close and loving relationship. She made him happy. Soon he began to realize he needed a secure job to make her life more comfortable.

Around this time Gopal, who had bought *Palaniappan* and now owned a drama company called Dravida Actors Company, invited Karunanidhi to act in plays that would propagate Dravidian ideology. He agreed on the condition that he would only act in the plays he scripted.

Karunanidhi and two of his friends now moved to Villupuram where *Palaniappan* was to be staged. They reached a month ahead to rehearse. Karunanidhi describes in his memoirs what a miserable life it was, with little money, little food, just one set of clothes and scarcity of water to bathe. They had to walk a great distance to the paddy fields where there was a tap, bathe and quickly wash their shirts and dhotis. He recalled later: 'During those times, the tears that flowed from my eyes would mingle with the water from the tap.' They would tie a small towel around their waists, the washed shirt thrown over one shoulder and the washed veshti held over their heads like an umbrella and walk back in the hot sun. The clothes would dry by the time they reached their room. They would wear them and go for a meagre and unappetizing lunch. 'Do you believe,' he wrote later, 'that I rarely slept those days?'[1]

When *Palaniappan* was staged they were in for a shock. The play didn't attract more than a handful of people, even though Periyar and Anna came to watch on different days. The title was changed to *Shantha*, a woman's name, in the hope that it would draw bigger crowds. But that didn't make a difference. Karunanidhi soon found out why people were staying away when he overheard a conversation in the streets of Villupuram. He and the rest of the Dravida Actors Company were described as a paraiyan troupe. 'Let their own caste fellows see the play!' they said.

Karunanidhi writes that in those days, people thought 'Dravidian' stood for scheduled caste and paraiyan was a generic word for Dalits.[2] Karunanidhi and his friends wound up the play in Villupuram and left for Pondicherry.

In the meantime, Periyar, leader of the Justice Party, had withdrawn the party from electoral politics and changed its name to Dravida Kazhagam at a conference in Salem. Two important resolutions were passed, which annoyed the more affluent party members. Periyar asked those who had been given titles and honours by the British government to relinquish them and stop using the name of their caste – Mudaliar, Pillai, Naidu, for instance. Annadurai read out the resolutions, as if to protect Periyar from the wrath of his detractors, many of whom left the party in a huff.

The Dravida Actors Company fared better in Pondicherry. Here they found bigger and more enthusiastic audiences, and Karunanidhi became something of a hero. People began addressing him as Sivaguru – the name of the character he played. Karunanidhi also started writing articles in a paper called *Thozilalar Mithran*, meaning 'friend of workers'. For this he would get free cups of tea but not a single paisa. One of his articles criticizing Gandhi angered the Congress. He followed it up with another one mocking Gandhi with the question 'What if Gandhi became the Viceroy?' The furious Congress supporters waited for an opportunity to settle the score with the fellow who had abused their leader.

At this time, the DK held a conference in Pondicherry, in which Periyar, Annadurai and Pattukkottai Azhagiri Samy participated. A huge crowd came to hear them, but among them were Congress workers waving placards and shouting, 'Dravidian leaders, go back!'

Annadurai started his speech with his usual panache. 'To say vaa, come, is Tamil culture. To say po, go, is not in our tradition. How can such a negative word enter here?'

As Annadurai continued speaking, the Congress workers kept heckling him. When they pulled down the DK flag that was hoisted at the conference, Karunanidhi and his friends hurriedly helped smuggle the speakers out to a safe place. Then he left the conference venue with the poet Bharathidasan. As the two friends walked along a deserted, dimly lit street a group of Congress supporters confronted them. Karunanidhi fled and the men chased him. He tried to hide in a house, but they dragged him out and thrashed him mercilessly until he lost consciousness. They then threw him into a gutter and left him for dead.

When he came to a few hours later an old woman took him home, fed him and tended to his injuries. She gave him a kurta and a skullcap so that he could reach his home in disguise. Late that night DK workers found him and escorted him to where Periyar was staying. Karunanidhi was deeply touched when he learned that Periyar and Anna had not gone to bed, worrying about him. Periyar applied medicine to his bruises and wounds with his own hands. He then asked Karunanidhi to accompany him to his home town, Erode. Moved by his affection, Karunanidhi agreed.

Periyar made him assistant editor of his magazine *Kudi Arasu* where Karunanidhi's friend Karunanandan also worked. The monthly pay was Rs 40 but Periyar deducted Rs 20 for the lunch and dinner the men had at his residence, Rs 10 for breakfast and tiffin in the evening and Rs 5 for miscellaneous expenses. Karunanidhi sent the remaining Rs 5 to Padma by money order. 'Even that amount gave much happiness to people at home,' he notes in his autobiography.

Periyar had some strange fads. He considered bathing a waste of time and did not believe in daily baths. Karunanidhi, however, began his day with a bath and wore fresh clothes every morning. 'How will you work if you waste time bathing?' an annoyed Periyar asked him. 'Bathing is also work,' replied Karunanidhi. Periyar was an exacting taskmaster, giving Karunanidhi no time to relax. But there were some rewarding moments. The old man would ask Karunanidhi and Karunanandan to sit with him after dinner on the open terrace and talk to them long into the night about the political changes unfurling around the world. The extent of Periyar's knowledge and his radical views on social issues made a lasting impression on Karunanidhi's young mind.

Karunanidhi had worked at *Kudi Arasu* for a year when he received a call from A.S.A. Saamy of Jupiter Films, a famous production house in Coimbatore. Saamy wanted him to write scripts for films under their banner. Karunanidhi was commissioned to do the screenplay for their next film titled *Rajakumari*.

Karunanidhi was thrilled. Writing scripts was his forte and the money was attractive. Periyar did not object to his departure from *Kudi Arasu* – the young man deserved a better standard of living.

~

Joining Jupiter Films marked a turning point in Karunanidhi's life. Not only did it bring him fame and money over time, it also brought about his acquaintance with a young actor called M.G. Ramachandran. MGR was an attractive man, a little effeminate, with an easy smile. He wore khadi clothes and a chain of tulsi beads around his neck. He was an admirer of Gandhi. Karunanidhi took an instant liking to him. He gave him books written by Annadurai, and Ramachandran in turn gave him books by Gandhi. Karunanidhi, with his compelling arguments, soon converted Ramachandran to Dravidian ideology and the latter joined the DK.

Karunanidhi missed Padma and wished they could spend more time together. Now that he was earning well, he took a small house on rent at Singanallur near Coimbatore and brought Padma over from Thiruvarur. Those were the happiest days, living with his beloved Padma, writes Karunanidhi, though the place was like a 'sparrow's nest'. The memory of that time never dimmed even when he grew old. He vividly recalled one incident when he had a tiff with Padma and left home in the evening without drinking his coffee. It was past six-thirty and dusk had fallen. Standing in the queue at the bus stop to catch a bus for Coimbatore, he was surprised to hear a voice gently saying, 'Look this side, please.' Was that Padma's voice? He turned and found her standing there, head covered with her sari pallu. She was holding a brass cup of hot coffee, wrapped in a piece of cloth. The bus stop was two furlongs away from the house. His heart melted on seeing her and they went back home. He writes in *Nenjukku Needhi* that he never got angry with her again. He wished he could spend more time with her and give her a better, more comfortable life.

When the film *Abhimanyu*, for which he had written the script, released, Karunanidhi proudly took Padma to watch it, telling her to look out for his name in the credits. But it was not there. Karunanidhi was deeply humiliated, though Padma tried to comfort him. He went to the producer and demanded to know why his name had been omitted. The producer replied, 'You become more famous, we will do that.' Karunanidhi was too furious to think straight. He left Coimbatore and went back to Thiruvarur with Padma.

Soon after he wrote the play *Manthiri Kumari*, which was later made into a film and became a big hit.

Around the same time *Murasoli* started being printed at a press. It earned praise, but it was losing money and Karunanidhi sold Padma's gold chain to pay off his debts.

The press was in a place called Vijayapuram. The printed issues had to be transported across the river to Thiruvarur and delivered to the subscribers and distributors. Karunanidhi could not afford to engage anyone for the task. He and the manager Kanakasundaram would walk on a bamboo bridge with the printed load on their heads, sit in the *Murasoli* office all night and stamp the addresses and send the weekly for delivery in the morning. Karunanidhi wondered how long this could go on.

Now Padma became pregnant. He was worried that she was pale and weak, and he was unable to take proper care of her.

Yet this was also a time when he wanted to immerse himself in his writing because India was approaching its independence and he didn't want to miss a moment of history in the making.

On 15 August 1947, as the whole country celebrated India's freedom from British rule, Periyar called it a day of mourning. He said it would be better if the white man's rule continued instead of the country going into the hands of the north Indian Aryans. But Annadurai demurred, saying it was a day of celebration because the humiliation, the curse of foreign domination had been wiped out.

For some time now, disagreements between Periyar and Annadurai had been out in the open. Karunanidhi, intending to bring about a rapprochement between the two, wrote an article in *Murasoli* titled 'Last Days' in which he attacked 'the opportunists' who stood in the way of their reconciliation. It incensed members of the Kazhagam and copies of *Murasoli* were burnt.

Karunanidhi was so caught up in the political turmoil that he could not be present for the birth of his son. When he rushed to the hospital to see the baby, a tired and weak Padma smiled at him; the complicated delivery had been made worse by fever. Karunanidhi did not know this was the last time she would smile.

Padma and the baby came home from hospital, but her fever did not subside. Karunanidhi left for a two-day tour and when he returned her condition had worsened. His heart ached to see her suffer and he did not want to leave her bedside. But there were people waiting at his front door to accompany him to a political meeting he had committed to address.

By the time he got back, Padma had breathed her last. He knelt before her body, tears streaming down his cheeks. He bent and kissed her forehead. 'That was the only thing I had left to give her. She finished her chapter in my life when she was just twenty,' he writes in *Nenjukku Needhi*. His blissful three years of married life ended in grief and guilt. He could not forgive himself for failing to provide her better medical care and not being by the side of the woman he loved so dearly in her last moments.

3

Periyar vs Annadurai

Nineteen forty-eight was a year of mourning for both Karunanidhi and the country. It was the year Padma died and the year Mahatma Gandhi was assassinated by Nathuram Godse. For all his ideological differences with the Congress, Karunanidhi deeply admired Gandhi and wrote a poignant passage on him in his autobiography:

> Gandhi fought and led several non-violent protests against the might of the foreign rule. He underwent fasts and almost reached the gates of death . . . No one thought of snuffing out his life when he courageously fought a moral war; but when the nation became free from foreign yoke and attained the independence that he desired, he was killed. Not by an outsider. A man born on Indian soil snatched away that sacred life.

It was also a year of new beginnings in Tamil Nadu politics as well as in Karunanidhi's personal life. On 15 September 1948 the family arranged a second marriage for him, since the newborn,

Muthu, needed a mother. They chose a young girl named Dayalu, who was the daughter of a middle-class farmer from Thanjavur. Her brother was also a member of the DK and therefore there was no ideological inconsonance between Karunanidhi and his new bride's family. Karunanidhi gave his mother, Anjugam, the Rs 800 he had received for his play *Thookkuththooki*, as marriage expense.

On the wedding day the bride's side was busy welcoming relatives and guests who had come from neighbouring villages and towns. The melodious and auspicious notes of the nadaswaram filled the air and the ceremony was due to start any moment. As the bride stood waiting for the groom, a group of student protesters marched in the street, shouting, 'Long live Tamil! Long live Periyar! Down with Hindi!' Karunanidhi forgot he was the bridegroom. As if in a trance, he left the marriage hall and joined the march. After an hour-long frantic search, with both families worrying that Karunanidhi and the students had been arrested, he was brought back. Luckily no one was arrested in Thiruvarur that day. Since Annadurai could not come to preside over the Self-Respect wedding ceremony, Karunanidhi did it himself. He gave a short speech and put the garland around the slender neck of a bewildered Dayalu. For Dayalu, waiting for an often-absent husband would become a regular feature of life. This husband whose comings and goings were so unpredictable would subsequently father her four children. Dayalu remained a simple housewife who took no interest in her husband's public life. And, as Karunanidhi explains in his autobiography, 'It is good that she got used to waiting for me from the very first day . . .'

~

Meanwhile, the crisis in the DK was coming to a head with the ongoing clash between Periyar and Annadurai. Karunanidhi, who at first had tried to bridge the gap between them, was forced to choose between his two mentors: would it be Annadurai over Periyar?

Periyar's movement had begun to languish even before India became independent. Though it had undoubtedly made a broad impact, it was his refusal to enter electoral politics that created restlessness among his young, intelligent but ambitious lieutenants. Commenting on the differences between the two DK leaders, RMV, who came under the influence of Periyar as a young boy points out:[1] 'Anna admitted that Periyar's movement was a very necessary movement. But we all agreed with him that we could not just remain a band of reformers and Brahmin-bashers under such a formidable leader as Periyar, who behaved like an autocrat.'[2]

RMV continued: 'Anna said, "Periyar came to break and he has done it, and it is for us to build anew." He said the same to the Congress: "You brought Independence. But the mason cannot say, 'I shall remain in the house. You have to make way for the new occupants.'"

Annadurai was a prolific writer and he was open about his differences with Periyar. The last one was in 1947, when he chided Periyar for dubbing Independence Day as a day of mourning.

'Anna was very clear that you could not achieve anything without political power,' says RMV, 'that if a system was to be attacked it had to be attacked politically and not with reference to any individuals or any particular community.'

Periyar, however, was firm in his resolve to stay away from political power. Perhaps the type of social grievances that he articulated could not have been tackled at that time from a political plank. But while the movement can be said to have diverted people from national issues, it created a strong impact and won broad-based support. As N. Ram observed, 'Periyar was able to broad-base the movement, even bring in very radical views – on women, against landlordism, etc. He was a very remarkable figure who held a mirror to his age. He was smart enough not to enter electoral politics.'

The feminist activist V. Geetha agrees: 'It is clear that the generation of the 1930s, forties and fifties were genuinely moved by Periyar's atheism even if they did not practise it. They felt it was something very powerful that enabled them to challenge hierarchies in their personal lives as well as in their social milieu.'[3]

~

Annadurai was already known for his oratorial skills both in English and Tamil before he came under Periyar's wing. Periyar, spotting his potential, engaged him as a clerk, writer and interpreter. Annadurai wrote articles, plays and speeches, giving powerful literary expression to Periyar's atheism and Brahmin-bashing. But the distance between him and Periyar arose mainly because the latter was difficult to deal with, authoritarian, unrelenting in his dislike for plays and actors, and with extreme and uncompromising views on both personalities and policies.

Periyar, on his part, perhaps felt uncomfortable with Anna's growing popularity. Thousands flocked to hear Anna, admired him and even looked upon him as a leader long before he showed signs of coming to power. And the Tamil language acquired a new status and appeal when Annadurai and his very talented young friend

Karunanidhi skilfully used it in satirical, politically propagandist plays.

A new language of evocative prose combined with convincing logic evolved through plays and cinema and caught the imagination of the masses. The language of their discourse, with its combination of politics and entertainment, became increasingly influential. It was clear that the Dravidian movement was growing and evolving beyond Periyar's control.

On 24 October 1948 Periyar organized a large public meeting in Erode with Annadurai as the chief guest. Periyar put forth his demand for a separate Dravida state.[4] Periyar also announced at the meeting, 'I have given the keys to the box in Anna's hand,' indicating there would be a change in leadership of the movement. But despite such placatory attempts, the DK members knew the rift between Periyar and Annadurai remained.

Karunanidhi believed in following your star to reach your destination, and instinct told him Anna was his star. It was almost like the pull of destiny. He made his choice known. He protected and defended Annaduari in public, which offended the seniors in the movement. He recounts an incident in *Nenjukku Needhi* to illustrate how kind Annadurai was even to those who always attacked him in public forums. Pattukkottai Azhagiri Samy's health was failing. At the Erode conference convened by Periyar, Azhagiri Samy, who had been a staunch supporter of Periyar and a sharp critic of Annadurai, announced that it would be his last rally because of his illness. Anna was concerned and immediately took him to a hospital in Tambaram, Chennai, for treatment. Anna also announced that whoever invited him to speak would have to send Rs 100 to Azhagiri Samy's family. But the doctors could not cure Azhagiri and suggested that he return home to Thanjavur. At the station, lying on a stretcher, a bleary-eyed Azhagiri said to a friend who was with him, 'Tell Anna Azhagiri has finally understood who his friends and who his foes are.' A few months later Azhagiri died penniless. Annadurai and his followers organized a massive cultural festival in his honour and collected Rs 6000, a big amount in those days, and handed it over to the bereaved family.

At a students' meeting in Thanjavur, Karunanidhi criticized Periyar, saying he had 'neglected to take care of Azhagiri Samy during his last days'. Periyar in turn issued a statement saying Karunanidhi should not be invited to any event or meeting. He also said that Anna must have asked him to say so. Karunanidhi writes that he was appalled at Periyar's statement but did not respond to it.

DK members wondered how this war would end. The answer, however, came from unexpected quarters.

~

Periyar, the Brahmin-basher, was a very close friend of the Vaishnavite Brahmin C. Rajagopalachari, even though they were sworn political enemies. When Periyar broke clay idols of Ganesha in the middle of the street, Rajaji, at that time chief minister of the Madras Presidency, ignored it. When Rajaji died in 1972, Periyar, old and confined to a wheelchair, went to the cremation ground and sat till the end, grief writ large on his face.

When Rajaji became Governor General of India, it was rumoured that Periyar and Rajaji had had a secret meeting at Thiruvannamalai in May 1949. Members of the DK were intrigued: what had the two met to discuss? Periyar kept mum for a few weeks.

On 19 June 1949, he published a statement in his paper *Viduthalai* (Freedom) that the meeting had been held to discuss his potential heir, for he was no longer able to travel and work as before and he could not see anyone taking on that responsibility.

Nine days later, on 28 June, he dropped the bombshell in a statement in *Viduthalai*: 'It is necessary and urgent for me to create a legal heir for myself and for my wealth and property. I have therefore decided to hand it over to Maniyammai, whom I have known for the past six years and who has gained my trust.'

It became clear that the seventy-two-year-old Periyar wanted to marry his thirty-one-year-old personal assistant Maniyammai. Kazhagam members were scandalized. The news of the marriage created a big furore.

Rajmohan Gandhi, grandson of Gandhi and Rajaji, writes in his book *Modern South India*:

> Some critics accused CR [Rajaji] of encouraging the marriage to discredit and divide the Dravida moment, but the truth was very different. Three months before the Thiruvannamalai meeting, EVR [Periyar] had written to CR announcing his intention of marrying Maniyammai and requesting CR to participate in the wedding as its sole witness.
>
> In a letter of 21 February marked 'Confidential' CR replied that he did not think that as Governor General he could quite play the proposed role, and he added some advice: EVR should consider, said CR, whether Maniyammai was capable, once EVR was no more, of looking after his estate as he would want her to.[5]

Just what happened between the two at Thiruvannamalai remains unknown. But Rajaji sent his best wishes when Periyar went ahead with his marriage on 9 July.

K. Veeramani, current president of the DK, says that Periyar's decision to marry Maniyammai was purely pragmatic – he needed someone in his old age who would be a loyal and trustworthy companion – and that their relationship remained platonic till the end.[6] Be that as it may, it brought matters to a head in the DK.

The members of the DK were now ready for the inevitable split. It is true that they were scandalized by Periyar's decision to marry a woman forty years younger but their main objection was that he had announced her as his heir and handed over the party funds to her. Many leaders had dedicated their lives to Periyar's movement and worked hard to raise funds for the party and they felt betrayed.

The first to leave the DK was Periyar's nephew E.V.K. Sampath. Many others followed his lead. Some in the Kazhagam wanted Periyar to be suspended. Anna pacified them, but after much consultation he and his supporters resolved to break away from the DK and form their own party DMK, based on the ideals of Periyar, but with an agenda to move forward on various issues.

On 17 September 1949, under torrential rain, the DMK was born at Rayapuram Robinson Park, marking the historic split with the DK. Launching the organization, Anna declared: 'Our very first duty is to oppose any government which attempts to suppress freedom to write and freedom of speech. In this, the Dravida Munnetra Kazhagam must be at the forefront and fight like an army. Come all of you!'

It was a momentous day. The members felt enthused and inspired but were still clueless about what the future held. They would rule the land where for decades the Congress had wielded power and the communists had strong support in several pockets.

Influenced by Periyar, and in an effort to crystallize a distinct linguistic and regional identity, Annadurai had at first sought to rally the Tamils around him on the planks of separatism,

Brahmin-bashing, playing up the glorious past of the Tamils and the exploitation of the south by the north. But by 1962, when Annadurai became a member of the Rajya Sabha, he had mellowed, his vision had widened and many could discern a broadening perspective full of promise. When war with China broke out and the nation's security was threatened, Annadurai gave up his demand for secession. But he was for a long time regarded as a secessionist by his detractors.

Says RMV, an ardent follower and admirer of Anna, 'When you read his writings and speeches now you may think he contradicted himself. But you must see it as an evolution in his thinking. In the 1930s, because of his association with Periyar he may have said certain things. But after 1945, you will see the change towards more mature politics. When you are starting a political campaign or a movement you do things more out of compulsion than out of conviction.'[7]

In 1945, one Narayana Pillai asked Anna, 'Do you think this separate Dravida nadu is possible?' Anna replied, 'As long as Nehru is alive it will not happen. After Nehru we do not know what will happen to India. So we should keep this issue alive.' But in 1962, he gave up the demand for a separate state. RMV says, 'Basically he was not an anarchist at heart. Periyar, on the other hand, said that only by severing the north's hegemony would the south benefit. But for Anna, the liberties of an individual could be achieved only through a well-entrenched constitutional nationhood.'

Annadurai later said in an interview that he believed 'the democratic setup envisaged by the Indian Constitution would be the safest'.

'After our association with Anna, we started realizing that Periyar's extremist approach to issues was not right,' says RMV.

'Atheism in Tamil Nadu will not work. That is why when Anna broke away from him in 1949 and started a new party, he stressed on the saying *Onre kulam oruvane devan*, [One community, one God] a line he took from the ancient Tamil text *Thirumandiram* by the Nayanar saint Thirumular.'

There were, of course, other reasons why Annadurai decided to part ways with his mentor. As mentioned earlier, Anna and his friends felt there was no point in agitation if it did not lead to political power. They wanted to contest elections and Periyar violently opposed the idea. Annadurai disagreed with Periyar's anti-national posturing like declaring Independence Day as a black day of mourning. The DK members were also unhappy with Periyar's autocratic style of leadership. When the historic split came and many members crossed over to Annadurai, Periyar chastized them as mere 'teardrops' that would sooner or later evaporate into thin air.

But Periyar was woefully mistaken. The DK had about 50,000 members, three-quarters of whom joined the new party, the DMK. Although the split had provoked bitterness, Annadurai declared that the two organizations would operate like 'a double-barrelled shotgun'. The office of party president was symbolically left vacant for Periyar. Despite such gestures to promote affinity, the ideas and ideals propagated by the DMK were in time to diverge quite significantly from Periyar's rigid views.

~

If the 1930s and 1940s involved a radicalization of the regional movement, the following two decades witnessed the opposite trend. The DMK softened its approach in most fields except language, which became the rallying point for regional sentiments.

Expressions of radical atheism were abandoned. The late Dr Parimalam, adopted son of Anna, said, 'Appa was practical. He said I do not run a party to prove that there is no God.'[8] The harsh rhetoric and actions against Brahmins gave way to a critique of Brahminism as an ideology and practice. When secessionist parties were declared illegal in India in 1963, the DMK publicly gave up its demand for a separate Dravida Nadu. Instead it chose to plead for more autonomy for the states. The time was ripe for the DMK's rise to political power. The momentum was again provided by the language issue.

4

The Rising Sun

In the two months after its founding in September 1949, the DMK saw an astonishing growth. The rising sun, its symbol, seemed appropriate as 700 branches with a total of 50,000 members sprang up all over Tamil Nadu. Karunanidhi was made a member of the propaganda unit of the party by Anna. He plunged into the task with great enthusiasm, but it was also an adventure that entailed considerable hardship. He had to travel a great deal, often with no money for even a cup of tea. He describes a train journey when he and his friend Kannadasan, a well-known poet, sat penniless and ravenously hungry, watching a fellow passenger in the opposite seat munching apples without offering them a piece.

On 2 May 1950, Madhava Menon, a minister in Tamil Nadu's ruling Congress government, announced that Hindi would be a compulsory language from classes one to six in all schools. A massive agitation began all over again, stronger than the earlier ones. The DMK had turned into an army. The government was rattled by their vigorous protests; many DMK members were arrested, beaten and jailed. But the protests continued unabated.

Within two months the government had to relent and modify its stand: Hindi would only be an optional subject.

It was their first victory, the DMK said. But protests continued in railway stations against the use of Hindi on trains and on the signboards of shops owned by north Indians. DMK and DK men applied tar over Hindi words written in railway stations. They could be seen working together at times. In Tiruchi, Karunanidhi and even Periyar blacked out Hindi words on the trains and railway stations. Periyar wished Karunanidhi well at one point during this campaign, saying that even if they had parted ways 'the affection remained'.[1]

To Karunanidhi, it was bliss to be alive during those days, charged with passion and a sense of mission. People, the young and the student community in particular, flocked to join the fledgling DMK despite the support the Congress and the Communists still enjoyed. With Annadurai as their leader, Karunanidhi worked tirelessly to build the party from the bottom up.

It was not easy, however, managing and controlling a party that grew so fast and so big. Factions and differences cropped up soon enough. Karunanidhi with his shrewd intelligence, was quick to address them, winning over people with a personal and conciliatory touch. The close relationships forged with the members during this period were an asset that would help him throughout his political career.

The Tiruchi branch of the DMK was particularly problematic. It was not expanding or working the way other branches did because of internal fighting. Anna was upset and refused to attend any public meeting in Tiruchi until the issue was settled amicably.

Karunanidhi and the others pleaded that it would be resolved only if Anna went to Tiruchi and addressed a meeting. Anna suggested that Karunanidhi be sent instead and if he succeeded, and if there was an indication that the branch was alive, only then would he go to Tiruchi.

Karunanidhi rushed to Tiruchi with his team and managed to bring the two warring camps together, telling them how hurt the leader was because of their quarrel. He reminded them of their goal, of the vision they had for Tamil Nadu, of their dreams to see Dravidian rule. They could achieve this only with the leadership that Anna alone could provide.

The reconciled groups came together and shouted in unison, '*Anna vazhga*!' Long live Anna!

The Tiruchi branch began their activities with renewed vigour and organized several meetings across the district. DMK flag-hoisting functions were held. Within a year the branch showed remarkable progress. A major problem they tackled was that of unsold handlooms. To help the poor weavers they had decided to buy the stock and sell it themselves to collect funds for the party. Anna volunteered to go to Tiruchi for the sale. Handloom goods that hardly had a market till then found a new market now with the help of the DMK. Later, in 1956, it was in Tiruchi that Annadurai decided the DMK would enter electoral politics, an important departure from Periyar's stand. It was also decided that the members must wear handloom clothes. Karunanidhi was assigned the responsibility of raising funds for the party.

~

Karunanidhi's family had now shifted to Salem. Life was a little more comfortable because he was once again earning through writing scripts for films. The owner of Modern Theatres,

T.R. Sundaram, said he wanted to make a film based on Karunanidhi's play *Manthiri Kumari*, and Karunanidhi was asked to write the script. The film was a box office hit, running for several weeks. Karunanidhi featured prominently in the credits, earning him renown in Tamil cinema for the first time. N.S. Krishnan, a famous actor who visited Salem and saw the film, was so impressed that he met Karunanidhi and requested him to write the screenplay and dialogues for his forthcoming film *Manamagal* (Bride) and also paid him an advance of Rs 10,000. The actor and the scriptwriter became very good friends. Krishnan persuaded Karunanidhi to shift to Chennai where he would get more opportunities to work in films. In 1951 Karunanidhi moved to Chennai.

~

The DMK did not contest the 1952 Parliamentary elections but extended their support to 'any candidate not belonging to either the Congress or the Communists, who has a progressive, intelligent bent of mind'. The Congress did not get a majority but formed a government under Rajaji, aligning with the Labour and Common Wheel parties.

In 1953 the DMK proceeded to fiercely oppose the government. The DMK was smarting from Rajaji's boast that he would crush the DMK like a bug. The DMK attributed this comment to his Brahmin arrogance. As it happened, Rajaji now announced a grand education project that smacked of casteism, according to the DMK. It was a modified scheme of elementary education called kulakkalvi thittam wherein students would go to school for half a day and learn the profession of their parents for the rest of the day,.

Rajaji told the Assembly, 'It is a mistake to imagine that the school is within the walls. The whole village is the school. The village polytechnic is there, every branch of it: the dhobi, the wheelwright, and the cobbler.'

It was his pet idea that this kind of education would lighten the child's burden while getting him equipped with his 'birth' skills. But this turned out to be a ball of fire handed over to the 'black shirts' (DK). Periyar ran with it across the country declaring: 'Here is proof from the old Brahmin's mouth. He wants to perpetuate the caste system.'

Rajaji refused to alter or withdraw. Annadurai and his DMK men took to the streets and Congress MLAs began to desert CR, quietly at first and then openly'.[2] They said that Rajaji's 'persistence will only sound the death knell of our party'. Most Congress MLAs now wanted K. Kamaraj, a humble Congress politician from Virudhunagar (he would later become president of the Congress party and also chief minister of Tamil Nadu), to replace Rajaji. Kamaraj too pleaded with him to give up his pet education scheme.

Finally, on 25 March 1954, Rajaji, rendered weak and pale by bronchial pneumonia, read his five-minute-long statement of resignation in the Assembly 'in a calm and clear tone'.[3]

Kamaraj took over and the education scheme was shelved.

~

The DMK also protested against 'Nehru's Delhi Sultanate' which had dismissed the Tamils' protests as 'nonsense'.

Another important protest was against the name of a small town in Trichi district, Dalmiyapuram, named after the Marwari industrialist Ramkrishna Dalmia. The DMK demanded that it be changed to its original Tamil name, Kallakudi, because they viewed the north Indian name as a sign of the north's economic oppression.

Karunanidhi geared up for this campaign with a dramatic plan and on 15 June 1953 led a group of twenty-five DMK members to the railway station. There they pasted the name Kallakudi on the station signboards, undeterred by the presence of armed policemen. The police did not try to stop them. Around ten in the morning, a train approached the station. Karunanidhi and four others lay down on the tracks, shouting, 'Tamil vazhga!' Long live Tamil! The police asked them to get up but they refused. Karunanidhi writes in *Nenjukku Needhi* that the train came very close before stopping and they were in real danger of being crushed under its wheels. The police pulled them off the tracks and detained them. Other DMK men then took turns lying on the tracks until they were lathi-charged a couple of hours later. Karunanidhi was sentenced to two months in jail and slapped with a fine of Rs 35. He went to jail but did not pay the fine.

Karunanidhi was hailed by DMK cadres as 'Kallakudi veerar', Kallakkudi's hero, and he must have felt like a real hero after the high drama of that day. But he writes that Annadurai was very annoyed with him for going beyond his brief and did not speak to him for days.

After he came out of prison Karunanidhi once again immersed himself in party work, constantly travelling and meeting members across the state. During one such journey, returning from a public meeting late at night, he met with a car accident. Perhaps the driver fell asleep; the car hit a milestone and overturned. Karunanidhi sustained a severe blow to his nose, which started bleeding. His right eye was hurt and his whole face began to swell. He proceeded to the next meeting but the pain was unbearable. His friends took him to Vellore Hospital. He was treated and advised not to read, write or attend public meetings for six months. But Karunanidhi could not abide by this for more than two months. There was a deadline to finish a play and he started writing again, which worsened the pain. He was again admitted to hospital and underwent no less than eight surgeries in the eye. The vision in that eye was almost 75 per cent gone.

To conceal that eye and also to protect it from the glare, he started wearing dark glasses. The north Indian media always made fun of the Dravidian leader with his trademark dark glasses, not aware of his medical problem. MGR – the matinee-idol-turned-politician – also started wearing dark glasses to hide his wrinkles, but Karunanidhi was singled out as the 'wily' Karunanidhi hiding his expression and his thoughts behind those impenetrable black lenses.

In 1957 the DMK entered the poll fray. N.S. Krishnan joined the election campaign and made three visits to Kuliththalai, from where Karunanidhi was contesting. Karunanidhi writes that the DMK was never under the illusion of defeating the Congress: 'The intention was to create a few cracks in the arrogant dictatorial fortress of the Congress.' The DMK won fifteen Assembly seats, including Kuliththalai, and two Lok Sabha seats. Annadurai became the leader of the Opposition and Karunanidhi an active and colourful member of the legislative party. The DMK's achievement was commendable, especially since the party had no experience of electoral politics and no financial backing.

Karunanidhi soon charmed the members of the Assembly, including those from the Congress, with his eloquence, wit and biting sarcasm. The reporter's gallery, which used to be almost empty because of the dullness of Assembly sessions started overflowing with journalists who now never missed the proceedings, especially when Karunanidhi spoke. At the end of the day there was always fun and laughter and friendly banter with him.

In 1959 the DMK emerged as the single largest party in the Madras Municipal Corporation elections, winning forty-five seats, and A.P. Arasu became the first DMK mayor of Madras. Karunanidhi writes in his memoirs: 'When he heard that forty-five DMK men had won, Anna looked at me and said, "But I have lost to you!"' The story was that Anna was not convinced when Karunanidhi, who was in charge of the selection of candidates, had said that the DMK would win forty-five seats. Karunanidhi challenged him: 'What if I prove what I say? What will you give me?'

'Anna smiled and said, "I will give you a sovereign worth of a gold ring." As promised, he presented me with a gold ring.'

Karunanidhi never removed that ring from his finger. It was still there on his finger when he died and was buried along with him.

But his detractors spun quite a few stories around that ring. Many in the party, less versatile and less hardworking, were extremely jealous of Karunanidhi's rise and also of the proximity he enjoyed to Anna. E.V.K. Sampath and Kannadasan had already accused him of diverting party funds to produce films. They felt that they had worked for the corporation elections as much as he had, and yet were not rewarded by the leader. Kannadasan writes in his book *Vanavasam* that when he complained to Anna that he was partial to Karunanidhi (by gifting him the ring), Anna said, 'Why don't you also buy a gold ring and bring it to me, I will present it to you!'

Karunanidhi's enemies believed Kannadasan's words.

But the truth now lies buried in the sands of Marina in Chennai, inside the casket where the man in dark glasses and yellow shawl rests.

When Karunanidhi's eye was badly damaged, the doctors advised him to travel by car with well-cushioned seats to prevent sudden jerks that could harm the eye. Karunanidhi, famous scriptwriter now, could afford to buy an expensive car. Sampath and Kannadasan said that he had bought it out of the party's funds. They also said that he was poisoning Annadurai's mind against them. Annadurai countered their charges as false and tried to bring them round but Sampath and Kannadasan left the party in 1961.

It was during those days of internal factions and rivalry that *Murasoli* became a daily. Karunanidhi felt the need to have a daily dialogue with the party cadres. He started writing a letter every day to the party brethren whom he called udanpirappukal (his blood brothers) – a practice he continued for fifty years. It was a strategy to make every DMK supporter feel that the DMK was a family, all born of the same womb, and sharing the responsibility for maintaining the family's honour and prestige. It was an emotional bond that he forged with the members, who came to regard him as the ultimate patriarch. The anti-Hindi agitation, in which he played such a dramatic and effective role, further cemented his bond with DMK members, and hugely enhanced his stature among the people of Tamil Nadu.

5

The Anti-Hindi Conflagration

While Periyar's Self-Respect Movement was primarily for 'personal liberation from ideas of caste', the language agitation that began as early as the 1930s was a potent expression of Tamil nationalism.

Periyar's movement brought social and cultural consciousness to large sections of the Tamil people and gave them a sense of common political identity.

It was, however, the DMK, which broke away from Periyar in 1949, that transformed Tamil nationalism into an ideology of mass mobilization.

Although the DMK had abandoned its secession demand during the India–China war in 1962, the party forcefully carried the message of Tamil nationalism forward and associated itself closely with Tamil pride. The concept of maanam (honour) was central to its discourses.

The 1960s saw terrible food shortages, for which the state's Congress government alone could not be blamed. But the DMK took maximum mileage out of it. Its message was simple and powerful. While the Communist Party raised the question of whether it was food or honour that was more important to human beings, the DMK argued that if a morsel of food and a strip of cloth were given to a naked and hungry captive on his release, he would go for the strip of cloth to cover his shame and preserve his honour, and only then look at his stomach.

The impact of this cultural and political message was reflected in the language riots of 1965, sparked off by a decision by the Central government to switch to Hindi as the sole official language in the country from 1965.

~

On the night of 25 January 1965 Chennai was busy preparing for Republic Day celebrations. But the air was tense with the news that the DMK would be staging protests against the imposition of Hindi on the Tamils by the 'insensitive' Central government. Late that night, all DMK leaders who had declared that Republic Day would be a mourning day were arrested as a precautionary measure and sent to jail by the state's ruling Congress government.

A couple of hours past midnight, people in the local office of the DMK in Virugambakkam in Chennai woke up with a start. Someone was screaming, '*Tamizh vazhga! Hindi ozhiga*!' Long live Tamil! Down with Hindi! It was like the scream of a wounded animal.

It took a while for them to locate where the sound was coming from. They rushed to the garden across their building, to see a man in flames. It was a horrific sight – a writhing, screaming human ball of fire. Before they could rush to his aid, the figure collapsed lifeless in a charred heap.

That was thirty-four-year-old V. Ranganathan of Perumal Koil

Street, a Post and Telegraph employee and an active member of the DMK. He was married and had three children. According to his friends, he had told them that on Republic Day he would do something 'peaceful' to protest against the 'Hindi imposition'. In the dead of night he soaked himself in petrol and set fire to his body.

The same night a few kilometres away in Kodambakkam, T.M. Sivalingam, a twenty-four-year-old DMK worker, immolated himself in much the same manner in a maidan. There was a letter near the body that said he was putting an end to his life as a 'protest against the imposition of Hindi and as a sacrifice at the altar of Tamil'.

The next morning, while all the agitating DMK leaders were behind bars, the students took over. They set fire to jeeps, buses, piles of Hindi books, a 20-foot effigy of the 'Hindi demon' and pandals decorated for the Republic Day celebrations. They picketed Congress offices and stoned the cars of ministers. The police tear-gassed processions in Chennai, Madurai, Coimbatore and Nagerkoil. Hundreds of students and DMK members were arrested. But the agitation continued and reached its peak on 10 February when two sub-inspectors were burnt alive by a frenzied mob in Tiruppur, a sleepy town near Coimbatore. The state had never witnessed such an orgy of violence before. Outside Chennai, on a single day twenty-four people were killed and twenty-five injured.

The Tamil Nadu government under the Congress chief minister M. Bhaktavatsalam felt justified in crushing the anti-Hindi agitation with brutal force. He accused the Opposition of instigating and misleading the students with its 'anti-national and communal' propaganda. The police opened fire on protesters in many locations, killing sixty-six, and attacked even peaceful public 'mourning day' gatherings. The excessive force deployed by the state government to quell the anti-Hindi agitation evoked widespread anti-Congress feelings and boosted support for the DMK, even among students.

In Delhi, Prime Minister Lal Bahadur Shastri was taken aback by the passions the issue aroused, terming the immolations 'new to this country'. He argued, 'By saying Hindi is the national language, I have not said anything new. It was decided in the Constitution that it would be so from the year 1956.' He failed to see why people were so agitated.

Shastri had not understood the Tamil psyche nor had he anticipated the violent reaction against the imposition of Hindi as the official language. He hastened to calm the situation. He assured the Tamils that they were free to use English or promote their own language and that no one would be forced to learn Hindi.

But despite the glorification of the Tamil language during these agitations, it was not love for Tamil alone that aroused the student community. During the first two decades post-Independence, the ruling Congress party was persistent in its efforts to introduce Hindi instruction in schools (Hindi was taught in all state-aided schools in Tamil Nadu under the Congress regime). The Tamil Congress members considered learning Hindi a mark of patriotism and an integral part of the 'Congress culture'. They argued that since, according to the Indian Constitution, the official language was to be Hindi by 1965, it made sense to learn the language early in non-Hindi-speaking areas. The Tamils felt they faced a unique problem – Tamil, unlike other Indian languages, was not derived from Sanskrit and was therefore very different from Hindi.

The compulsory introduction of Hindi was looked upon as a symbol of the devaluation of Tamil culture and language, which they felt was 'far superior' to the language and culture of the north. Many Tamils, who took pride in their language and culture, but who were also nationalists, desired indefinite retention of English as an official language along with other Indian languages. But the Congress government at the Centre was not going to accommodate such a request.

There were enough safeguards in the Constitution against any autocratic decisions taken by the Central government against the wishes of the people of non-Hindi-speaking regions. The Official Languages Act of 1963 provided for the continued official use of English by the national government, and for an assurance that Hindi would not be forced on non-Hindi-speaking people.

But the Tamil Dravidianists pointed out that the act contained enough clauses that indirectly pushed people to learning Hindi. Knowledge of Hindi was a qualification for recruitment to national government employment and a prerequisite for promotion, though not for recruitment; it introduced government service recruitment examinations in Hindi, but not in other Indian languages. The Tamils felt this gave an unfair edge to Hindi speakers over the non-Hindi-speaking Tamils and was a subtle means of persuasion to make Hindi instruction compulsory in non-Hindi-speaking areas whereas Hindi-speaking people were under no compulsion to learn any other language.

These provisions angered the students, most of whom were already under the spell of Tamil nationalism and Dravidianist rhetoric. When they took to the streets, the Centre, convinced the agitation was instigated by the narrow regional chauvinism of the Opposition (DMK), slammed it as unpatriotic and anti-national.

The Centre's inability to understand the Tamilians' frustration and anger and their pride in their own language and culture was to have a huge impact on the modern history of Tamil Nadu. And Karunanidhi, a rising star in the DMK, had already proved his courageous commitment to this issue in Dalmiyapuram in 1953 when he lay down on the railway tracks.

'Those who want to impose Hindi on the Tamilians must be made to realize their folly,' thundered Annadurai. He realized the great political gains the anti-Hindi agitation would bring to his party. It was a potent weapon that could be sharpened with the powerful rhetoric that he and his colleagues were so good at. He went on, 'They say making Hindi the common language in India would pave the way for unity in the country. I ask, can you say a common language spoken in Ireland, Scotland and England has helped create unity there?

'Is Hindi comparable to the richness and antiquity of our mother Tamil? Yet they have the audacity to impose it on us, a language which has neither history nor literary merit, and make us inferior to the north! How will a Tamilian be on a par with the north Indian by learning a language that he cannot master? Imposition of Hindi is a cultural invasion. A scheme to keep us subordinate to the north. Tamil is our life and breath. So let us prepare ourselves to give up our lives to save the honour of Tamil. Tamil is our birthright. It is a holy war that we are waging. Come all of you. Join this war!'[1]

~

The anti-Hindi agitation, coupled with the rise in the price of rice, catapulted the DMK to power in 1967 and changed the history and political culture of Tamil Nadu thereafter. None of the journalists or political pundits at that time even imagined that 1967 would be a watershed moment for Tamil Nadu. But the Assembly election results that year announced the rout of the Congress party which won just forty-nine seats, and the thumping victory of the DMK which won 138 seats, a clear majority. It came as a surprise even to the DMK. On 6 March 1967 Annadurai took oath as the first DMK chief minister of Tamil Nadu. Karunanidhi was sworn in as the minister for public works, housing, highways transport and sports. After 1967 the Congress would never again come back to power in the state.

The mood in the DMK camp was euphoric. Anna's first important act was to fulfil his poll promise to distribute three measures of rice for one rupee. Subsequently, laws were passed to change the name of the state to Tamil Nadu from the Madras Presidency to replace the three-language formula with a two-language formula – English and Tamil – which effectively banished the Hindi language and Hindi education from the state. Anna also made Self-Respect marriage legal. During Anna's chief ministership Karunanidhi, as transport minister, nationalized transport corporations, paving the way for cheaper and more effective connections within the state.

The DMK had delivered on its promises – and some more. Its victory was in essence the victory of the backward classes in a prescriptive and regimented society. Now, not only the DMK but the entire lower-caste Tamil society, including the Dalits, felt empowered.

~

The Congress, desperate to come back to power, stopped at nothing to criticize the DMK. It spread the story that the members of the

DMK had no morals; they were womanizers, and for them, having two wives, with one kept in the 'back lane', was the norm. The term 'chinna veedu' (small house), a metaphor for 'other woman', became a term of abuse and ridicule. Karunanidhi fell victim to such an attack.

According to common gossip Karunanidhi had a number of girlfriends. Women who heard him on public platforms adored his oratory skills, clever double-edged wit and easy laugh. He was famous as a scriptwriter. He was respectfully called Kalaignar. He and a young woman named Dharmambal, known as Rajathi, who was a theatre artiste, developed a close relationship. And the secret could not be hidden when Rajathi became pregnant. Karunanidhi brought her to Chennai from her home in Pennaadam in South Arcot district, took a house on rent and installed her there.

On 5 January 1968 Rajathi gave birth to a baby girl at the Durgabai Deshmukh Maternity Hospital. When the hospital asked the name of the father, she told the truth – M. Karunanidhi, minister for public works, Government of Tamil Nadu. The hospital authorities were rattled and informed government officials.

They in turn informed the chief minister. Annadurai was embarrassed. He was worried this would damage the reputation of his government and the party. When the Congress got wind of it they decided to create a storm in the Assembly. A Congress member interrupted the session with a dramatic question: 'Who is Rajathi?' It soon grew into a chorus, with Congress members drumming the desks and asking, 'Who is Rajathi?'

Annadurai took Karunanidhi aside and said, 'You either resign or admit the truth.'[2]

As the Congress continued their chant, Karunanidhi got up

and said, 'Rajathi is the mother of my daughter Kanimozhi.' The words, in Tamil, are in the state Assembly records.

The Congress members, perhaps taken aback by his blunt and unabashed statement, fell silent.

Annadurai must have been relieved that Karunanidhi came forward to admit to the relationship, and also that he had taken care of Rajathi and not forsaken her. He understood their relationship was not a casual one. Karunanidhi too was relieved that he had faced the belligerent Opposition members in the Assembly and quietened down about his private life. He felt he owed it to Rajathi to assuage any feelings of insecurity she may have had and declared publicly that she was his thunaivi (partner) while Dayalu was his manaivi (wife).

The entry of Rajathi into Karunanidhi's life must have caused shock and grief to his wife Dayalu, who had borne him four children. It must have been a stressful time for Dayalu, as well as for Karunanidhi who had to manage living with two women in two different houses. Karunanidhi split his day between the two women. He spent his afternoons and evenings in the CIT Colony house where Rajathi and Kanimozhi lived and went back at night to Dayalu and their four children in the Gopalapuram home, a modest, old-fashioned house, which would also be his official residence when he became chief minister.

Perhaps time helped all of them to come to terms with the situation, but it must have been hard for Kanimozhi as she grew up to bear the stigma of being the daughter of a man who was not legally wedded to her mother. She later revealed, 'A lot of people use it to hurt you. It is used as a weapon.'[3] She was a sensitive child, interested in poetry and literature. The relationship with the family in the other house was understandably not easy. But Kanimozhi, a Rajya Sabha MP from 2013 to 2019 (and now the

DMK's Lok Sabha MP from Tuticorin) seems to have evolved into a self-assured politician. She managed to rise above the hurt and prejudice she had faced earlier, to become a dependable supporter of her half-brother Stalin, now leader of the DMK, and the articulate voice of the party in the capital. This was possible, she says, because, 'My father has never made me feel alienated. He has never let my mother down either . . . There are many politicians who make mistakes and they try to hide it under the carpet or even hurt the person. Their children are neglected. I know children who do not have the courage to say who their father is because they may not live for another day if they did.'

Karunanidhi went out of his way to ensure his daughter felt loved and secure and was protected as much as possible from the jeers and slurs of Tamil society.

~

To the DMK party workers, Annadurai was the very epitome of the DMK's goals and ideals. He was admired as aringyar anna (the scholar) and peraringyar (the genius). For many, Annadurai was what drew them to the DMK and also the reason they remained in the party. They admired his wisdom, his warm personality and also his good governance policies. Annadurai did not live long to fulfil his promise. He died of oesophageal cancer, aged just sixty, in 1969, less than two years after he became chief minister.

When the government machinery and the Cabinet were almost paralysed with anxiety over Anna's life-threatening illness, the news came of a heinous atrocity in the remote village of Keezhvenmani in Thanjavur district. On the night of 25 December 1968, a mob descended upon a hamlet of Dalit agricultural labourers in Keezhvenmani and set fire to their huts.

The labourers had been demanding higher wages since 1966. The landowners refused, arguing that the harvest had been poor. When the labourers struck work, the landowners brought in men from other districts. Workers in Keezhvenmani protested and tried to prevent the outsiders from entering the area. This resulted in clashes between the two sides. The landlords were aware that the Communist Party of India-Marxist (CPI[M]) was backing the Keezhvenmaṇi workers. As the clashes continued, three members of the CPI(M) were killed. P. Ramamurthy, district secretary of the CPI(M), wrote a letter to the chief minister asking for police protection. Annadurai's response, at a public meeting, was: 'What threat can there be in this regime to the lives of Ramamurthy's partymen?'

The CPI(M) felt that this was a flippant, irresponsible statement, and the situation was indeed more serious than Annadurai thought. When the landowners' agent Pakkirisamy was killed, they were outraged. According to an eyewitness account the landlords surrounded the Dalit colony from three sides, cutting off escape routes and setting huts on fire. Forty-four men, women and children were burnt alive.

An ailing Annadurai was horrified and sent Karunanidhi and S. Madhavan, minister of law, to Keezhvenmani. It was Annadurai's first acid test as chief minister and his failure to judge the situation must have shaken him. After the report from Karunanidhi and Madhavan, he set up an enquiry commission under Ganapathiya Pillai, a retired judge. The commission recommended the government should make efforts to raise the wages of the farm labourers. Accordingly, the Tamil Nadu Farmworkers' Fair

Wages Act was passed in 1969, 'following which,' recalls Justice K. Chandru, retired judge of the Madras High Court, 'the farm workers in the western part of Thanjavur district got higher wages fixed than others in the state. And the farm labourer system was also abolished.'[4]

Though a number of people on both sides were arrested and jailed; the prosecution did a shoddy job in court, while the government remained preoccupied with Annadurai's health which had become critical. He died on 3 February 1969.

Keezhvenmani would remain a big blot on Annadurai's regime in the annals of Tamil Nadu.

6

Inheriting Annadurai's Mantle

'It was Anna's wish that Kalaignar take over after him.' K. Anbazhagan, a senior member of the DMK, was addressing a large crowd at Villupuram after Annadurai's death. 'Having seen Kalaignar's hard work, his writings, his service, his sacrifice, his sharp wit, his power of argument,' he continued, 'Anna had no doubts that Kalaignar would succeed him.' Anbazhagan then narrated an incident to prove his point: 'During a public meeting when Anna had to speak, he said, "I will speak first since I have to leave for some urgent work, and Karunanidhi will continue after that. I have written the opening history of this movement and he will write the latter part of it."'

'Why did Annadurai mention only Karunanidhi's name?' Anbazhagan asked the crowd. Why indeed, thought the crowd, unless Annadurai wanted Kalaignar to be his successor?

One of the jokes about the DMK and its highly disciplined cadres is that if Muthuvel Karunanidhi were to tell a party colleague to stand on his head in a corner, the latter would not ask why, but 'which corner'! Such was Karunanidhi's influence in the party, even before he became chief minister. But whenever there was a crisis, a challenge to his leadership, his dominant position had to be legitimized, and the only way of doing this convincingly was to emphasize Karunanidhi's standing with Annadurai, the founding father of the DMK. It was left to Anbazhagan, therefore, to convince the party of the legitimacy of Karunanidhi's leadership by invoking Annadurai's name. Perhaps this constant effort to establish the closeness between Annadurai and Karunanidhi arose from the fact that Annadurai had not explicitly named Karunanidhi as his successor, even when he knew his end was near. Annadurai may have preferred to let the party decide that democratically. He may also have felt that naming his successor would create a bitter feud in the party.

Actually the party's general secretary, V.R. Nedunchezhiyan, (who was also called Navalar [good speaker] by party workers) one of the five so-called founding leaders, was considered the number two in the party. A college-educated Vellala (a backward caste of people who were traditionally agriculturists), given to long-winded, meandering speeches, he stayed aloof from the party activists. In 1965, at the party conference in Tiruchi, Annadurai resigned from the post of general secretary of the DMK (it was at this conference too that the DMK decided to contest elections for the first time) and welcomed Nedunchezhiyan who succeeded to the post with the words, 'Thambi [younger brother], come. Come, to take over the leadership. We shall listen to your commands.' Many therefore interpreted this to mean that he regarded Nedunchezhiyan as his successor. But Annadurai habitually used hyperbole while referring to those who worked with him. He had, for example, described Nedunchezhiyan as a walking university and MGR as his idhayakkani (fruit of his heart).

Generous and voluble in showering praise on his colleagues though he was, he kept silent on the succession issue. When Annadurai was undergoing treatment for cancer and immediately after his death, Nedunchezhiyan was the acting chief minister. In the succession battle that followed Anna's death, however, MGR and Karunanidhi joined hands to keep Nedunchezhiyan out of the leadership race.

While Nedunchezhiyan appeared to enjoy Annadurai's favour, Karunanidhi had the support of all the district secretaries of the party, thanks to his organizational talents. Karunanidhi had displayed his matchless skills in building the party, raising funds, conducting election campaigns and directing agitations. As the party treasurer, Karunanidhi staged a number of plays written and scripted by him in all the districts, on behalf of the party. He was instrumental in collecting Rs 11 lakh during the 1967 general elections by charging an entrance fee during party meetings and election rallies. A portion of the collection was distributed among the party secretaries as a token of appreciation for their work. This helped him build a group of loyalists within the party.

Karunanidhi thus had the party under his control and reaching the chief ministerial chair turned out to be a cakewalk for him: 300 of the 383 members of the DMK's general council pledged their support to him. A number of party MLAs and ministers then arrived at Karunanidhi's house and insisted that he take over. Karunanidhi writes in *Nenjukku Needhi*, that he did not wish to take up the post. 'For me, who had been opining that Navalar should be the next chief minister, this sudden turn of events was painful.'

MGR, who would later become Karunanidhi's sworn enemy, was a major support for Karunanidhi during the succession battle. He invited the members over for lunch to his Ramavaram Gardens residence and convinced them that Karunanidhi would be the best choice for the post.

~

On 10 February 1969 Karunanidhi became chief minister of Tamil Nadu. He was forty-five years old, ambitious, with unbridled energy and a head full of dreams. Periyar, Rajaji, Prime Minister Indira Gandhi and several other leaders sent him their congratulations and good wishes. But, as Karunanidhi wrote in his autobiography, the English papers from the north, like the *Mail*, *Amrita Bazaar Patrika* and others, wrote highly damaging editorials calling him a 'terrorist', a secessionist and an anti-national who had led protests against the imposition of Hindi.

Karunanidhi felt uncomfortable starting his tenure with rumblings in a section of the party because he had superceded a senior like Nedunchezhiyan. The latter did not hide his resentment either. Karunanidhi pleaded with him to join the ministry. But Nedunchezhiyan wanted nothing less than the chief minister's chair. Then Periyar stepped in to help.

On 11 February 1969 Periyar wrote an open letter of advice to Nedunchezhiyan and the cadre of the DMK in Viduthalai, 'In this situation, what should not have happened is Navalar's discontent. If this discontent increases, it will be bad and result in enmity within the party. The chief minister's post does not belong to Kalaignar or to Navalar. That is the property of the Tamils. Navalar and Kalaignar are only trustees. I request both of them to understand this. I believe that no one should look upon this post with a sense of right or with ego. In public life, looking upon something as a right or with ego amounts to selfishness.'

In subsequent open letters in Viduthalai, he praised Karunanidhi, expressing his complete faith in him and asking Nedunchezhiyan to relent. Finally the latter gave in. After all, Periyar was his mentor too. Nedunchezhiyan became the minister of education and health and also the leader of the House.

In 1972 MGR disclosed what had transpired at a party meeting in April 1969 in which they discussed who should be the next chief minister. The majority, including him, said Kalaignar. Karunanidhi, however, expressed no such desire, even sending his nephew Maran to convey the news to them. His wife too sent the same message. He became chief minister because they did not give him a choice.

Nedunchezhiyan, however, charged that it was Karunanidhi's strategy to give the whole episode such an appearance and that he desired to become chief minister even when Anna was fighting for his life.

Bitter words from a disappointed man. Karunanidhi, though, was undoubtedly aware he was the party's favourite and there was no way he could lose the battle, especially when his dear friend MGR proposed his name. There would later be a bitter parting of ways between MGR and Karunanidhi. As R. Kannan writes, 'It was only a matter of time before competitive politics, ego, ambition and mutual distrust would turn these two friends into foes, allies into opponents.'[1]

On 26 July, 320 of the 326 newly constituted general council members chose Karunanidhi as the party's first president, a post that had been kept vacant since the DMK's formation in honour of Periyar. Nedunchezhiyan was chosen as general secretary and MGR as treasurer. On MGR's elevation as treasurer, Periyar remarked in private that Kalaignar had taken a step that he should not have. Periyar's remark would prove prophetic.

~

Once the dust had settled, Karunanidhi got actively involved in governance and speeding up reforms.

On 2 September 1969 he established the Justice Rajamannar Committee to formulate proposals for the state's relations with the Centre. This was an issue close to Karunanidhi's heart and one he pursued energetically. As a follow-up, on 22 February 1970, a meeting was held in Tiruchi at which Karunanidhi made 'five great declarations', one of which was autonomy in the state and federalism at the Centre.

On 15 September 1969 his government announced the Manu Needhi Thittam (justice for petitions). Under this scheme officials went directly to the people, collected their petitions and resolved their complaints on the spot. The success rate of the scheme was reported to be 92.2 per cent! The project helped the bureaucracy get in close touch with the people, thereby bringing in a culture of accessibility in the government.

The state's first Backward Classes Commission, the A.N. Sattanathan Commission, was set up on 13 November 1969.

Talking about Karunanidhi's early achievements, Justice K. Chandru says the most impressive was the amendment to the Tamil Nadu Land Reform Act of 1961. Quite a few industrialists and landowners supported the Congress party, which did nothing about land reforms. The Tamil Nadu Land Reform Act was passed in 1961, following massive agitations. According to the act, the maximum landholding of an individual was fixed at 30 standard acres. However, far too many of the landless and small landholders did not benefit from the reforms. Then, in 1970, Karunanidhi's government boldly reduced the cap to 15 acres. 'As a result, a large amount of land was taken over and distributed to agricultural labour and small landholders.'

On the economic front Karunanidhi declared that setting up industries was crucial for the state's prosperity. In March 1970 Karunanidhi managed to get the Centre's sanction to start the Salem steel plant in Tamil Nadu, thanks to an alliance with Indira Gandhi, the prime minister. When Karunanidhi became chief minister, Indira Gandhi had exclaimed, 'Who, Karunanidhi is the chief minister? Will he cooperate with the Centre? I have heard that he is a confrontationist.' Her apprehensions about him were to prove prophetic, but only a few years later. For now, they would be allies.

In 1971, acting on the recommendations of the Sattanathan Commission, Karunanidhi hiked the reservation for backward classes from 25 to 31 per cent and for scheduled castes and tribes from 16 to 18 per cent, taking the total reservation up to 49 per cent.

When Indira Gandhi came to Chennai few months later, to unveil Annadurai's portrait at Rajaji Hall, Karunanidhi addressed her concerns, famously saying, '*Uravukkuklai koduppom, urimaikku kural koduppom.*' Let us join hands in cooperation, let us lend our voice for rights. He proved his point by supporting Indira Gandhi's nationalization of banks, her candidate for president of India and the abolition of privy purses.

Meanwhile, trouble had been brewing between Indira Gandhi and senior Congress leaders. When it was time to elect the president of India in August 1969, after the death of Zakir Hussain midway through his term, Indira Gandhi wanted to support independent candidate V.V. Giri over the Congress party's official candidate Neelam Sanjiva Reddy. She had gone ahead with the nationalization of banks without consulting the finance minister, Morarji Desai. A split between Indira Gandhi and her rivals in the party seemed imminent, with two parallel Congress Working Committee meetings convened for the first time. When Nijalingappa, president of the Congress party, suspended Indira Gandhi from the party, the party split into two – the Indira-led Congress-R (Requisionists) and the Nijalingappa–Kamaraj-led Congress-O (Organizational).

Most Congress MPs went over to Indira Gandhi's side. But to sail through, she needed the support of regional satraps. Karunanidhi, quick to smell an opportunity, offered his support to Indira Gandhi, and also in the ensuing general elections, with a rider – the Lok Sabha seats would be fought by the Congress in alliance with the DMK, while the Assembly seats would be fought by the DMK without the Congress. Karunanidhi showed his extraordinary ability to bargain and arm-twist.

This was a turning point in Dravidian politics, which had so far been bitterly against the Congress party. But, keen as Indira Gandhi was for Karunanidhi's help, she was less eager to support his claim for state autonomy, something the members of her Cabinet did not appreciate either.

The perception that he was a secessionist was deep-rooted.

~

There was one DMK member who was increasingly causing Karunanidhi trouble – the man who had insisted that Karunanidhi should succeed Annadurai as chief minister. MGR's popularity was growing at an astonishing rate and he played a crucial role in the party's electoral success in 1971. Once Karunanidhi's friend and staunch supporter, MGR now often seemed disgruntled and questioned many of Karunanidhi's decisions. While it was easy for Karunanidhi to effectively undercut others in the party, MGR's appeal and mass base made him a formidable rival.

'In 1971 there was a party mahanadu in Madurai,' recalls RMV. 'MGR spoke, followed by Karunanidhi. More than a lakh people had come. After MGR finished his speech, the crowd started to leave. Karunanidhi was the president of the party. He was so shocked to see that his speech could not hold the crowd that he faltered and then fainted. This hard evidence of MGR's popularity over his own was too much for him to bear.'[2]

In the DMK culture, there are always a dozen speakers or more, and at all the public functions in which Karunanidhi participated, his speech was always the last. The faithful cadres were expected to clap and applaud whenever his name was mentioned by other speakers, and they were also expected to remain seated till Karunanidhi finished his speech, no matter how late it was. Going by the norms of that same culture, there could be only one thalaivar. RMV continues, chuckling at the memory, 'But MGR would deliberately come late to the venue and distract the crowd's attention. He loved to see the audience cheering him.'[3]

RMV says Karunanidhi was initially reluctant to invite MGR to campaign during the 1971 elections, believing that the DMK would win anyway. The Congress leader Kamaraj had hit the campaign trail, announcing that the DMK would not win and even if it did, it would only be by a slim margin.

'I impressed upon Karunanidhi that MGR should be roped in to campaign,' recalls RMV. 'MGR toured the state for fifteen days and that made a big difference. Kamaraj was right. In almost a hundred places the DMK won just by 2000 votes.'[4]

The DMK front, called the Progressive Alliance, included seven parties and won 205 out of 234 seats in the Assembly elections. The DMK captured 184 seats. Karunanidhi became the chief minister once again.

MGR believed Karunanidhi was beholden to him for this landslide victory and expected an important Cabinet portfolio. But Karunanidhi was in no mood to oblige. MGR was not happy with the post of party treasurer, which was largely nominal as Karunanidhi controlled party finances. There were quite a few people around MGR to goad him to demand what was his due as an idolized actor and a highly influential figure with immense mass following. Members of his fan club were restless, expecting political posts if he became a minister. When the election results were announced, MGR was shooting a film in Kashmir. Karunanidhi writes in his autobiography that MGR called him from Kashmir, shared his happiness about the party's victory and also expressed his desire to join the Cabinet. 'Come, we will speak in person,' said Karunanidhi.

By the time MGR reached Chennai – his arrival was delayed because he could not get connecting flights – the list of ministers had been released. Karunanidhi writes that MGR asked for the health ministry. MGR was still a busy actor. Karunanidhi was always eager to show that all the decisions were taken democratically by the party. He invited the members of the party high command and asked their opinion. Shanmuganathan, who was Karunanidhi's personal assistant till his death and was witness to the meeting says, 'The senior members said MGR could be inducted into the Cabinet if he gave an assurance that he would not act hereafter. I took the message to MGR and read it out to him. MGR was visibly angry and said, "That means they will not give me a Cabinet berth, doesn't it?"'[5]

Karunanidhi knew MGR would not give up acting since that was what connected him to the masses.

Playing characters who were generous, virtuous, valiant, strong, chivalrous and invincible for two decades was actually an image-building exercise for MGR, and people had begun to view MGR and his screen image as one. When the audience cheered him in movie theatres, he felt they were cheering him not just as an actor but also as a political leader.

MGR concealed his anger for a long time. In fact he praised Karunanidhi at every meeting. So Karunanidhi was puzzled when MGR's tone changed suddenly and he became belligerent in his attacks.

Karunanidhi writes in his autobiography that he felt betrayed and could not understand why such a good friend had turned against him. It was like a stab in the back. He writes that he understood later that it was the Congress working from behind the scenes, furiously scheming to create a split in the DMK.

To undermine MGR's base in 1972 he persuaded his eldest son, M.K. Muthu, to act in films he scripted, with the hero's character fashioned after the roles MGR played in his films. When Muthu imitated MGR's gestures in his films, people found him ridiculous. Muthu fan clubs were formed to rival those of MGR.

Karunanidhi's loyalists tried to pressurize some MGR fan clubs to turn into Muthu fan clubs, using financial inducements and police repression. Outraged MGR fans took to the streets and about 800 clubs threatened to disaffiliate themselves from the DMK, forcing Karunanidhi to disband the Muthu fan clubs. Muthu was a disaster as an actor anyway, and in the end he became bitter about the way his father had used him to challenge MGR.

On the governance front, Karunanidhi, in fulfilment of the DMK's vow to improve the lives of the poorest citizens of Tamil Nadu, continued introducing various schemes such as building tenements for slum dwellers, banning hand-pulled rickshaws and replacing them with cycle rickshaws, as well as a Rs 10 crore drinking water scheme.

But there were growing complaints about the government's arrogance and corruption in high places. Karunanidhi dismissed three of his ministers who were charged with corruption, but the complaints continued and reached the gates of Delhi.

~

The Congress, the CPI and the CPI(M) found their presence and influence eroded in the state after the DMK came to power with a brute majority. Members of the Congress party in Tamil Nadu especially felt a sense of shame and loss of face before the party high command.

Congress leaders from Tamil Nadu who held ministerial berths at the Centre, like C. Subramaniam and Mohan Kumaramangalam, launched a vicious tirade against Karunanidhi's corrupt government.

Karunanidhi writes in his autobiography, 'Delhi's eyes fell on my friend MGR. They needed someone who was strength for the DMK, but at the same time weak and incapable of handling hardships. MGR fitted the bill. They got in touch with him. Coaxed him with threats and also blackmail. MGR was confused. He would certainly not act against the Kazhagam. But he had to act as the Centre's puppet.'

Mohan Das, former DGP of Tamil Nadu, in an article he wrote for a Tamil journal in 1992, threw light on the Congress strategy at that time:

> We enacted a big drama in 1971 to wean MGR away from the DMK. DMK had fifteen MPs. Politically Karunanidhi was very powerful. He was fiercely advocating state autonomy. He also claimed that his was the best-administered state. All this reached Indira Gandhi's ears. She needed the support of the DMK MPs. But she also wanted Karunanidhi under her control. She decided that if the DMK were to split, it would ask for the support of the Congress. She asked her senior intelligence officials to work towards this. An important Congress official was sent to assist them. He sat with them and gave them a plan.
>
> When we looked at the DMK's top leaders, MGR was at the forefront. MGR was acting in a number of films and his income was high. Bearing this in mind, authorities such as the Income Tax Department, and the Enforcement Directorate targeted MGR and started their raids. He had just returned from abroad after a film shoot [*Ulagam Sutrum Valiban*]. They questioned him on his accounts in relation to this as well. He did not, however, know that there was a huge agenda behind these moves questioning him. I was sent to speak to him. He was depressed and worried when I met him. I drew him into conversation and suggested that to resolve his problems he should go to Delhi and meet

> with madam [Indira Gandhi]. I also suggested the name of a Congress functionary through whom he could meet the PM. MGR accordingly went to Delhi in the company of his lawyer and auditor.[6]

MGR went to Delhi and returned a changed man. He demanded control over the party's finances and in his capacity as the party treasurer asked for explanations of discrepancies in the party accounts. His request went unheeded. He publicly criticized the growing corruption in the party's ranks and challenged ministers and legislators to disclose the assets of their families and close relatives.

The DMK government had lost its idealistic sheen. Many of its leaders, at all levels, were looking after their own interests, and their activities went unchecked by the leader. MGR, more than anyone else, was aware of this and decided to embarrass Karunanidhi at public forums. He had thrown down the gauntlet.

The DMK executive, loyal to Karunanidhi and outraged at MGR's open criticism of him, demanded that MGR should express 'regret' for publicly shaming their leader. They would take no further action against him if he apologized. MGR refused to apologize, saying he had stayed true to Anna.

In response, the executive committee expelled MGR from the party on 10 October 1972.

Shanmuganathan, witness to these events as they unfolded, narrates what happened that day: 'Many in the Executive Committee wanted to expel MGR. Thalaivar [Karunanidhi] was very disturbed. He was obviously not in favour of that. The meeting went on and on and he said, "Let the matter cool down a little. We will decide tomorrow." Navalar then said, "I knew you would dilly-dally on the issue and therefore I have sent the news. I informed the pressmen standing outside that we have taken action against MGR. We have expelled him from the party." Thalaivar was shocked and said, "Why did you do such a thing?" and asked me to run and stop the news. But then the PTI [Press Trust of India] reporter Venkatraman said the news had already been sent to Delhi.'[7]

Navalar had seized the opportunity to hit back at MGR, who had prevented him from becoming the chief minister after Anna's demise.

According to Shanmuganathan, Karunanidhi felt Navalar should not have been so hasty. 'But Thalaivar realized that even if we had not expelled him, MGR would not have remained for long in the party. There was a Congress conspiracy in bringing about the split.'[8]

Now that news of MGR's expulsion had appeared in the press, Karunanidhi, as president of the party, announced at a public meeting that MGR had been 'thrown out of the party' for 'indiscipline'.

A week after his expulsion, on 18 October 1972, MGR announced the formation of a new political party, Anna Dravida Munnetra Kazhagam (ADMK), with his supporters and burgeoning rasigar manrams (fan clubs). The ADMK flag would have the same red and black colour of the DMK flag but with a picture of the founder leader of the DMK, Annadurai, in the Centre.

Karunanidhi put up a brave front, saying no party 'formed without any sacrifice, principles and basic organizational structure' could last long. The DMK, he said, was a fortress that could not be threatened by anybody.

Whether Karunanidhi realized it or not, MGR's expulsion would change the political landscape of Tamil Nadu for decades to come. 'It was an act of blunder,' wrote Cho Ramaswamy in *Thuglak*. 'Hereafter the votes will be with MGR and the party will be with Karunanidhi.'

Cho Ramaswamy had predicted what would happen.

'Karunanidhi underestimated his [MGR's] appeal', said Cho. 'I have travelled all over Tamil Nadu with MGR, and seen the crowd and its devotion to him. They saw him as a good man whose intentions were good.'[9]

Thereafter, politics in Tamil Nadu revolved around the rivalry between Karunanidhi and MGR and after MGR's death, between him and Jayalalithaa. And after Jayalalithaa's death, between the DMK and the AIADMK, as the ADMK came to be known.

7

MGR vs Karunanidhi

Karunanidhi was distraught over the fallout with his old friend MGR, though he tried not to show it, saying in public that MGR's new party was just an 'illusion'. He was too shrewd and seasoned a political player to underestimate MGR's phenomenal popularity – the man had transformed into an almost mythological figure.

Karunanidhi now became obsessed with devising ways to nullify the MGR challenge. Taking their cue from him, DMK leaders began to disparage MGR in every way they could. Karunanidhi did not stop them. They said MGR was a Malayali born in Kandy, Sri Lanka; he was not a true son of the soil, so how could he understand the aspirations of the Tamils? If he became the chief minister, they warned, Tamil Nadu would in no way be different from Kerala. Karunanidhi himself joked in the Assembly, 'We will not allow two Keralas in south India.'

The Tamizhar Pathukaappu Peravai (Forum for the Protection of Tamils) was launched to protect Tamils from the threat of Malayali dominance. It was commonly believed that its members were from the DMK. Though there were some incidents of violence against establishments owned by Malayalis, the group primarily targeted ADMK activists and theatres screening MGR's films. Karunanidhi insisted the DMK was not involved in these incidents, but no one believed him. And all the DMK's efforts to derail the growth of the ADMK failed. The violent activities of the DMK cadres or of the lumpen elements encouraged by them only damaged the image of the DMK and its leader. The anti-Malayali tirade did not gain currency. It was obvious even to the man on the street that it was directed against MGR.

Karunanidhi suspected that MGR had painstakingly formed and built up his fan clubs over the years to wrest political power from him. The members of MGR's fan clubs were not merely his film-crazy fans but also members of the DMK. They swore allegiance to their hero, ready to die for him. What if he hailed from Sri Lanka? What if he was born to parents who spoke not Tamil but Malayalam? He was one of their own, speaking their language and voicing both the anguish and joy of the poorest, most marginalized Tamilian. He had shown them, like no one before, how to combat everyday oppression. Watching him on the screen, his fans would personally experience their hero's trauma, his struggles and his ultimate triumph.

How carefully planned was MGR's strategy to win over the masses? How much political thinking was behind the creation of the myth?

The phenomenal rise and success of MGR as an actor and later as a politician, and the emotions that his name continues to evoke among the common people in the state, so many years after his death, remains the subject of much analysis.

~

Maruthur Gopalan Ramachandran was born on 17 January 1917 in Kandy, Sri Lanka. MGR's father Gopala Menon died when he was a child and left the family penniless. Ramachandran's mother, Sathya, moved to India with her children and settled in Kumbakonam, Tamil Nadu. The family was so destitute that hunger claimed the lives of his two sisters and an elder brother. Driven by extreme poverty, MGR began his acting career as a theatre artist at the age of seven and joined the Madhurai Original Boys Company, owned by M. Kandasamy Pillai. After a long struggle M.G. Ramachander, as he was then called, got a break doing small roles in mythological films, and then moved on to action films that became his forte. Though critics never thought much of his talent as an actor, his films broke records at the box office. He also won the national award for *Rickshawkaran.*

The social scientist M.S.S. Pandian attempts to explain MGR's extraordinary popularity and support among the poor in *The Image Trap*. Pandian argues that MGR carefully created a screen image that corresponded to 'the cultural presuppositions' of the subaltern, manifested in the folk-hero ballads. The typical MGR hero is a low-status underdog who acquires the power to dispense justice, uses education or literacy as a tool of his struggle to escape his circumstances, and defends women's honour. 'Given his carefully constituted image MGR effectively manipulated it to his own political advantage.'[1]

MGR projected himself as one of the oppressed on the screen but with the cinematic licence that he had he could dispense justice and even resort to violence and yet remain invincible. The audience never doubted his invincibility. Just as religious myths blurred the line that demarcated life and legend 'the cultic power of MGR films caused cinema and reality to merge'.[2]

The importance of MGR's association and identification with the DMK can hardly be underestimated. There is more to his tremendous popularity than his star status and his convincing portrayals of the invincible good guy with a winning smile that charmed the female audience.

The film producer RMV hints at how he and others close to MGR meticulously built his image and tried to place him on a pedestal as someone different from and more elevated than other leaders like Karunanidhi. 'All of us knew MGR's faults but we chose to ignore them. We were keen to project the positive side of him. Why is Karunanidhi alone thought of as a womanizer and not MGR? Because of the negative propaganda we did against Karunanidhi. It was also Karunanidhi's mistake to have underestimated MGR's importance to the party. MGR was not just a star riding on the DMK. He was an asset to the party, a colossal figure. And people did not take kindly to Karunanidhi attacking MGR. Such a colossal figure could not be challenged.'[3]

MGR's heroic image was strengthened by acts of charity off screen. He earned fame and adoration for his generosity and helpfulness. He was always the first to donate to disaster relief. He was always in the news for his donations to orphanages and schools. He had the ingenuity to distribute raincoats emblazoned with the DMK insignia to 6000 rickshaw pullers after torrential rains in Chennai. Sure, his generosity was well advertised. Poor and old women would be planted on the roadsides along the routes that MGR took and he would stop his car, hug them, pose for the camera and ask his assistant to put some currency notes into their outstretched palms.

Sara Dickey, an anthropologist, highlighted another factor behind MGR's political success: his support base in the network of his fan clubs. Dickey argues that the fan club activities helped to operationalize his image as a benefactor and friend. The fans were committed to promoting his name and fame and did so by advertising his films, engaging in election work, raising funds, and providing neighbourhood services. The clubs operated as a sort of volunteer corps of community service, 'advising authorities of fires, crimes, or electrical outages, cleaning blocked drains and dirty streets, providing shelter for flood victims, and handing out food and clothing to local residents'.[4]

They also served as mediators between local citizens and party officials. MGR himself said that the fan clubs and the party were not different. There were 15,000 MGR manrams with 18 lakh members enrolled. The fan clubs' work thus added substance to MGR's image, strengthened his altruistic reputation and solidified support for him.

RMV was right. Such a man could not be challenged. Karunanidhi realized this too late.

~

MGR, like one possessed, launched attacks against the Karunanidhi government for corruption at all levels. MGR's obsession appeared almost personal in the relentless way he pursued it. Justice Chandru narrates an incident during that period. Chandru was then a student leader in the Students Federation of India (SFI). There was a students' revolt in Tiruchi when two buses were burnt and the police was in search of two SFI students. They escaped to Chennai and approached Chandru for help. Since MGR was seriously attacking Karunanidhi, the three students sought his help to escape arrest. MGR heard their story. He asked them, 'How many buses did you burn?' The students nervously said, 'Two, sir.'

MGR said, 'You burnt just two? Go, burn more buses. Create more damage! Karunanidhi's government must be damned! Karunanidhi must go!'

Taken aback at MGR's response, the three knocked on the Governor's door for help, who immediately spoke to the police on their behalf.[5]

The ADMK organized meetings all over Tamil Nadu, demanding an enquiry commission to look into the several charges they levelled against the DMK government. They also demanded the dismissal of the government.

In November 1972 MGR went to Delhi and gave a memorandum to the President of India, seeking the appointment of a commission of enquiry against the entire Cabinet of the Tamil Nadu government, against all the district secretaries of the DMK, against officials who were specifically mentioned as corrupt and against officials who were involved in abetting corrupt ministers.

In just two months, MGR had shaken up the DMK. On 14 December Karunanidhi came up with a response to the charges and tabled it on the floor of the Assembly. Denying the allegations in toto, he described the charges as 'extremely frivolous, vexatious and false'. With his usual flair for catchy rhetoric he said, 'On hearing the loose talk of a washerman, Ram sent Sita to the forest; can Ramachandran send the DMK to the forest?' He further held that 'the state Cabinet is not accountable to the Union Government'.

Karunanidhi then went a mile further and declared that he conceded probity was an important issue. On 12 February 1973 he introduced the bill for Public Men's Conduct Enquiry Act.

The bill provided for a jail term of up to seven years if the person charged was found guilty. Any inauthentic complainant would be awarded three years in jail. The bill brought everyone, from the chief minister to members of the corporation council, former and present, under its purview. MGR understood that Karunanidhi was trying to checkmate him. He described it as a smokescreen for corruption even as the Jana Sangh's L.K. Advani, *The Hindu* and *Swarajya* lauded it. The bill was passed on 5 April. The ADMK voted against it.

It so happened that at this time the differences between Karunanidhi and Delhi were growing. Karunanidhi's participation, together with Opposition parties, in the Depressed and Backward Classes Conference held in Allahabad in October 1973, and his links with Jayaprakash Narayan (JP) who was bitterly opposing Indira Gandhi, were discomfiting to the Centre. On 29 January 1974 Karunanidhi complained that he was not consulted by the Centre on the India–Sri Lanka agreement on stateless people.

He also reiterated that Katchatheevu, the uninhabited islet in the Palk Strait between Sri Lanka and Rameswaram, was part of Tamil Nadu. Fishermen from both countries went there to catch shrimp. On 28 June 1974 Indira ceded Katchatheevu to Sri Lanka. It was agreed that 'the island falls under the Sri Lankan maritime boundary'. Karunanidhi recorded his opposition to this and conveyed the feelings of the people of Tamil Nadu to the foreign secretary. MGR, however, blamed Karunanidhi for 'failing to protect the rights of the fishermen of Tamil Nadu' and said he should resign.

To this day the AIADMK blames Karunanidhi for 'gifting away' Katchatheevu to Sri Lanka, as a result of which the Tamil fishermen forfeited their right to fish in the surrounding area and risked getting caught or shot at or imprisoned by the Sri Lankan navy when they strayed beyond the international maritime limits.

~

By 1974 the Centre was becoming alarmingly authoritarian. As MGR was busy acting in films, Karunanidhi was upping the ante against Indira Gandhi. Soon the battle lines between Karunanidhi and MGR became more sharply drawn. In April 1975, at a public meeting with the CPI(M) and CPI Karunanidhi called on 'all parties to come forward to prevent Indira Gandhi's attempts to silence all political parties and establish dictatorship'. His arch-rival MGR, on his part, had joined hands with Indira Gandhi and her Congress party.

Karunanidhi invited JP, who was spearheading the Opposition against Indira Gandhi, to declare open the Rajaji Memorial. On the eve of JP's visit, MGR published an open letter requesting JP to advise Karunanidhi to either consent to an enquiry into the corruption charges or conduct a referendum on Karunanidhi's governance. Karunanidhi responded that if JP were to point out the shortcomings of his government, the DMK administration would take corrective action.

On 6 May 1975, at a public meeting at the Marina in Chennai, JP described the language of MGR's charges as low and bitter, saying that it was easy to make accusations but difficult to prove them. Besides, JP added, Karunanidhi was willing to discuss the charges with the Opposition and was ready for an impartial probe into them. After all, he had enacted the Public Men's Conduct Enquiry Act.

On 12 June 1975 the Allahabad High Court struck down Indira Gandhi's election from Rae Bareli, citing campaign irregularities. While her opponents demanded her resignation, Karunanidhi said he would appreciate it if she quit voluntarily. MGR, on his part, issued a melodramatic filmy style statement: 'Should this fate befall the mother in the cradle of democracy?'

On 25 June Indira Gandhi imposed a state of national Emergency, justifying it as necessary to protect the country from a conspiracy by reactionary forces.

Karunanidhi was alarmed, though he had had a hunch that something ominous was about to happen. On 27 June the DMK executive passed a resolution expressing its 'anguish' and termed the Emergency as 'the inauguration of dictatorship', which Karunanidhi himself had drafted in the early hours of that morning.

The next day two presidential ordinances denied judicial recourse against arrests and exempted the Central government from providing reasons for an arrest. A number of Opposition leaders were arrested and put behind bars.

M.K. Stalin, Karunanidhi's son, who was twenty-three years old at that time, recalled later at the fortieth anniversary of the Emergency, that two emissaries from Indira Gandhi informed Karunanidhi that even if he did not support the Emergency, he should not oppose it and if he did so his ministry would be dismissed. Stalin said, 'Our leader gave a categorical reply, "I am a student of Anna and Periyar. I will never support dictatorship. The DMK will always stand for democracy," and he sent them away.'

Soon thereafter, Karunanidhi and senior DMK leader Nedunchezhiyan met K. Kamaraj of the Congress(O). Kamaraj was a highly respected leader in Tamil Nadu, and he was extremely upset by what was happening under the Emergency. Karunanidhi recalls

Kamaraj exclaiming in despair, 'The country is lost! The country is lost!' When Karunanidhi asked Kamaraj if his government should resign in protest, Kamaraj advised him against quitting. He said that Tamil Nadu and Gujarat were the only places in the country where one could still breathe the air of democracy.

On 6 July 1975, at the Marina in Chennai, Karunanidhi delivered a hard-hitting speech. He asked the mammoth crowd assembled there to take a vow to defend democracy and called on the prime minister to release the Opposition leaders and restore press freedom.

On 31 January 1976 President Fakhruddin Ali Ahmed signed an ordinance dismissing the DMK ministry. Just that evening, hours before the ordinance was signed, at an event at the Don Bosco School in Chennai, Karunanidhi, ever the astute reader of political undercurrents and omens, forewarned that this would possibly be the last event in which he would participate as chief minister.

8

The Emergency and the Rise of MGR

Karunanidhi recounted the events of that day in graphic detail in *Nenjukku Needhi*.

After the event at Don Bosco School, Karunanidhi went to his home in Gopalapuram. When he alighted from the car he saw his sister's sons Amirtham and Selvam standing at the entrance of the house, each holding a piece of paper in his hand. They said to him, smiling, 'They have dismissed the government.' The paper they held was a printout of the news of his dismissal from the PTI. Karunanidhi smiled too and said, 'The big suspense is over!' He immediately sent his official car back to the secretariat. His administrative staff at the house were upset, many of them in tears. He pacified them and went upstairs to call his friends and colleagues to inform them of his dismissal. He found the phone had already been disconnected.

The relationship between the DMK and the Congress-ruled Centre had never been easy. Indira Gandhi continued to hold that the DMK was a secessionist party. Karunanidhi, on his part, couldn't see why the democratically elected state government needed Delhi's permission even to repair a ceiling in the secretariat building. For years he had demanded greater autonomy for the states, and in 1969 he had gone to Delhi for the same.

The Rajamannar committee that his government set up to study the matter, had, after consulting various agencies from all over the country, submitted its report in May 1971, which concluded that the demand for greater autonomy by the states was justified and not a threat to India's integrity and sovereignty.

Karunanidhi engaged with the other chief ministers of the south to strengthen the case for state autonomy. To work out a strategy for Tamil Nadu's development projects he formed a planning commission, much like the one at the Centre. He obtained the right for the chief minister to hoist the Indian flag at Fort St. George, Chennai, on 15 August. Until then it was the Governor who had hoisted the flag.

Such displays of regional assertiveness disturbed Indira Gandhi, who was looking for reasons to dismiss Karunanidhi's government. She resurrected the corruption charges that MGR had listed in his memorandum some years earlier and asked the Governor of Tamil Nadu to investigate the issue.

Governor K.K. Shah's report charged the DMK administration with maladministration, corruption and misuse of power for partisan political ends. The most glaring charges in the Governor's report appeared in his references to the DMK's shrill demands for autonomy and its leadership's militant speeches. 'Some of the DMK leaders have already given a threat of revolution in Tamil Nadu if the life of the state Assembly is not extended.'

India Today reported in its cover story that fortnight, 'When some of his [Karunanidhi's] more foolish supporters began to describe him as another Mujibur Rahman it was time to call his bluff.'

Not surprisingly, MGR hailed the dismissal of the Karunanidhi government as a 'courageous act' that was welcomed by the AIADMK. But almost the entire media in Tamil Nadu denounced it as murder of democracy. Several DMK members were taken into custody under the Maintenance of Internal Security Act (MISA). The army was posted at Fort St George to prevent any files from being removed.

The police came to Karunanidhi's house looking for Stalin but he was in Maduranthakam, acting in a propaganda play. The next day Karunanidhi himself called the police to come and take his son into custody. The police also wanted his nephew Murasoli Maran – his sister's son, who was an active member of the DMK and Karunanidhi's close confidant. And when Murasoli Maran arrived in Chennai from Delhi the following day, Karunanidhi once again told the police to come and get him.

Karunanidhi appealed to his party workers to maintain peace in the spirit of duty, dignity and discipline, even as 500-odd DMK leaders were arrested, many of them brutally beaten up. Stalin later said in an interview that they could not approach the courts for relief because MISA was a draconian act. He was thrown into jail with Maran and former state electricity minister Arcot Veerasamy. They were forced to sign letters stating that they were no longer DMK members and attacked when they refused. This went on for three months. DMK MP Chitti Babu died in prison. Arcot Veerasamy lost his hearing in one ear and Murasoli Maran sustained a back injury that never healed completely.

On 3 February 1976, Annadurai's death anniversary, Karunanidhi wrote an article in *Murasoli* titled 'Those Who Could Not Place Wreaths at the Anna Mausoleum'. It was his allusion to the 25,000-odd DMK members who would normally have come to the memorial but were not there because they had been arrested after the dismissal of his government.

This was surely a traumatic period in Karunanidhi's political and personal life. The Governor's report was a devastating indictment of his administration. His son Stalin, Maran and several close associates were in prison. Within the DMK, many started seeing him as a liability. S. Ramachandran, who later joined the AIADMK, claimed that a sizeable section of the party wished Karunanidhi and some ministers would resign from the DMK, to prevent the party from disintegrating. 'Give me poison instead,' said a pained Karunanidhi. 'I must thank Indira Gandhi for having made me aware who my friends are.'

Justice Chandru had started practising as a lawyer around that time. As a student he had been a human rights activist. He went to see Stalin and the CPI(M) members who were in jail, documented the miserable conditions in which they were kept and submitted his report to the authorities, following which some basic amenities were given to them.

Justice Chandru says, 'The Emergency changed the CPI(M)'s views about Karunanidhi. They saw him as a true democrat, not afraid to raise his voice against dictatorship. Since the Emergency provisions were more strictly and severely imposed in the rest of the country, it was only in Tamil Nadu that the CPI(M) could continue with their activities. It became a place of refuge for many political fugitives. During Emergency Karunanidhi regained the reputation he had lost.'[1] The Opposition parties all over India, including the Rashtriya Swayamsevak Sangh (RSS), regarded him with new respect.

But in Tamil Nadu, humiliation continued. One day as he was leaving his Gopalapuram residence, officials from the revenue department stopped him and asked him if the house had been purchased after he became chief minister.

Hurt and angry, Karunanidhi simply replied, 'This house was bought in 1956. Doesn't MGR know that?'

The *Murasoli* office was raided. Then Rajathi's house was raided. When he entered the house where Rajathi and Kanimozhi stayed, officials who knew him very well were now asking, 'Who are you? What is your name?'

The Emergency had emboldened the police and the Enforcement Directorate, the latter because of the Sarkaria Commission enquiry. N. Ram speaks about the farce that took place in the name of the Sarkaria Commission:

> Soon after MGR submitted a memorandum to the President in November 1972, asking for the appointment of a commission of enquiry to look into his allegations of corruption against Karunanidhi, MGR's ally, M. Kalyanasundaram, a CPI veteran, submitted two more memoranda containing further corruption charges. Nothing much happened by way of follow-up until the promulgation of the Emergency and the dismissal of the DMK government on 31 January 1976, ostensibly on the issue of corruption. Barely two months before the dismissal, two former DMK leaders who had joined MGR's camp had submitted a fourth memorandum. Within days of the undemocratic dismissal, a Supreme Court judge, Ranjit Singh Sarkaria, was appointed to function as a one-man commission to enquire into the twenty-eight allegations of corruption and misuse of power. Most of these charges had been gathering dust for more than three years.

> The whole exercise, carried out under the authoritarian Emergency regime and featuring selective leaks spiced up by official propaganda, turned out in the end to be a futile affair.[2]

The twenty-eight allegations ranged from irregularities in allocating tenders for government projects to non-payment of tax. A few charges stood out prominently. One concerned Anbil Dharmalingam, minister for local administration and agriculture in Karunanidhi's Cabinet. Prior to becoming a minister, he was allegedly not an income tax assessee, as he did not own any property. But he became noticeably wealthy after he became a minister. Wealth and a number of properties had been accumulated in the names of Dharmalingam's relatives, sons and wife. The main charge against him was that Nathan Publications, in which he was a partner along with another DMK member, received the contract for printing school textbooks in certain districts of Tamil Nadu. From 1970 to 1976 Nathan Publications did big business, despite lower bidders in the same district with more experience. It was said that Nedunchezhiyan, who was education minister, facilitated the contract.

Karunanidhi was accused of receiving bribes for signing off on murky deals, including for the sale of the Samayanallur thermal power plant, the aerial spraying of pesticides for crops and other such schemes that favoured his cronies.

In none of the cases, however, was the Central Bureau of Investigation (CBI) able to produce any valid documents to prove that the deals were illegal, or that money had been given to Karunanidhi.

One much-talked-about case was the Cuddalore Veeranam Drinking Water Project. It was alleged that the project was given to the Sathyanarayana brothers who did not have any prior experience and that one of the brothers was a close friend of Murasoli Maran. A huge advance was paid to them but the project did not take off. When MGR came to power the project was completely dumped and buried. The Sarkaria Commission said that while there was no evidence that Karunanidhi had accepted a bribe, allegedly to the tune of Rs 45 lakh, he must be held responsible for the loss to the exchequer.

When MGR was questioned by the commission, it emerged he was not aware of the list of allegations in the memorandum that the government had sent in his name.

In its first report submitted on the eve of the 1977 Lok Sabha elections, the Sarkaria Commission held that six of the seven allegations it had looked into had been proved, wholly or in part. The Indira Gandhi government, which was facing an election debacle, let it be known that it would institute legal proceedings against Karunanidhi and his colleagues. Sarkaria had reportedly labelled the dismissed chief minister and his close associates masters of 'scientific corruption', a phrase Jayalalithaa would later pick up during her successful campaign for the 2011 Tamil Nadu Assembly elections.

When the four volumes of the final reports of the Sarkaria Commission were eventually published in 1988, most of the remaining twenty-one allegations were held to be groundless or unsubstantiated. As N. Ram says, 'They turned out to be a damp squib. Now the prejudicial political circumstances, the haste with which the 1976 exercise had been conducted, the inconclusive and laboured nature of evidence turned up, the public perception that all this was a political vendetta enacted through a command quasi-judicial performance, and above all the electoral rout of the

Emergency regime, ensured that the corruption charges against the DMK and its top leaders were buried. The whole exercise only served to undermine the credibility of enquiry commissions.'[3]

~

Just as suddenly as the Emergency was declared it was brought to an end by Indira Gandhi on 21 March 1977. She announced that general elections would be held.

Karunanidhi aligned with the socialist group of political parties which came together under the name Janata Party. The DMK was in no shape to face the Assembly elections. The people of Tamil Nadu, it seemed, did not think much of the DMK's and Karunanidhi's ideological opposition to the Emergency. Because of press censorship, they were not aware of the large-scale arrests, or the suffering the arrested went through in prison. In the elections that followed, the state chose to place its faith in their matinee idol. MGR swept to power with his AIADMK winning 144 of the 234 seats. The DMK managed to get just forty-eight seats in the Assembly. In the Lok Sabha elections, the DMK–Janata Party–Congress(O) won just five seats while the AIADMK–Congress(R) combine won thirty-four seats. But the Congress lost at the Centre and the Janata Party came to power.

MGR continued in power till his death a decade later in 1987 except for a brief period of six months when Indira Gandhi came back in power and dismissed his government on 31 January 1980, along with other state governments that had aligned with the Janata government.

For the next thirteen years the DMK remained out of power in Tamil Nadu, only coming back in 1989. For those thirteen years

Karunanidhi performed his duty as the leader of the Opposition diligently, but many top DMK leaders crossed over to MGR's party. Yet the DMK did not disintegrate.

~

In the run-up to the elections in 1977, MGR had successfully discredited the DMK and Karunanidhi. His campaign revolved around the Sarkaria Commission report and its interim findings, which stated that Karunanidhi and his ministers were indeed guilty of corruption.

MGR worked his charisma on his besotted audiences, who believed what he said about Karunanidhi. They made no distinction between MGR the politician and MGR the film hero and his onscreen image – the kind, compassionate friend of the poor, protector of damsels in distress. They worshipped him blindly, mesmerized.

MGR's first tenure, from 1977 to 1980, was by all accounts corruption-free. He picked up the former Congress chief minister K. Kamaraj's idea of the midday nutritious noon meal scheme for children studying in government schools, which gave children hot, cooked lunch at school every day. The idea was to increase the enrolment of children in schools by poor parents who would otherwise send their children out to work. MGR's government expanded the scheme from rural to urban areas as well. Attendance at primary schools reportedly went up to 96.2 per cent among the six to eleven age group and to 66.03 per cent in the eleven to fourteen age group. So popular was the scheme that successive governments built upon it. Jayalalithaa once famously said MGR should be given the Nobel Prize for introducing such a far-sighted humanitarian scheme. MGR also distributed free tooth powder and free footwear for the children. The poor deified him.

But the clean government proved too good to last. The MGR government relaxed prohibition on liquor consumption. The creation of the Tamil Nadu State Marketing Corporation (TASMAC), vesting it with a monopoly on the wholesale supply of Indian-made foreign liquor, was widely perceived as a brilliantly innovative way of financing the state's welfare schemes, especially MGR's ambitious midday meal programme which in time became a model for other states to follow. Less known at that time was the stream of illicit revenues that began to flow from the favoured owners of distilleries and breweries into a political fund that was now at the disposal of MGR who as chief minister ruled his party and Cabinet with an iron hand, suppressing any stirrings of dissent.

Karunanidhi often wondered at MGR's ability to emerge unscathed from allegations of corruption. He wrote in his autobiography, 'However much the Opposition shouted about the alleged scams under his rule – the rectified spirit scandal, the shipping scandal, corruption in the selection of district wholesale arrack dealerships – nothing stuck to MGR.' Justice Chandru recalls that MGR, and later Jayalalithaa, repeatedly described Karunanidhi as theeya shakthi (evil force) at all public forums, and such was their charisma that people believed what they said.

Comparing the governance styles and achievements of MGR and Karunanidhi, Justice Chandru says, 'There is absolutely no doubt that Karunanidhi was a great administrator. He was genuinely concerned about social justice. When legislative amendments were proposed he studied them carefully, and once he took decisions he immediately carried them out. I say this from my own experience. MGR and Jayalalithaa stand nowhere near him for administrative skills.'[4]

~

Karunanidhi's life during his years out of power carried on as usual. His private secretary Shanmuganathan recalls, 'He would get up at four-thirty every morning whether he was in power or not. Before I reached his residence at seven-thirty, he would have finished reading all the newspapers, practised his yoga, had his bath and written his daily letter to the cadres that he published in *Murasoli* . . . Throughout the day he would be busy with work or meetings till he went to bed at eleven at night. He would read till midnight. When the Assembly was in session he would prepare for the debate like a school student. He would pore over documents, often through the night. During such times it would appear as if another spirit had entered his being. He looked more excited and creative when he was the leader of the Opposition.'[5]

Even after the DMK's thumping defeat, Karunanidhi was not disheartened. As leader of the Opposition, he would debate and argue in the Assembly with his trademark wit and quick repartees, his answers well researched, whatever the subject under discussion. Records of Assembly proceedings of that time provide ample evidence of his oratory prowess and sharp intellect.

All through MGR's successive regimes Karunanidhi never let MGR rest, yet underneath his combativeness, vestiges of the decades-old friendship and affection remained. 'He had no enmity towards MGR,' says Shanmuganathan. 'I have seen it myself. When

MGR was ill and hospitalized, he wrote in *Murasoli*, "I am also praying," and when he dictated it, I saw tears in his eyes. When MGR died he cried all night.'[6]

Durai Murugan, senior member of the DMK, narrates an incident from 1985–86, when MGR was the chief minister, and Madras University decided to honour him with a doctorate. Durai Murugan was a member of the syndicate of the university and all honorary doctorates had to be approved by the syndicate. Even one veto would mean that the doctorate would not be given. 'Thinking that I would not agree, the principal planned in secret to get the signatures of the syndicate members just a few hours before MGR arrived [when it would be difficult for Durai Murugan to veto it]. I heard about this plan the night before. So around 1 a.m. I went to Kalaignar's house, woke him up, told him what the principal's plan was, and asked him what I should do.'

'Kalaignar did not pause to think. He said, "There is no enmity between me and MGR. Only a difference in opinion. Don't oppose the doctorate, which is being given to him for his good deeds."'[7]

On the advice of his leader, early the next morning, to the astonishment of the principal, Durai Murugan himself proposed the honorary doctorate for MGR at the syndicate, which was approved unanimously.

AIADMK leaders too speak of how MGR demonstrated his respect for his arch-rival. MGR once slapped an AIADMK leader when he took Karunanidhi's name. (Calling a revered person by name is regarded as disrespectful in Tamil Nadu.) 'Who are you to call him by his name? What status do you have? I myself call him Kalaignar.' Another time when MGR was in a car with some of his trusted friends, Jeppiar, who went on to become a liquor and education baron, allegedly used foul language to describe Karunanidhi. This angered MGR so much that he stopped the car on the highway and asked Jeppiar to get out and walk back to Chennai.

~

In the 1977 general elections the Congress lost miserably and Indira Gandhi was defeated. The Janata Party came to power in Delhi with Morarji Desai as prime minister. But his regime did not last long, due to the contradictions within the party and the clashing ambitions of the socialist and Jana Sangh factions. His government was reduced to a minority as the faction led by Chaudhary Charan Singh, who had prime ministerial ambitions, broke up the government with the help of the socialists and declared open revolt. There were also allegations of financial irregularities against Morarji's son Kanti Desai. Morarji's reluctance to act against his son baffled his own supporters. During the heated debate in Parliament on the confidence motion, Desai submitted his resignation even before the vote of confidence. Chaudhary Charan Singh took over as the prime minister in July 1979. He had to prove his majority within forty days. He courted MGR's eighteen MPs and offered them ministerial positions. MGR agreed, saying that he was in favour of stability at the Centre. He always supported whichever government was in power at the Centre. But Charan Singh's government fell in less than two years, in January 1980.

General elections were held again in 1980. Angered by MGR's support of the Janata Party under Charan Singh, Indira Gandhi now turned to the DMK for an alliance in Tamil Nadu.

She sent a feeler to Karunanidhi asking him to forget the past. Karunanidhi now did a somersault. Just a few months earlier, when Indira visited Madurai, the DMK had staged a huge protest rally, waving black flags. In the mayhem that ensued the DMK was charged with an attempt to murder Indira. Moreover, the party still nursed the wounds of the physical and mental torture that many DMK members suffered during the Emergency. As Karunanidhi said in his autobiography, lakhs of the DMK cadres tended the bloody scars caused by the Indira government's cruelty with one hand and held black flags in their other hand.

But now Karunanidhi was quick to see the benefit of befriending Indira Gandhi, who he calculated would be back in power.

His opponents criticized him when he went to Delhi to apologize for the DMK's protests in Madurai. Karunanidhi's response was to unabashedly declare that one should forget and forgive since Indira herself had openly apologized for the excesses committed during the Emergency. Karunanidhi now reached out to her at a public meeting in Chennai, with the words, 'Nehru's daughter, come! Give us a stable rule!' The words in Tamil were delivered with his usual panache as a catchy rhyme: '*Neruvin magale varuka! Nilaiyaana aatchi tharuga.*' Not everyone approved of Karunanidhi's new support for Indira. Cho Ramaswamy said Karunanidhi did it to smartly wriggle out of the Sarkaria Commission enquiry. Some of his party members disapproved too. But Karunanidhi was right in his prediction that Indira Gandhi would win the elections.

Fed up with the succession of unstable governments, the voters brought Indira Gandhi back to power at the Centre. In Tamil Nadu, the DMK–Congress(R) alliance won thirty-seven out of the thirty-nine Lok Sabha seats, while MGR who had aligned with the

Janata Party came a cropper, winning just two seats. Karunanidhi said MGR had lost people's confidence. He pressed the Centre to dismiss MGR's government.

Indira Gandhi never forgot nor forgave MGR's betrayal. It was now time for vengeance. She dismissed all the state governments that had aligned with the Janata government. MGR's government was dismissed on 31 January 1980 on charges of corruption and abuse of authority.

Indira Gandhi continued her alliance with Karunanidhi in the May 1980 Assembly elections, perhaps thinking their victory in the parliamentary election was an indicator that MGR had lost his appeal. But both she and Karunanidhi were proved wrong when the voters of Tamil Nadu brought MGR back to power with a massive mandate.

It was during this period, starting from the early 1980s, that the Sri Lankan Tamil problem drew the attention of Tamil Nadu politicians. Both the leading players, MGR and Karunanidhi, felt it was their bounden duty to extend their support to fellow Tamils across the Palk Strait. Karunanidhi did not realize then the serious consequences this would bring. As the saying goes in Tamil, 'it became like a snake coiled round his feet'.

9

The Long Shadow of Sri Lanka

When Karunanidhi became chief minister for the first time following Annadurai's death in 1969, he proudly announced that he had chosen a hymn in praise of Tamil Tai (Tamil mother) to be sung at all government functions. The song, *Neerarum Kadaluduththa*, composed by Professor Sundaram Pillai, became in effect the anthem of the state.

The metaphor of the Tamil language as mother and the Tamils as her children strengthened the emotional appeal of the language issue, evoking feelings of devotion to the mother tongue and serving to unite all Tamils, irrespective of caste, gender and even borders. The involvement of Tamil Nadu and its political leaders in the Sri Lankan Tamil issue should be seen in this context.

Before the 1980s, there was little popular concern in Tamil Nadu about discrimination against Tamils in Sri Lanka. But 1981 onward, the harrowing stories narrated by Tamil refugees arriving in Tamil Nadu, the burning down of the famous Jaffna Public Library over 31 May–1 June 1981 and the week-long anti-Tamil violence in Sri Lanka aroused widespread anger and sympathy for the Sri Lankan Tamils. Soon thereafter, MGR and Karunanidhi met Indira Gandhi separately in Delhi, urging the prime minister to protect Sri Lankan Tamils.

Several militant Tamil groups sprang up in the Jaffna area to fight the Sri Lankan government. The ethnic issuc took a more serious turn in 1983, when hundreds of Sri Lankan Tamils were killed in a systematic pogrom that shocked the world.

The Dravidian party leaders competed with each other in supporting and patronizing the rival militant Sri Lankan Tamil groups, many of whom took refuge in Tamil Nadu. To many observers, both in Delhi and in the state, the demand for eelam (a separate homeland for the Sri Lankan Tamils with full statehood) was reminiscent of the demand for Dravida Nadu.

Activists of the DK, the DMK and smaller Tamil parties forged close links with Sri Lankan Tamil militant groups and conducted an extensive drive throughout Tamil Nadu to build public awareness and support for their cause. The DMK demanded protection of the civil rights of Sri Lankan Tamils and came out in support of eelam in its manifesto. Karunanidhi asked pointedly, 'If the Centre can support the Palestinian struggle for a homeland, why does it not back the movement for a Tamil eelam?'

The AIADMK under MGR also spoke up for their Tamil brethren in the island nation, and they supported agitations for the Sri Lankan Tamil cause, at least partly in order to contain Karunanidhi who tried to project himself as 'thamizhina thalaivar' (leader of the Tamil community). The Congress government at the Centre too aided MGR's efforts. As chief minister MGR could give more patronage to the militants and had thus won over the Liberation of Tamil Tigers for Tamil Eelam (LTTE). He got them to promise not to take any help from the DMK. But though MGR did not officially support their demand for Eelam, he reportedly provided armed support to their secessionist movement.

There were, however, limits to the empathy with which people of Tamil Nadu regarded Sri Lankan Tamils. Though Dravidian activists referred to Sri Lankan Tamils as 'blood of our own blood', this was perceived by the general public as mere rhetoric, since there were historical and cultural differences between the Tamils of India and Sri Lanka. The ancestors of the Sri Lankan Tamils had migrated from India more than a millennium ago. Even the Tamil spoken in Sri Lanka was different. Moreover, the Sri Lankan Tamils felt superior to the Tamils of Tamil Nadu and had scant respect or sympathy for the Indian Tamils living in Sri Lanka's hill country, who had been sent to the tea estates of Kandy by the British as indentured labour two hundred years ago.

Gradually, sympathy in Tamil Nadu declined because the Sri Lankan refugees brought violence and unrest along with them. Suddenly, country bombs began exploding in rural areas of Tamil Nadu, while thefts and loot were on the increase in urban areas. The Sri Lankan guerrilla groups were engaged in a fratricidal war. There was general public apprehension at the speed with which the groups, especially the LTTE, were spreading their network all over the state by the late 1980s.

Karunanidhi had been disillusioned with the militant groups even earlier, soon after he convened the Tamil Eelam Supporters Organization (TESO) conference on 4 May 1986 in Madurai, inviting leaders from all over India. The idea was to advise all the militant groups whose goal presumably was the same – to strive for a separate Eelam or for greater autonomy in governance – to come together. N.T. Rama Rao, chief minister of Andhra Pradesh, Atal Bihari Vajpayee, H.M. Bahuguna and leaders from Punjab,

Kashmir and Karnataka attended, all with one pertinent question. They agreed that the Sri Lankan government's repressive actions needed to be condemned and they must all jointly impress upon the Indian government to take this up with seriousness. But were all the militant groups together?

Karunanidhi assured them of having categorically told the groups to work together. They had given him their word and he believed them.

On what basis did Karunanidhi give this assurance? He had no direct contact with Velupillai Prabhakaran, leader of the LTTE. It was MGR who was his patron – he allegedly gave Prabhakaran Rs 4 crore and forbade him to have any dealings with Karunanidhi. All the journalists in those days knew the assurance given by Karunanidhi at the Madurai conference was merely to play to the gallery and not based on any substance.

The Sri Lankan Tamil militants believed the Indian Tamil leaders would help them realize their cherished dream of a separate eelam. But beyond giving covert assistance in kind and cash, the leaders of Tamil Nadu had no power to decide the fate of Tamils who were subjects of another sovereign country with its own democratically elected government. Still, both MGR and Karunanidhi tried to score points over each other as champions of the Sri Lankan Tamil cause and viewed the eelam campaign with an eye on the elections.

Though Karunanidhi was genuinely concerned about the plight of the Tamils in Sri Lanka, he felt the LTTE had betrayed his trust more than once, by resorting to violence. He recalled, 'We were all moved by the Tamils' plight. Those boys, Prabhakaran and his companions, looked so innocent and gentle in their manner. But when their violent deeds came to light, I was absolutely shocked and repulsed.'[1]

Karunanidhi knew Sri Sabaratnam, leader of the Tamil Eelam Liberation Organization, and had become fond of him. When he got information that Sabaratnam had been captured by the LTTE and was to be executed, Karunanidhi urgently called up 'Baby' Subramaniam, the head of the LTTE's education division, to tell him that Sabaratnam was like his brother, even closer than his brother, and he should not be killed. Soon thereafter, he was shocked to learn that Sabaratnam had been tortured and killed on 6 May 1986, just two days after his TESO conference in Madurai. He was all the more outraged because the LTTE had done so even though he had interceded on Sabaratnam's behalf, and this led to a loss of face before all the leaders who had attended the TESO conference out of respect for him.

~

Rajiv Gandhi, then prime minister, wished to solve the problem by persuading the militant groups and the Sri Lankan government to come to the table for a dialogue. Sri Lankan President J.R. Jayewardene didn't like the Tamil Nadu chief minister MGR and other leaders giving arms and cash to the LTTE. The LTTE, the most ruthless of the groups, was the stumbling block. Since Prabhakaran had received a lot of help from MGR, he was expected to listen to him. But Prabhakaran was not amenable to holding any talks, and MGR asked the Tamil Nadu IGP Mohan Das to confiscate all the weapons given to Prabhakaran. In protest, Prabhakaran went on a fast. Fearing it would upset prospects of a peace accord the Centre announced it was neither consulted nor informed. Karunanidhi too joined the bandwagon and criticized MGR's orders against Prabhakaran.

While Karunanidhi had often spoken against the LTTE's violence, he was against the arms being taken back from them, which according to him had been given for their self-defence in the civil war in Sri Lanka.

Faced with criticism from the Centre and fearing the consequences of Prabhakaran's fast, MGR retreated and the weapons were handed back to Prabhakaran.

India then held talks with the Sri Lankan government to try to negotiate peace between them and the militant groups. MGR, as chief minister of Tamil Nadu, was called for the talks, and asked to negotiate with Prabhakaran. Prabhakaran remained steadfast in his refusal to participate in the peace talks, and MGR returned to Chennai disappointed. Nevertheless, the Indo-Sri Lanka Peace Accord was signed on 29 July 1987 in the presence of the other militant groups in Colombo.

Four days later, at a meeting convened by the Congress party at the Marina in Chennai, MGR (his party was once again an ally of the Congress) lauded the decision to send the Indian Peace Keeping Force (IPKF) to Jaffna for the protection of the Tamils. The same week, on 5 August, MGR left for the US for medical treatment. MGR had been ailing for more than three years and it was clear he would not live much longer.[2]

Delhi believed that MGR would eventually succeed in persuading Prabhakaran to agree to the accord, but this did not happen. When MGR died on 24 December 1987, a month after his return from the US, Prabhakaran issued a note of condolence:

'He was like a brother. We could not have grown so much without his help.'

~

What the Indian government did not expect was that the LTTE and the IPKF would battle each other. Prabhakaran and his followers were convinced that the IPKF had been sent to undermine their position. The general public in Sri Lanka had initially welcomed the IPKF, but with constant conflicts between the IPKF and the LTTE, they were now wary about its presence. The LTTE's news bulletins carried horrifying accounts of army excesses. Human rights activists and pro-LTTE Tamil nationalists took to the streets of Tamil Nadu.

Under pressure to react, Karunanidhi, once again chief minister, spoke critically of the Indo-Sri Lanka accord and severely condemned the excesses of the IPKF. He had once requested the Centre to send the Indian army to protect the Tamils of Sri Lanka. Now he demanded that it be called back.

In 1989, V.P. Singh became the prime minister, heading the Janata Dal coalition government after Rajiv Gandhi and the Congress were defeated in the general elections held that year. V.P. Singh realized that sending the IPKF to Sri Lanka had been a mistake and asked them to return to India.

One of the greatest disasters of Indian diplomacy came to an end on 24 March 1990. IPKF commander Lieutenant General A.S. Kalkat said, 'We came as a proud force and are leaving as a proud force.' But in reality the Indian soldiers came back unsung and unwanted, demoralized and disheartened. For over two protracted years the IPKF soldier had fought a war he did not want to, a war he did not understand, a guerrilla war he was not trained to fight. Many saw their colleagues blown to smithereens by landmines. As many as 1155 soldiers were killed and 2984 wounded, according to official figures. In no war had the Indian army lost so many personnel. And it was no longer an official secret that the IPKF was also caught in the crossfire of petty ego battles between the Intelligence Bureau and the Research and Analysis Wing.

The withdrawal of the IPKF was the LTTE's moment of glory. They had convinced the then president, Ranasinghe Premadasa, that they could talk peace only after the IPKF left. Premadasa fell for the ruse and asked the Indian troops to leave. Clearly the LTTE was back in control. In fact, they were in control even before the IPKF quit. The jawans who returned said they had been holed up in their camps for many days before they left. The Sri Lankan army helplessly looked the other way as aggressive LTTE cadres patrolled the streets.

When the IPKF troops landed in Chennai in 1990 Karunanidhi, who was chief minister, refused to go and receive them. He felt compelled to keep up his image as 'the protector of the Tamil community'. Though he had expressed his disapproval of the LTTE's ruthless killings of fellow militants and Sri Lankan leaders, it was a grave misjudgement on his part to have encouraged the LTTE to roam freely and spread their wings in Tamil Nadu, not realizing it would be a threat to the security and sovereignty of the country as a whole. N. Ram observes, 'There was no love lost between Kalaignar and Prabhakaran' as he was 'very moderate and was against violence'.[3] Yet why Karunanidhi hesitated to take strict action to curb the militants even when he was in power is a question that remains unanswered.

To many Tamil nationalists in Tamil Nadu, Prabhakaran became a cult figure; Sri Lankan Tamils became the 'blood of our blood'; Tamil Tai shed copious tears over the misery of her children in Sri Lanka, and it was the duty of every Tamilian worth his salt to wipe her tears. Karunanidhi was wrong to assume this was the prevailing public sentiment. Armed Sri Lankan Tamil militants of rival groups roamed the streets of Tamil Nadu and broke into brawls and gun-fights in the open. All these militant groups had their own camps, virtually prohibited zones for outsiders. Their internal feuding on Tamil soil continued unchecked until Karunanidhi's government was jolted out of its delusions by the murder of a rival militant leader, Padmanabha of the Eelam People's Revolutionary Liberation Front (EPRLF), and thirteen others in a flat in Kodambakkam, one of Chennai's busiest areas, on 19 June 1990.

The Congress and the AIADMK now clamoured for Karunanidhi's resignation. It was widely believed that the murderers were allowed to escape with the full knowledge and support of the chief minister. Karunanidhi's weak assurances that he had condemned the killings did not hold much water. Nor was his riposte that all those who wanted his resignation should also demand that Sri Lankan President Premadasa ensure the safety and security of innocent Tamils who were being killed by the Sri Lankan army every day. 'If Mr Premadasa concedes the demand of Sri Lankan Tamils and proclaims the constitution of separate Eelam,' he declared, 'I might consider the demand for my resignation.'

Six months later, on 30 January 1991, the Central government invoked Article 356 and dismissed Karunanidhi's government. Among the reasons cited for imposing president's rule was that 'it perceived [the situation] as the DMK ministry's failure or reluctance to act against Sri Lankan Tamil militants, who apparently have a free run of the coastal areas in Tamil Nadu. The Centre's repeated efforts to prod the DMK government into firm action against the extremists yielded no results.'

The Tamil Nadu press reacted sharply to the dismissal, calling it a partisan decision. And DMK party workers gathered in large numbers in front of Karunanidhi's house, shouting slogans against the Centre's action. But when just a few months later, in May 1991, Rajiv Gandhi was assassinated during his election campaign by an LTTE suicide bomber at Sriperumbudur, thirty-eight kilometres from Chennai, Karunanidhi must have felt relieved he was no longer chief minister. Nevertheless, a section of the Jain Commission report on the assassination indicted Karunanidhi for having created a conducive atmosphere for the terrorists in Tamil Nadu to carry out their murderous schemes.

Whenever Karunanidhi was interviewed and there was a reference to the Sarkaria Commission that had enquired into the charges of corruption against him, he would get irritated, but whenever there was a reference to the Jain Commission report on the assassination of Rajiv Gandhi he would look disturbed and nervous. He felt the LTTE, whom he had vociferously supported, had betrayed his trust, and he was ashamed for being taken in by their false assurances of not carrying out acts of violence on Tamil Nadu soil.

During a private conversation a few years later, he confessed how shocked he was when Prabhakaran and his gang had killed Padmanabha of the EPRLF and his men. 'I trusted them,' he said. 'We were all genuinely moved by the Tamils' plight. I was too shocked when such a massacre happened right here in our streets.

From then on I decided to have no more truck with Prabhakaran and his associates. I stopped seeing or talking to them.'

In the 1991 elections to the Lok Sabha and the Assembly following Rajiv Gandhi's assassination, the DMK was handed a humiliating defeat. The voters brought to power the Congress at the Centre, and Jayalalithaa of the AIADMK in Tamil Nadu, giving her a massive mandate. Her detractors attributed her victory to the sympathy wave generated by Rajiv's assassination. A sympathy wave may have swept other parts of the country, but as far as Tamil Nadu was concerned it was a vote against terrorism and the DMK, which the people thought was indirectly responsible for Rajiv Gandhi's murder.

~

Some six years later, in 1997–98, the dark shadow of Sri Lankan Tamil terrorism continued to fall on Karunanidhi and the DMK, and even on the government at the Centre. When the Jain Commission's interim report was released, the DMK was part of the United Front government under Prime Minister I.K. Gujral. The Congress, which supported the minority United Front government from outside, was unwilling to support the DMK's participation in the Central government if the interim report held it responsible for their leader's death. The Congress firmly believed that Rajiv was killed as a result of the DMK's politically motivated laxity towards the Sri Lankan militants. When the Congress sent its ultimatum to Gujral to drop the DMK ministers from his Cabinet or face withdrawal of its support, he waited for the DMK ministers to resign. When they didn't, he sent in his resignation to the president and the government fell.

To view Karunanidhi or Justice M.C. Jain as responsible for the Central government's fall would be an oversimplification. The findings of the interim report did not come as a real surprise to those who were following the proceedings. Jain's indictment of the DMK was not taken seriously even by its worst detractors. Besides, the indictment could not be taken as proof of the charges. Karunanidhi therefore had no reason to succumb to the Congress's pressure and withdraw his men from the Gujral Cabinet. The Jain report, in a sense, was merely a convenient pretext for the Congress to unsettle a fragile coalition. A sordid game of bluff and brinkmanship, with Karunanidhi as its pawn, led to the collapse of the United Front government. The country headed for a snap general election in 1998 that the majority of the Lok Sabha did not want.

The final report of the Jain Commission absolved Karunanidhi of all the charges it had made earlier, saying there was no valid proof that he had helped the LTTE. But the interim report had done enough damage, and turned the public against him.

The Sri Lankan issue was indeed a tricky wicket on which Karunanidhi had to play. He realized he had made mistakes – most notably, he had failed to understand the minds of the terrorists, had seriously misjudged them, and rather naively trusted them. There were a few in his own party who had direct dealings with the LTTE, but this was without his knowledge. He bore many wounds of betrayal and must certainly have feared meeting a violent end himself.

Gopal Gandhi, in his obituary essay on Karunanidhi, recalls that during the height of Sri Lankan Tamil militancy Karunanidhi had had his hands more than full, dealing with competition from Jayalalithaa even as he almost single-handedly ran the government. And to make matters more complex for him, explaining to the people of Tamil Nadu how and why India–Sri Lanka relations were a foreign policy matter and foreign policy was the prerogative of the Central government was just about impossible. He was on the cusp of India's federal dilemmas. A lesser politician could have played politics on that fluid crest, but Karunanidhi as chief minister was going to do nothing of the kind.[4]

Gopal Gandhi quotes Karunanidhi as privately saying to him that he was perplexed by Prabhakaran: 'Nobody knows Prabhakaran's mind. Nobody from our side is in touch with him. Nobody can be. We used to know his deputies . . . now they are all dead . . . assassinated. But militancy is no solution. Secession will never be countenanced by Sri Lanka . . . And it will never be given up by Prabhakaran . . . he will never have a change of heart. We grope in the dark . . . Yet, we have to keep trying for our Tamil kin's urimai [rights] there.'[5]

The Tamil nationalist pro-LTTE groups and the AIADMK held Karunanidhi responsible for the killing of thousands of innocent Sri Lankan Tamils by the Sri Lankan army during their civil war with the LTTE, saying he did not put enough pressure on the Centre to stop the bloodshed when the DMK was part of the United Progressive Alliance (UPA) government from 2004 to 2009. They alleged that the UPA government headed by the Congress supplied arms to the Sri Lankan army and Karunanidhi was party to it. These allegations are unfair.

The Centre's archives reveal that the UPA government had indeed made serious efforts to bring the war to an end in their discussions with the Sri Lankan government and Norwegian peace negotiators. Representatives of various human rights organizations were also present. It was proposed that if Prabhakaran surrendered, he and his family would be assured safe asylum. But even when the

LTTE had become weak due to the prolonged war, Prabhakaran did not agree. Had he, thousands of lives would have been saved, including those of his family's.

'Since this was classified information it was not made public,' says MP Ravi Kumar, human rights activist and spokesperson of the Dalit party Viduthalai Chiruthaigal Katchi. Karunanidhi was well aware of the offers made to Prabhakaran, but 'as chief minister, Karunanidhi was bound by the oath of secrecy he was under. He did not speak about it or defend himself when he was cornered by his opponents,' explains Ravi Kumar. [6]

~

To see how the Sri Lankan Tamil problem continued to dog Karunanidhi in his final years, one must jump ahead by a decade. The civil war in Sri Lanka became intense in 2008–09. Karunanidhi again appealed to Prabhakaran to accept a settlement through dialogue as the problem could never be solved militarily. But Prabhakaran did not comply.

Karunanidhi was eighty-five years old, mentally and physically exhausted. When news came of the huge massacre at Mullivaikkal in Sri Lanka on 18 May 2009 in which thousands of Tamils were killed, he was devastated. He went on a hunger strike, sitting at Anna's mausoleum. The Centre was worried and within a few hours Pranab Mukherjee, then finance minister, called to persuade him to give up the fast since the war was over and President Rajapakse had promised that no weapons would be used against the Tamils.

The Opposition ridiculed Karunanidhi, saying that he started his fast after breakfast and ended it before lunch.

The very next day, on 19 May 2009, Prabhakaran was killed in an ambush at Mullaitheevu.

Shanmuganathan says that Karunanidhi 'was devastated when he heard the news'. He admired Prabhakaran's passion for his cause, even though he abhorred his violent means which included terror attacks and assassinations and led to the deaths of thousands of innocent civilians.

The Sri Lankan government fought the final battle against the LTTE with single-minded determination, disregarding human casualties and human rights violations. The cry from President Rajapakse to the man in the street, was belligerent and unequivocal: 'The Tigers/Prabhakaran should go!'

As the civil war in Sri Lanka reached its endgame, Karunanidhi was eighty-six and powerless to do anything to mitigate its brutality. His opponents screamed that he had betrayed the Tamils. It was hard to bear. Worse, he could not now claim to be thamizina thalaivar (leader of the Tamils).

That sorrow came to Karunanidhi in the last decade of his life, but the decade before that had been a turbulent one, when he had had other problems to contend with. So we must now roll back to December 1987 and the events that unfolded after the death of Karunanidhi's close-friend-turned-main-political-rival, MGR.

10

A Woman Scorned

MGR, the founder of the AIADMK, did not give any thought to the future of his party, which he had founded and completely dominated. He had started his party to oppose Karunanidhi, to hit back at the man whom he had helped so much and yet who did not give him a ministerial berth, to show Karunanidhi that MGR, his bête noire, would be his nemesis. He went on to be the chief minister for a decade and more, and sent Karunanidhi into political oblivion. His goal achieved, MGR did not seem concerned about who his successor would be nor about the chaos his death would create. He might well have said to himself: 'After me, the deluge!'

But despite their enmity, Karunanidhi was grief-stricken at the death of his old friend.

R. Kannan writes that Karunanidhi heard the news early in the morning when he was on a train returning from Periyar. He went straight from Chennai's Egmore station to MGR's house, his heart full of grief and poignant memories of their time together at Singanallur, the suburb of Coimbatore where they had been such close friends. The news had still not spread widely, and Karunanidhi was allowed in to bid his emotional personal farewell to MGR. Karunanidhi was right when he later wrote that if he had not gone to MGR's house immediately on hearing the news, he would never have been allowed to pay his respects, for the enmity between the two parties had become so deep.

As the news of MGR's death spread, Chennai succumbed to grief and anarchy. Crowds began pelting stones, burning buses and vandalizing images of Karunanidhi. The sight of their venerated leader in his trademark fur cap and dark glasses lying lifeless on the flower-bedecked gun carriage hit the surging, sobbing crowds like a hammer blow. '*Thalaivar, nee sollame poittiye*,' they wailed. Leader, you have gone without telling us.

Doordarshan cameras also captured a young woman, grief clouding her lovely face, making a desperate attempt to climb on to the gun carriage to place a wreath, and being pushed aside rudely by some AIADMK men, their words spitting venom – go, prostitute, out with you!

It was as if Tamil Nadu had stepped into a cinema screen and become part of an MGR movie.

This public humiliation would be a catalysing moment in the young woman's life.

~

A sordid political drama now began to unfold. The AIADMK split vertically as MGR's wife Janaki, a novice in politics, was propped up by MGR's trusted lieutenant R.M. Veerappan aka RMV, to be installed as the state's first woman chief minister. The other faction too was led by a woman, MGR's favourite film star, Jayalalithaa Jayaram. Jayalalithaa declared: 'When Karunanidhi expelled MGR in 1972, the former had the MLAs but the latter walked away with party workers. The same thing is happening now.'

Tamil Nadu Governor Sundar Lal Khurana hastily accepted Janaki's claim to form the government but also gave her three weeks to prove her strength in the Assembly. The factional fighting that now came out into the open was the worst in Tamil Nadu's political history, with each faction holding MLAs hostage in five-star hotels. On the appointed day, the warring groups turned so violent that the Assembly had to be adjourned sine die. A state of emergency was declared and President's rule imposed for six months, and again extended for another six months, for no reason except perhaps to conduct the Assembly polls along with the Lok Sabha elections in 1989.

The electoral battle following the lifting of president's rule was fought by four fronts: the Janaki and Jayalalithaa factions of the AIADMK, the DMK and the Congress.

The Congress decided to go alone and suffered a humiliating defeat. Prime Minister Rajiv Gandhi made a tactical blunder when on his dozen campaigning visits to Tamil Nadu he unwisely declared that the parliamentary elections, held alongside the Assembly elections, were a battle between the Dravidian 'regional' tradition and the 'national' political culture that the Congress(R) represented. The Tamil voters responded to him by rejecting the Congress. The split in the AIADMK into the Janaki group and the Jayalalithaa group divided the votes as well and the people of Tamil Nadu went for a less confusing choice. They opted for stability and voted for the DMK and its experienced leader, Karunanidhi, who had been languishing in the political wilderness since 1977.

The DMK won 151 seats while Jayalalithaa's AIADMK won twenty-seven and the Congress twenty-six. Jayalalithaa became the leader of the Opposition. The Janaki faction failed miserably and MGR's widow quit politics altogether, announcing the merger of her faction with that of Jayalalithaa.

The merger gave Jayalalithaa the popular two leaves electoral symbol and she became the undisputed leader of the AIADMK. And lest anyone still had any doubts, Jayalalithaa, at a post-election conference in Chennai, declared, 'I am the leader of this party and it is my utterances alone that are to be considered, not irresponsible statements made by others in the party.'

In by-elections to two constituencies that followed soon after, the AIADMK won with a big margin, signalling that Jayalalithaa was a force to reckon with, even though her party had fared poorly in the main polls.

Many AIADMK leaders were unhappy at the way Jayalalithaa was consolidating her position, and they worried about their own future. But they did not revolt since the election results had clearly shown that she was the only vote catcher in the party.

~

Karunanidhi now understood that he would have to drive Jayalalithaa out of politics. A case was foisted on Jayalalithaa and her aide Natarajan, implicating them in fraud and attempt to murder. It was alleged that the deposit money collected before the Assembly elections from the ticket seekers who were left out of the fray was not refunded, and that Natarajan threatened to kill them when they demanded their money back. Some of them lodged complaints and the DMK played it up. Lack of funds was a serious issue in the AIADMK. Finally, police harassment over these charges forced Jayalalithaa to announce that she was resigning from the state Assembly. She even wrote a resignation letter to the Speaker but later said she never actually sent the letter. Meanwhile, news appeared in the press that she had resigned. The letter had mysteriously reached the Speaker who confirmed the news. Jayalalithaa sent a letter to the Speaker claiming that since she had never dispatched the resignation letter, he need not take cognizance of the letter he possessed. The Speaker therefore announced that she remained the leader of the Opposition in the Assembly.

The public, however, was not able to figure out who was speaking the truth, and the ruling DMK spread the word that Jayalalithaa was mentally unstable.

When the budget session began on 25 March 1989, Chief Minister Karunanidhi, who also held the finance portfolio, stood up to begin his budget speech. Before he could start speaking, the deputy leader of the Congress, Kumari Anandan, rising on a point of order, said that the police had acted undemocratically and in a high-handed manner against the leader of the Opposition, Jayalalithaa, which amounted to a breach of privilege towards a member of the House. Karunanidhi, who was home minister as well, was responsible for the police, and so Anandan sought the permission of the House to discuss the matter.

Jayalalithaa then sprang to her feet and alleged that at the instigation of the chief minister, the police had acted against her and her telephone was tapped, and these acts amounted to a breach of her privilege as a member of the House and leader of the Opposition. She also charged Karunanidhi with misuse of power to deny her democratic rights. She urged the chair to discuss the motion of breach of privilege against the chief minister and the police commissioner, P. Durai. P.H. Pandian who was then in the

Janaki faction (he would later fall at Jayalalithaa's feet when she became the chief minister) objected to her motion. He used foul language that was expunged by the Speaker. But Pandian's words sparked off a heated argument by Jayalalithaa's supporters and the Speaker was unable to permit a discussion on the privilege motion. Pandemonium broke out as angry AIADMK members occupied the well of the House, shouting and gesticulating wildly.

When Jayalalithaa repeated that a person charged with 'criminal acts' should not be allowed to present the budget, Karunanidhi, according to a reporter present, made a rude remark directed at Jayalalithaa, which too was expunged. An AIADMK member charged towards Karunanidhi. He lost his balance and his spectacles fell to the floor. Several DMK ministers rushed to protect him. Missiles flew from both sides and mikes were pulled out and used as weapons. An AIADMK member tore up pages of the budget. Chappals and books landed on Jayalalithaa's head. The Speaker adjourned the House, and the chief minister was escorted out of the House by his MLAs even as the mayhem continued. Jayalalithaa sat in tears, with her head in her hands. After a while, when she attempted to leave, Thirunavukkarasar, an AIADMK member (now in the Congress) alleged that Durai Murugan, a DMK minister, pulled the end of her sari pallu. No eyewitness came forward to support this but the allegation spread fast among the public.

Durai Murugan to this day vehemently denies the charges made against him.

'Nothing of the sort happened in the Assembly,' he says. 'I have clarified this many times. It was a yarn spun by Thirunavukkarasar. Moopanar [Congress leader] was sitting next to Jayalalithaa, right in front. I was at the back of the hall. When violence broke out

I moved forward and saw that Veerapandi Arumugam [DMK member] was bleeding from the forehead. He was hit with a mic. I saw Kalaignar's broken spectacles on the floor. I escorted Veerapandi to safety. I then went to look for Kalaignar. He was sitting in another room outside the Assembly hall. I gave him the broken spectacles that I had picked up from the floor and stayed with him. How could I do such a thing to Jayalalithaa when I was not inside the Assembly hall?'[1]

Whatever the truth, people believed Jayalalithaa's story when she came out of the Assembly, teary-eyed and with dishevelled hair.

Enraged and humiliated, Jayalalithaa left, swearing never to step foot inside the House 'until conditions are created under which a woman may attend the Assembly safely'.

Assured of its strength, the DMK probably concluded that the shame and humiliation would make Jayalalithaa flee from active politics. Little did they know they had given her a magnificent obsession and a burning ambition – to come back as chief minister of Tamil Nadu.

~

Jayalalithaa was becoming inured to insults from her own party workers and betrayal from trusted relatives and friends. She had learned the hard way what it was for a former actress to be a political leader in a sexist and violent culture. She had seen the worst side of it the day MGR died. Jayalalithaa had rushed to his house at Ramavaram Gardens when she heard about his death. She was not allowed to enter the house. When MGR's body was kept in Rajaji Hall for public viewing, she stood beside it for nearly two days. As she herself said in an interview to *India Today*, at Rajaji

Hall she stood 'for thirteen hours the first day' and 'eight hours the second day'. Wasn't that physically exhausting? 'There was no physical strain,' she said. 'I suppose it was my willpower. But there was mental and physical torture.' Several women stood next to her, she said, and started stamping on her feet, driving their nails into her skin, and pinching her. During the rituals around the body she was not allowed inside. Later when she tried to place a wreath on the body when it was being carried to the gun carriage, Janaki's nephew Deepan, an actor himself, was among those who rushed forward and pushed her down. K.P. Ramalingam, now in the DMK, was in the AIADMK then and confesses he was totally opposed to Jayalalithaa. He was in the gun carriage and claimed that it was he who pushed her down when she tried to climb into the carriage, cursing her violently. He had no hesitation in recalling the incident. There was a tinge of pride in his voice, in fact.[2]

He also recalls that back when he was a brash young man, who had joined the AIADMK because he was a huge fan of MGR, he once met Karunanidhi during a train journey. Being in the rival party he did not have a high opinion of Karunanidhi but greeted him nevertheless, saying vanakkam. He was surprised when Kalaignar smiled and said he would like to say something to him. 'I notice that you speak very harshly about that lady Jayalalithaa. You are free to have your opinion but you are young and have to move forward. I feel it is not good for you to express your opinion so openly about a person who is a member of your party. Your leader will not like it. Just think about it.' Ramalingam was irritated by his advice and mumbled to himself, 'I don't need your advice.' But he later realized how gracious it was of Karunanidhi to advise him for his own good even if he was a member of the rival party. When Jayalalithaa came to power, Ramalingam quit the

AIADMK and joined the DMK. He became an MP and also an MLA and a minister subsequently, and became a loyal supporter of Karunanidhi. Little surprise, then, that he now smiles broadly and says with pride, 'I pushed her down with rage and cursed, "Down with you ****. Never raise your shameless face again!"'

Too shocked to react, red in the face, Jayalalithaa walked away with a police cordon round her and reached home where there was no one to comfort her. She must have felt totally isolated and rudderless with her mentor gone. She confessed in public later that she was so grieved by MGR's death that she wished to enter the funeral pyre along with him like the 'satis' in olden days. This went down well with her admirers and the rural folk, but invited a lot of criticism from women's groups and ridicule from the DMK.

After the incident, Jayalalithaa sent identical telegrams to the Governor, the chief secretary and the DGP about how she was manhandled and insulted by her political rivals. The episode had received prominent coverage on Doordarshan. And the public assault on her produced an outpouring of popular sympathy. The AIADMK cadre realized the party desperately needed a charismatic figure to lead it, and as Shahul Hameed, who was student chairman of the AIADMK, Karur, said, 'Jayalalithaa was the only person with charisma.' This was the most important ingredient to win in Tamil Nadu politics.

~

For all his shrewdness, Karunanidhi ignored Jayalalithaa's growing popularity, firmly believing that the Dravidian psyche would outright reject Jayalalithaa's leadership. Wasn't she a former actress, not initiated into the Dravidian movement and its ideology? Above all, wasn't she a Brahmin, a symbol of ridicule in the eyes of the Dravidian movement? A Brahmin woman and an actress – how could she ever challenge him, a seasoned politician and leader with a mass following in the state?

But what he thought was impossible began to take shape in the coming years due to Karunanidhi's overconfidence and his folly in allowing the Sri Lankan Tamil militant groups to carry out their activities unchecked on the soil of Tamil Nadu. As related in the previous chapter, his government was dismissed on 30 January 1991 and president's rule imposed.

Jayalalithaa had repeatedly complained to the Centre about the Karunanidhi government's callous disregard for national security by allowing the gun-toting militants, citizens of a neighbouring country, to freely indulge in ruthless fratricidal wars on Indian soil. When it became clear that Dhanu, the young woman who walked up to garland Rajiv Gandhi at his Sriperumbudur election campaign with a bomb strapped to her body, killing the former prime minister and fourteen others, was an LTTE militant, Jayalalithaa said, 'Didn't I warn you?'

In the Assembly elections the next month she won with a massive mandate. Tamil Nadu chose her, a political novice, to head the state, and at the age of forty-three Jayalalithaa became the youngest chief minister of Tamil Nadu. The DMK won just two seats in the Assembly. As Karunanidhi resigned from his own seat, admitting his moral responsibility for his party's shameful defeat, another shock lay in store for him – the DMK was heading for another split.

11

The Vaiko Affair

November 1993 saw a simmering crisis in the DMK boiling over. V. Gopalaswamy, better known as Vaiko, the rising star of the DMK, had just been expelled from the party by the high command.

Right after his expulsion, three young men, admirers of Vaiko, set fire to themselves in protest against the injustice done to their hero. Two of them died. The Vaiko affair had come to a head with a news leak, supposedly based on an Intelligence Bureau (IB) report that the LTTE was plotting to murder Karunanidhi, in order to pave the way for a new leader, a leader of their choice, clearly Vaiko, who was their friend and supporter.

Vaiko denied any knowledge of the matter, expressed unflinching loyalty to the party and its leader and declared he was willing to sacrifice his life to protect Kalaignar. After all, hadn't Kalaignar always referred to him fondly as his 'sword in the scabbard'?

Vaiko recalled the sequence of events that resulted in his expulsion from the DMK: 'On 3 November the IB sends an unconfirmed report. What is in the report? That the LTTE plans to assassinate Kalaignar. Why? To facilitate Gopalaswamy's

[Vaiko's] political ascendance! Kalaignar could have convened the general council to discuss the matter. If he had said, "My brother Vaiko would sacrifice his life for me – this is a conspiracy of the government," I would have felt my life worth living. Instead he releases the news to the press. Was it to see this that I toiled for so long at your feet?'

But Kalaignar was unmoved by Vaiko's declarations of love and loyalty. He wrote in *Murasoli* that there could not be 'two swords in the scabbard'. For Vaiko, this was the last straw. 'Karunanidhi is not my leader any more. I shall not think of anyone as my leader hereafter,' he thundered. More hysterical statements followed. And finally the expected happened. Vaiko was expelled from the DMK. In response he declared that it was *he* who represented the true DMK.

Karunanidhi's opponents said the LTTE factor was used as a ploy to oust Vaiko from the party because he feared Vaiko's growing popularity threatened his own son Stalin's political future. What Karunanidhi didn't doubt at all was that the LTTE would try to assassinate him. If they were audacious enough to kill a former Indian prime minister what would prevent them from doing the same to a former chief minister of Tamil Nadu?

Shortly after the expulsion, Karunanidhi told me, 'I have indeed praised Gopalaswamy as my "fighting sword". But he exploited the goodwill and for the past two years has been trying to usurp the top seat. Before that, in 1989, when the DMK was in power, violating party discipline he slipped away to Sri Lanka to meet the LTTE chief without informing me. I admonished him very strongly about this. We should have expelled him from the party at that time. Not doing so was a mistake. But then he said sorry and asked my forgiveness. Again and again for several other such mistakes he asked to be forgiven. To tell you the truth, after Rajiv Gandhi's assassination, we clearly said that we would be happy if the Sri Lankan Tamils got their eelam, but we never said that "support should be given to Tamil eelam'. But this man continues to embarrass us by openly speaking in favour of Tamil Eelam and the LTTE when it has been officially banned. So much so that in the last one year there has been an active campaign undermining my leadership in Tamil Nadu, in the pro-LTTE press abroad in Paris, Canada and Jaffna and also their website.'

Karunanidhi said he had not been aware of any threat to him until he received a letter from the IB informing him of reports of an LTTE plot to kill him, in order to facilitate Vaiko.

'I could not believe it initially,' he continued. 'But seeing how Vaiko behaves now strengthens my suspicion. Why didn't he call me then? Not only did he not contact me, he also sent a statement to the press that it was a plot to oust him from the DMK. I wanted to talk to him, but he did not respond. I waited for forty days before we expelled him. When I see those pro-LTTE papers printed in France and Germany criticizing me I do suspect that there must be some truth in the letter from the IB. He must be garnering support. Maybe there is a plan.'

This was his concern, a genuine one, that after Rajiv Gandhi *he* may be the next target. By expelling Vaiko from the party, he was sending a signal to the LTTE that Vaiko would never take his place.

'Your critics say that there is no democracy any longer in the DMK. And that it is your intention to promote dynastic rule,' I said to him.

Karunanidhi lost his cool. 'I have always said,' he responded agitatedly, 'that the DMK is not a Shankara mutt or a monarchy to pass on the mantle of power to an heir apparent. Prime

Minister Narasimha Rao's son is a minister in his state. Rangarajan Kumaramangalam's father and grandfather were ministers. Nobody thinks that to be odd. They pick on me because I am a Sudra . . . If I wanted any dynastic rule I could have done that even during 1989 when I was in power.'[1]

~

If there was an element of truth in that letter from the IB it would mean the LTTE had no real understanding of Tamil Nadu politics, and even less of the inner dynamics of the DMK. No one in the party thought Vaiko was second in line to become the president after Karunanidhi, especially since the leader had given no such indication. No one could dispute the fact that Karunanidhi had risen from the ranks and enjoyed widespread support from the DMK's MLAs and district secretaries when he succeeded Annadurai in 1969. He had created a large network of loyal cadres. In the organizational elections, all his supporters were elected to district secretary posts. It was by virtue of this support, and not because of electoral victories alone, that he could assume the chief ministerial post and, shortly after, be elected as party president. That Karunanidhi had earned his pre-eminent position in the DMK through his own skills and hard work lay at the bottom of his continued strength in the DMK, right until his death in August 2018. That the DMK under Karunanidhi's leadership survived two major splits and several election defeats was indeed proof of his managerial and leadership skills.

But the threat of expulsion from the party left little room for internal dissent in the DMK. The members of the DMK's executive council could, on the face of it, express and discuss conflicting views, but in the end it was Karunanidhi's decision that was always endorsed.

Since Karunanidhi was the face of the party, and his leadership most important for its survival, the party's executive council would elect his preferred person as his successor. It would not be bullied into electing somebody else, let alone someone favoured by a terrorist organization. This is what the LTTE had failed to understand.

~

Vaiko maintained that he and his followers were the true face of the DMK but after the Election Commission rejected his claim to the DMK flag symbol, he formed his own party – the Marumalarchi Dravida Munnetra Kazhagam (MDMK) in May 1994.

He began his political career in the DMK. He became an acclaimed orator and parliamentarian, who to this day remains quite popular in Delhi, across the political spectrum. There were separate Vaiko fan clubs in the DMK, until Karunanidhi in the early 1990s ordered that all associations formed in the names of living persons should cease.

Vaiko enjoyed a certain personal popularity within the DMK, without which it would hardly have been possible for him to establish the MDMK. He retains his image as a clean, honest politician, whereas the names of both Karunanidhi and Jayalalithaa have been tarnished with charges of nepotism and corruption. But for the fatal flaw of his obsession with the leader of the LTTE, Veluppillai Prabhakaran, and his cause to the point of risking his political future in Tamil Nadu, the Tamil voter would have probably given him a better deal.

Now an MP nominated to the Rajya Sabha, Vaiko is a bundle of contradictions. High-strung, given to shedding copious tears, he is a fiery orator, easily carried away by his own words. The predominant theme of the MDMK during the first years of its existence was to highlight the injustice done to their much-wronged leader, Vaiko, who his supporters maintained had been falsely accused and expelled from a party that he had long and faithfully served. Vaiko also hit out at the AIADMK and tried to lure dissatisfied AIADMK supporters by invoking MGR's name. He undertook an 1800 kilometre tour of the state on foot, making it his singular mission to speak against Jayalalithaa's regime. As for the split he created in the DMK, Vaiko was no MGR, who in 1972 had taken away a substantial part of the DMK's mass base. It was widely claimed that Vaiko was capable of attracting younger voters but that proved to be an exaggerated claim.

Though Vaiko and the MDMK never proved to be a threat to Karunanidhi and the DMK, Karunanidhi was deeply hurt by what he perceived as disloyalty and betrayal from a protégé he had trusted completely. First, MGR and now Vaiko had stabbed him in the back. This perhaps led Karunanidhi to introspect and agonize about whose loyalty he could count on. Perhaps he came to the conclusion then that it was only his own blood, his own family that he could ultimately rely on. It became a weakness he was accused of till the end of his days. But that was in the future. For now he had to contend with the rising power of Jayalalithaa.

12

The Prima Donna

The emergence of Jayalalithaa on Tamil Nadu's political landscape after her landslide victory in the June 1991 elections took Karunanidhi by surprise. How could she, a novice in politics and governance, cut the ground from under his feet? How did he so badly underestimate her power to cast a spell on the people of Tamil Nadu?

In 1991 the DMK was in disarray. To recap the events leading up to the DMK's defeat at the polls: in January of that year, Karunanidhi's government had been dismissed for creating a climate that allowed Sri Lankan terrorist groups to operate unchecked in Tamil Nadu. The assassination of Rajiv Gandhi in Sriperumbudur in May that year resulted in a wave of revulsion against the LTTE and strengthened public perception that the DMK was to blame for having done nothing to curb them. Karunanidhi now bitterly regretted not expelling the LTTE and cracking down on its supporters after the assassination of the EPRLF's Padmanabha and thirteen others in broad daylight in Chennai. Would he ever win back the trust and support of the people?

Jayalalithaa, meanwhile, was revelling in a victory in which she had completely trounced the DMK – winning 225 Assembly seats as against the DMK's pathetic showing of seven. And she didn't owe this victory to anyone else – she alone was the winning face of her party, adored by the masses as the leader of the AIADMK. Enthusiastic AIADMK cadres erected a 135-foot-high cut-out of her in Madurai. There could be no one taller than her, it seemed to proclaim.

Heady with power, she became increasingly dictatorial. Officials became mute in her presence; party members, even ministers, covered their mouths in reverence and fright when speaking with her; and many prostrated before her, whether in the dusty streets or on the granite floor of her house in Poes Garden. She seemed to enjoy every minute of this new avatar – the invincible Durga who could crush Mahishasura under her feet.

Her association with MGR had taught her never to trust the press. MGR had the reputation of slapping reporters or grabbing them by the collar when they displeased him. He had even put an editor of a popular Tamil weekly behind bars for carrying a cartoon censuring him on its cover. Jayalalithaa flirted with the press initially but after the brief honeymoon she turned totally intolerant of any criticism or even questioning of her actions and decisions. More than a hundred defamation cases were filed against journals that were 'unfriendly' to her. Some journalists were even beaten up by party cadres who wanted to prove their loyalty to her. Amma, as she was now called, seemed to condone their actions.

From 1991 to 1996 Karunanidhi and the DMK watched as Jayalalithaa along with her confidante Sasikala, whom she called udanpirava sagodhari (sister though not born of the same womb), ruled the state. Soon, stories of corruption at all levels of the

AIADMK, which presumably had her approval, began to circulate. Political thuggery too was at an all-time high as vengeance was wreaked upon DMK members for various slights, both real and perceived. In 1995 Jayalalithaa carried out a series of actions that shocked the people and embarrassed her party, and that soon brought about her downfall. She adopted Sudhakaran, the nephew of her live-in alter ego Sasikala. Then she announced the wedding of Sudhakaran with Sathyalakshmi, the granddaughter of the famous film actor Sivaji Ganesan, her former co-star and professional rival of her mentor MGR.

The sheer ostentation of that wedding, the vulgar display of wealth, watched by even the rural population, made Jayalalithaa an easy target for accusations of amassing wealth at the expense of ordinary people.

Karunanidhi was quick to point out the contrast with the modest wedding of his own daughter Kanimozhi when he was chief minister, performed quietly at a kalyana mandapam. The allegations of corruption against Jayalalithaa gained widespread credibility, thanks in no small part to Sun TV's videos of the crass extravagance of Jayalalithaa's adopted son's wedding.

Karunanidhi watched and waited. Jayalalithaa, he said, had a unique talent for destroying herself. Several cases of corruption were filed against her, notably one by Subramanian Swamy of the Janata Party, who filed the disproportionate assets case for which she was eventually convicted.

The writing was on the wall.

~

In the 1996 Assembly elections, the AIADMK failed miserably and the electorate went back to their old favourite, Karunanidhi. Jayalalithaa herself suffered a humiliating defeat at Bargur in Krishnagiri district. The DMK, in alliance with G.K. Moopanar's Tamil Maanila Congress (TMC), the CPI and the All India Forward Bloc, won all thirty-nine seats in the Lok Sabha and 221 out of 234 seats in the Assembly, with the AIADMK winning just four.

The DMK's return to power in 1996 was facilitated by two factors. Moopanar had broken away from the Congress to form the TMC because the Congress prime minister, Narasimha Rao, refused to accommodate the regional Congress party's demand to end the alliance with the corrupt and arrogant Jayalalithaa whose popularity had waned. Moopanar's new party walked away with the 20 per cent votes earlier commanded by the Congress. Then there was the decision of the actor Rajinikanth, with his immense fan following, to campaign in favour of the DMK: he declared that if the people of Tamil Nadu voted Jayalalithaa back to power even the gods would not forgive them. This statement was repeatedly telecast on Sun TV.

After their crushing defeat, Jayalalithaa and the AIADMK had to contend with the possibility of political oblivion and also political vengeance. AIADMK leaders murmured that Karunanidhi would move heaven and earth to destroy Jayalalithaa so that the throne of Tamil Nadu was left free for Stalin. And P. Chidambaram of the TMC, an election ally, who had been physically assaulted by AIADMK men, was now the Central finance minister and they expected him to work in tandem with the state government to destroy Jayalalithaa.

Karunanidhi in his election manifesto had vowed to attach the wealth and assets of Jayalalithaa and her associates, hold enquiries into corruption charges and mete out punishment to the guilty. He even had the judicial sanction to do so – the courts, while rejecting the anticipatory bail pleas submitted by Jayalalithaa also admonished the Karunanidhi government for the delay in taking action regarding the charges against her. Besides, the public mood had transformed from silent acceptance and simmering resentment during Jayalalithaa's rule to outright anger against the blatant corruption of her regime.

Karunanidhi knew that her arrest had the potential to turn into a vitriolic battle between the DMK and the AIADMK. If his government even appeared to victimize Jayalalithaa, the strategy could boomerang. His detractors pointed out that MGR did not arrest Karunanidhi when he came to power, despite the Sarkaria Commission's corruption charges against him. Karunanidhi himself would have preferred not to have Jayalalithaa in jail as that could set off a sympathy wave in a state where such events were known to provoke mass hysteria. Instead he would rather ensure that the string of cases filed against her (twenty-seven in all) would keep her running from one court to another, leaving her little time to attend to party matters and work her way back to power.

But his initial reluctance to arrest her began to evaporate, with his party cadres growing impatient and demanding action on the corruption charges against her, as had been promised in the DMK election manifesto. Jayalalithaa's arrest now became a political necessity for Karunanidhi. When the state Cabinet met on 5 December 1996 Karunanidhi discussed at length with his colleagues the political fallout of sending the AIADMK chief to jail. Halfway through the meeting they decided to proceed with it. Meanwhile, the newsrooms of all the dailies and weeklies alerted their photographers. Everyone waited with bated breath for the impending arrest of the imperious Amma who had seemed above the law.

On the afternoon of 6 December 1996 Justice C. Shivappa of the Madras High Court rejected seven anticipatory bail applications filed by Jayalalithaa, including the one in the Rs 8.53 crore colour TV case for which she was ultimately arrested. The next morning, as the police waited at Poes Garden, Jayalalithaa bathed, draped herself in a maroon sari, completed her puja, packed a suitcase and had her breakfast. Looking pale, she finally appeared at the portico and said to her followers who had assembled outside in pained silence – 'Nalai namathe!' Tomorrow is ours.

Aided by two grim-faced policewomen she stepped into the police van. She was produced before a city magistrate before being sent to Madras Central Prison as remand prisoner No. 2529. Within minutes Sun TV beamed the arrest.

The channel had found its golden moment. As the raids in her house and various other places ensued, the channel continued to air images for the common man to see the amazing collection of jewellery and other valuables amassed by the former chief minister. The blow-by-blow coverage of Jayalalithaa's arrest put off quite a few women viewers who wondered what the fuss was about – what was so surprising about a former actress owning so much jewellery, a thousand saris and hundreds of pairs of slippers? There were stray incidents of violence in which state-run buses were set ablaze and one person committed suicide. But with over 2500 AIADMK party activists being taken into custody even before her arrest, the protests seemed muted. A quick opinion poll conducted by a Tamil weekly showed that the overwhelming opinion was that she got what she deserved.

Jayalalithaa's government had earned the reputation of being extremely secretive and inaccessible, as well as the notoriety of being a 'cash and carry' government. The reports one heard of the bribes demanded at every ministry and department were mind-boggling. Some insiders in the AIADMK explained later that they had no option since they were under great pressure to donate to the party coffers. 'She knows that "money is power". That is why she allowed so much corruption,' explained Cho Ramaswamy.

Only select members of her Cabinet had access to Jayalalithaa's house. But meeting her directly was almost impossible. Many had to be content with talking to her on the intercom. Why her entire Cabinet and senior party members remained in such fear of her is part of her enduring mystique.

~

Karunanidhi insisted that the arrest was not an act of political vendetta. 'We only followed the court's directions. Sasikala, who ran an ordinary videocassette shop, managed to acquire property worth over Rs 1000 crore in less than five years. Her ration card and voter identity card reveal beyond doubt she was with Jayalalithaa in Poes Garden.'

Karunanidhi handed over to the press voluminous dossiers of colour pictures detailing evidence of the various properties, lands, farms and houses that had allegedly been bought during the previous five years in the name of Jayalalithaa and Sasikala. The dossiers were also sent to the Central government.

Jayalalithaa, for all her abilities as an accomplished actress-turned-politician, overlooked Karunanidhi's skills as a consummate scriptwriter, plotting drama and directing it to the finale. The master of the well-timed move took care not to appear vengeful. At first, he went for Jayalalithaa's closest Cabinet colleagues after prima facie charges of siphoning off funds from people's welfare schemes were established. Next, Chidambaram quickened the pace of investigations into cases against Sasikala. The arrest of former ministers, Sasikala and two of her nephews soon after the DMK came to power led to sensational disclosures of corruption during AIADMK rule.

To regain lost ground in the party, Jayalalithaa announced that she would have nothing further to do with Sasikala. However, while some of her former ministers turned against her, Sasikala proved remarkably loyal, refusing to speak against Jayalalithaa. Karunanidhi described Jayalalithaa as the queen and Sasikala as a pawn, and clearly tried to create a rift between the two when he said, 'A Tamil woman belonging to a backward community has been put behind bars because of the act of someone else,' meaning Sasikala, who belonged to the Thevar community was being victimized by Jayalalithaa, a Brahmin, who hailed from Karnataka. Years ago he had tried to arouse Tamil passions by calling MGR a Malayali, and failed. This time too he failed.

The material evidence collected by the Crime Branch in the colour TV case showed that in December 1995 Jayalalithaa had called for the file relating to the purchase of the TV sets and fixed the price of each set at Rs 14,500 – higher than the market rate. Considering that the order was for as many as 45,302 sets to be distributed to village panchayats, the investigating authorities argued that the government could have bargained for a hefty discount. Though there were six other cases filed against her by the state and Central agencies, the Karunanidhi government picked the TV scandal to nail her. According to top officials, the case met two criteria in investigations against former rulers – the necessity for custodial interrogation that the evidence unearthed warranted and direct personal involvement of the accused in finalizing the deal. Chief Secretary K.A. Nambiar said, 'The case has been made only on merit. There is nothing political about it.'[1]

The media had always felt uncomfortable dealing with Jayalalithaa and her government because of the secrecy that prevailed in the party and government circles, a total contrast to Karunanidhi's open and accessible style of functioning.

With Jayalalithaa's arrest the media was at ease, having faced threats from her government for even the slightest criticism.

Almost all papers predicted that in view of so many corruption cases, her political resurrection would be an uphill task.

Cho Ramaswamy, however, predicted, 'You cannot write her off!' He was not wrong.

13

Administrator Par Excellence

Karunanidhi's tenure as chief minister from 1996 to 2001 was remarkable for its innovative, efficiently executed administrative measures. Bureaucrats had always found him sharp and quick in taking decisions and implementing them, even when he was minister for public works under Annadurai back in 1967, and later as chief minister in 1969 and 1971 though his tenures then were short.

His first task on coming back to power in 1996 was to fulfil the promises he had made in the DMK election manifesto. Soon after taking the oath of office, he signed a government order to distribute rice for Rs 2 per kilo to all ration card holders. The economist J. Jeyaranjan of the Madras Institute of Development Studies points out that this act enabled a family to meet its major food requirement within Rs 40 per month.

Kerosene for cooking and sugar too were made available at heavily subsidized rates through ration shops under the public distribution system (PDS). In Karunanidhi's next term (2006 to 2011), wheat, pulses and palm oil came under the PDS.

Dr M.S. Swaminathan, the internationally renowned agricultural scientist, recalls that he would send his proposals to Karunanidhi before every budget, making recommendations to help farmers increase agricultural production. Karunanidhi would peruse them carefully and in his budget speech mention Swaminathan's name along with his recommendations that were to be implemented, and the funds allocated for them. 'He was very concerned about the farmers and was sharp in grasping the ideas proposed.'

In 1998 Karunanidhi appointed a committee to study marketing techniques for agricultural produce in other states. That is how he learned of the 'apni mandi' (farmers' own) market in Chandigarh, an idea that impressed him and led him to institute the 'uzhavar santhai' (farmers' markets in Tamil Nadu, where farmers could directly sell their produce without going through middlemen. From 1999 to 2000, 203 farmers' markets came) up across the state.

Karunanidhi also lent his focus to the knowledge industry.

As the *Hindu Business Line* noted in an article published in August 2018, 'The information technology and biotechnology sectors in Tamil Nadu owe the DMK government of 1996–2001 a great debt. Under M. Karunanidhi, the government took the first steps in policy and infrastructure to aid the development of both IT and biotech sectors. A separate IT department was set up in 1998, and a task force created to draw up a policy framework to attract investments to the IT sector. A thrust was given to computer education in schools, colleges and governance.'

Karunanidhi, a school dropout and now seventy-odd years old, became adept on the computer.

During this regime too Chennai's first dedicated software space, an IT park, was created. The Tidal Park, a joint venture between TIDCO and ELCOT, both state-run agencies, established the 1.2

million square foot facility at a cost of Rs 340 crore. The *Hindu Business Line* article continues: 'The Tamil Nadu Biotechnology Board was established in November 2000, and so was a 20-acre Women's Biotechnology Park in Siruseri for units to set up shop to produce processed agricultural products, food and medical products for the domestic and export markets.'[1]

The historian V.M.S. Subagunarajan notes, 'The young generation of Tamil Nadu today who play with words and ask on Facebook and Twitter: "what did Karunanidhi do for Tamil Nadu?" are not aware that it was Karunanidhi who introduced the computer and the internet in Tamil Nadu administration. For a start, electronic administration began in Thiruvarur and Tiruvallur districts.'

People close to him recall how excited Karunanidhi was to discover how with a click of the mouse one could enter libraries across continents and instantly read news from the other side of the world.

From women's emancipation to fighting for the rights of farmers and the poor and the marginalized, the schemes Karunanidhi launched were aimed at achieving social justice and equality in Tamil Nadu. Even earlier, in his days as a scriptwriter, Karunanidhi wrote passionately on these themes. Film buffs of that era knew his fiery dialogues by heart. Especially memorable were the passages in the cult movie *Parasakthi* (1952) spoken by the protagonist, Gunasekaran, portrayed by Sivaji Ganesan. In that script Karunanidhi, the crusader for social reform, highlights the oppression of women, the vices of so-called holy men and how avarice warped people's minds.

The most famous lines of the film have the protagonist stating why he killed the temple priest, how his sister was cheated by the rich and the holy and then had to run for her life. Here is a translation of his words, which were truly powerful and heartbreaking in the original Tamil: 'Society's high and mighty chased my younger sister; frightened, she ran; the rich chased her, she ran again; she sought refuge in the abode of the gods, but there was no refuge for her there; faith frightened her; she ran and ran and ran to the edges of life . . .'

These lines shook up the men and women in Tamil Nadu like few other words spoken in films had.

Decades later, when he came to power, Karunanidhi showed that his outrage at the social ills that powered his words as a screenwriter were not merely for the silver screen.

Karunanidhi's tenures as chief minister also saw reformative legislations such as the widow remarriage scheme, the intercaste marriage assistance scheme and financial assistance for widows. In addition, he ensured equal property rights for women, offered free education for backward castes and support to women's self-help groups. The legislation of 33 per cent reservation for women in local bodies was enacted by his government during 1996–2001, by which 44,143 women, including two women mayors, assumed office, one belonging to a scheduled caste.

Karunanidhi was instrumental in setting up welfare boards for workers in the unorganized sector and pensions for contract workers. Also to his credit are housing schemes for Dalits; electrification of villages; raising reservation for backward classes and scheduled castes; and strengthening the nutritional quality of the midday meals in schools by adding eggs to the menu.

Especially important among the long and impressive list of his achievements was the setting up of 24-hour primary health centres in all districts and villages, with trained, dedicated nurses.

'Karunanidhi was genuinely concerned about social justice,' says R. Nallakkannu, senior member of the CPI. 'Who else would have thought of Samathuvapuram, a project spanning across Tamil Nadu, under which all people, irrespective of caste or religion, would live as one in a village free of bias and prejudice. It was a manifestation of his dream to eradicate caste discrimination, of his deep-rooted faith in social equality.'

Samathuvapuram (Equality Village) was Karunanidhi's dream project. Utopian in concept, an answer to the serious caste clashes that the southern parts of Tamil Nadu had witnessed, it envisaged a housing complex where all communities could live without any discrimination and have equal access to civic amenities. Each village was to have a hundred houses, forty for Dalits, twenty-five for backward castes, twenty-five for most backward castes and ten for other communities. Each house was built at a cost of Rs 35,000. The title deeds were in the name of women. Beneficiaries had to give in writing that they would not install religious statues in the housing complex, not sell the house for fifteen years, not consume alcohol, and maintain cleanliness. By 2001, 145 Samathuvapurams were opened across Tamil Nadu. Critics wondered if such a government-imposed social engineering scheme would actually work. But Karunanidhi's motives were genuine. 'It is this that is important when assessing the man,' says Nallakkannu.

The establishment of slum clearance boards and building concrete houses for the slum dwellers was another of his initiatives, points out Nallakkannu, and adds, 'Before any other state did, he abolished hand-pulled rickshaws and introduced cycle rickshaws.'

Peter Alphonse points out a unique quality of Karunanidhi's – his respect and friendship towards members of other parties. An MLA during Karunanidhi's rule, Alphonse recalls how he invited them to discuss the problems the state was facing and listened attentively to their suggestions, even if they did not align with his thoughts. He was open enough to change his decisions if he saw merit in the other side's point. Peter recalls asking for the hospital that the government had planned to build in Tirunelveli to be shifted to his constituency, Tenkasi. P.H. Pandian of the Janaki AIADMK and a strong supporter of Karunanidhi had also requested that the hospital be moved to Seranmadevi, his constituency.

Karunanidhi studied both the requests and sent for Peter Alphonse. When Peter entered the chief minister's room, Karunanidhi stood up to receive him. He was going to sign the sanction for the hospital at Tenkasi and wanted to inform him personally before doing so. Peter, much younger than Karunanidhi, was overwhelmed by his warmth and grace. He chuckles fondly as he also recounts how lively the Assembly sessions were when Karunanidhi attended, his wit making the House roar with laughter.

N. Ram eloquently summed up Karunanidhi's administrative and cultural legacy.

> He was chief minister of Tamil Nadu five times. And uniquely, he won his seat every election he contested. His legislative career spanned six decades and his rhetorical skill marked by annotations, literary allusions, irony and a sense of history was a major asset to the party and the Dravidian movement. [He was] a politician who had a lot of time for ideas, for literature, for history and of course poetry. And he was a great reader also. His writings and interpretations of Tamil classics and his journalistic output for

many decades place him in a different league from most other Indian political leaders. Many things could be said about Kalaignar, the administrator. He was considered decisive. The most interesting thing was he struck an alliance in the sixties and seventies with the so-called national parties – in particular the Congress – permanently, as a junior partner. It was a very clever and shrewd move. No regional leader of another state did that at that time; no national party ever aspired again to lead in Tamil Nadu. Kalaignar had a major role in bringing this about. He remained true to state autonomy and state federalism. The party that had once espoused secessionism evolved and spoke of federalism. Whenever there was an encroachment on what is called cooperative federalism in India, during the Emergency for instance, we know how Karunanidhi raised his voice and even lost his government.[2]

~

Karunanidhi valued the role of the press in a democracy. Having been a journalist himself, he understood the needs and compulsions of the press better than MGR or Jayalalithaa, neither of whom had a good relationship with the fourth estate. Karunanidhi maintained direct contact with the editors of dailies and magazines. He read both English and Tamil dailies every morning. There was a special delivery system, with the papers reaching his house at 4.30 a.m., which is when he woke up. He would read every line from the first page to the last, and if he found any complaint about ministers, district collectors, or anyone in his administration he would call the concerned minister and official before they were out of their beds, asking for an explanation. If anything critical about him was published, he would call the editor directly and either explain his position in defence, or ask why such negative things had been written about him.

Remarkably, he took care to cultivate the editors and writers who were his severe critics. Cho Ramaswamy of *Thuglak* was his harshest critic. When Ramaswamy was critically ill in hospital, Karunanidhi, wheelchair-bound himself, went to the hospital to see him. The celebrated writer Jayakanthan was another scathing critic of the DMK and Karunanidhi. When he was ill and admitted to hospital, Karunanidhi, in power then, not only visited him but made the government cover all his medical expenses.

Karunanidhi was known for being a 'people's chief minister'. The doors to his house as well as his office in the secretariat were always open to the public. He consciously created an image of accessibility and openness, in sharp contrast to other politicians in the state, most notably Jayalalithaa.

N. Ram recalls his relationship with Karunanidhi: 'It went beyond that of a newspaperman and a politician. I have known him from the late sixties. What was remarkable was while he was a full-time politician, he was also a journalist and a writer every day . . . He was very warm, and accessible. Even if he was annoyed with what you wrote, you could always go and meet him and explain. There were times when he even changed his opinion and accepted yours.'[3]

~

The golden period of Karunanidhi's reign, from 1996 to 2001, ended amidst considerable drama.

The extracts from the Jain Commission's interim report published in *India Today* dated 17 November 1997 had said that the DMK and Karunanidhi could be blamed for facilitating an atmosphere in Tamil Nadu for the LTTE to carry out the assassination of Rajiv Gandhi. The DMK was an ally and partner in the United Front government led by I.K. Gujral. Karunanidhi dismissed the report as of no consequence, least of all to the United Front government at the Centre.

As has been narrated earlier, the Congress, which supported the United Front government from outside, felt 'it was totally unethical to support the DMK's participation in the government', with the interim report declaring it responsible for their leader's death. The Congress demanded the expulsion of the DMK from the United Front ministry or it would withdraw its support. Karunanidhi refused to bow out voluntarily, as this would imply that the report was correct. When the Congress Working Committee sent its ultimatum to Gujral, the inevitable happened. Gujral waited for the DMK to withdraw from the Cabinet and when that did not happen, he tendered his resignation and the United Front government fell in March 1998. The country now headed for a snap general election that the majority of the Lok Sabha did not want.

It was this political development that allowed the BJP to enter Tamil Nadu politics. The BJP's image in the south – a party that identified with the Hindi heartland – was somewhat altered by the quiet coup that Jayalalithaa and the BJP leader L.K. Advani engineered: Jayalalithaa declared that the AIADMK would fight the 1998 general election in alliance with the BJP. 'The Tamils,' according to the AIADMK general secretary T.M. Selvaganapathy, 'have always voted for the strongest party at the centre . . . that can ensure stability. Earlier, it was the Congress. This time it is the BJP.'[4]

On 14 February 1998, the eve of the general elections, Karunanidhi was dealt an awful blow, one that would taint his government once again for being negligent of national security.

14

Strange Bedfellows

For Karunanidhi, it was important not just to be secular, but to be seen as secular. He made it a point to display his closeness to Muslims and Christians, though he didn't make any effort to show any affinity to Hinduism. He attended Eid feasts but declined invitations to Hindu functions even as the chief minister. On several instances he hurt Hindu sentiments with his barbed and derisive remarks. He often criticized the Kanchi Shankaracharya, for example, for his 'retrograde' speeches.

In his preoccupation with projecting a secular image he failed to identify a situation brewing right under his nose. In the aftermath of the Babri Masjid demolition in Ayodhya in December 1992, a fundamentalist organization called Al Umma had gained a footing in Coimbatore. Under its general secretary Mohammed Ansari, it grew roots in Kottaimedu, a Muslim neighbourhood in the city. A number of unemployed, uneducated Muslim youth were attracted to Al Umma. When the police briefed then chief minister Jayalalithaa about their activities, she ordered the setting up of police checkposts in Kottaimedu, which Al Umma resisted.

During the 1996 election campaign, the DMK promised the Muslims of Kottaimedu that the checkposts would be removed once the DMK was voted to power. When the DMK did come to power, the pickets were indeed removed, though it was said that Al Umma activists removed them, and the authorities let them do so.

Kottaimedu became a haven for illegal activities. Almost every house was reportedly a godown of arms and ammunition and a shelter for militants. When reports of these activities reached Karunanidhi, he hesitated to take action, afraid of displeasing the Muslims. The police complained that the 'anti-social elements simply exploited the situation'. Karunanidhi ignored the frequent clashes that erupted between Al Umma activists and the police. He had to pay a severe price for this laxity when the DMK lost in the parliamentary elections that followed the fall of the United Front government in 1998.

On the eve of the elections in February 1998, the day L.K. Advani was to address a meeting in Coimbatore, a series of bomb blasts in thirteen places in the city left at least fifty people dead. Advani escaped because of a last-minute change in the time of his meeting. When Cho Ramaswamy asked the chief minister in an interview why there was such a security lapse, Karunanidhi's reply sounded weak. He said he had checked with the police commissioner about the security arrangements made in Coimbatore and the commissioner had categorically assured him that everything was fine and taken care of. 'I believed him, you have to trust your officers.'

'But why did you remove the checkposts that were kept by Jayalalithaa?'

'It cannot be denied,' Karunanidhi replied, 'that some terrorists infiltrated into Kottaimedu. But to conclude that all those who were there were terrorists and confine them within the checkposts would be like insulting the entire community, wouldn't it?'

Still, he was rattled by this grave security lapse and saddened at the loss of innocent lives. He was also aware that it would surely affect his party at the polls.

In the 1998 Lok Sabha elections the United Front comprising the DMK, TMC and CPI managed to win only nine seats, with the DMK winning just five, while the Jayalalithaa-led National Democratic Alliance bagged thirty out of the forty seats, with the AIADMK alone winning eighteen seats. The blasts had clearly taken their toll on the DMK, and Karunanidhi himself was so shaken that he showed little interest in the rehabilitation of Muslims affected during the riots that broke out after the blasts. The Muslim vote bank in Tamil Nadu would no longer be a deciding factor in an election.

When Jayalalithaa, as leader of the AIADMK, joined hands with the BJP, it was described as a natural alliance, considering her consistently soft approach on the Ramjanmabhoomi issue and her unabashed show of religiosity and visits to temples. But it soon became clear that Jayalalithaa's alliance with the BJP-led coalition that came to power at the centre was mainly for personal reasons and nothing more.

It was important for her to join hands with a national party that had the chance of forming the government at Delhi. By giving them the support of her eighteen members in the Lok Sabha, she could bargain for crucial ministerial posts that would help her wade through the numerous corruption cases in which she was embroiled. If she was lucky she might even charm the Centre into toppling the DMK government in Tamil Nadu, and pave the way for her return. During the election campaign she declared, 'We align with the BJP because under the circumstances today, the BJP alone can give a stable and strong government at the centre.'

Her party and the cadres knew better. Released from jail on bail in January 1997, she disappeared into self-imposed seclusion for eight months. The AIADMK cadres and members wondered if she was ill. Then suddenly one day, in the first week of October, she reappeared, addressed them at the party office and, to their relief, exhibited a renewed vigour and determination. They did not know that her hopes had been revived by the changes that were happening at the Centre, and that she was enthused by the Jain Commission report's indictment of Karunanidhi. She awaited the imminent fall of the United Front government of which he was a partner.

She told her party cadres that she was still in politics because she 'did not want it to be written in history that the AIADMK, a party that MGR founded in opposition to Karunanidhi', was wiped out by Karunanidhi. But in fact it was not her party's survival alone that motivated her – she could not allow Karunanidhi to wipe her out.

In her emotional, impassioned address to the AIADMK cadres she continued, 'Any other woman in my place would have committed suicide [for the kind of sufferings I have gone through] or would have become insane.'

But once the Lok Sabha election results were in, she constantly badgered the BJP coalition government with the quid pro quos she demanded for the support of her eighteen MPs. Having given 'unconditional support' to the BJP-led government, she evidently expected the prime minister to instantly dismiss the DMK government in Tamil Nadu. For twelve months Prime

Minister Vajpayee gave her the royal treatment. He surrendered to her his prerogative to choose his ministers and allocate their portfolios.

Her list of demands was long. First, bifurcation of the finance ministry and the appointment of Vazhappadi Ramamurthy of the Tamil Nadu Rajiv Congress (TRC), her ally, as minister for revenue and banking. Second, the AIADMK's M. Thambidurai was given the portfolio of law under pressure from her. Ram Jethmalani of the BJP was completely taken aback when he discovered that he had been allotted the portfolio of urban development and not law as he had expected.

The Sangh Parivar cried that Jayalalithaa had crossed the Lakshman Rekha when she objected to the removal of navy chief Admiral Vishnu Bhagwat by Defence Minister George Fernandes and demanded that Fernandes be dismissed.

Prime Minister Vajpayee humoured her to a certain extent, but did not agree to dismiss Karunanidhi's elected government even when Jayalalithaa hinted that she would withdraw support, and that she was not averse to supporting the Congress party to form the government.

And so, on the pretext of the government refusing to meet her demands, she withdrew her support. On 17 April 1999 Vajpayee's government was defeated by one vote in the dramatic no-confidence motion that followed. The DMK with its six MPs voted for the Vajpayee government, based on the logic 'my enemy's enemy is my friend'.

It was a momentous decision encouraged by Murasoli Maran, Karunanidhi's nephew and adviser on national politics, a pragmatic man who believed that being constrained by ideology at such a juncture was pointless. Here was a chance to beat his political foe and save the government.

General elections were declared but the BJP-led government was asked to continue as the caretaker government well through the Kargil war during May–July 1999.

~

In 1999, the DMK's golden jubilee year, the party had to take a major policy decision that went much against its cherished ideology. Karunanidhi, desiring a consensus, convened the executive council of his party which unanimously agreed that their current priority was to block the 'Jayalalithaa danger'. Ideology therefore had to take a back seat. Despite the historical enmity between the DMK and the RSS, the executive body therefore took the decision to support the BJP.

It put forth certain points in support of the decision. First, though the BJP had an alliance with the AIADMK and had indeed indulged Jayalalithaa in many matters, it had done nothing to harm the DMK. Second, it had taken a positive stance on the Kaveri issue, agreeing with Karunanidhi's constructive suggestions on having a monitoring authority to oversee the sharing of the Kaveri river waters between Tamil Nadu and Karnataka, a long-standing bone of contention between the two states. And most importantly, Vajpayee had refused to succumb to Jayalalithaa's pressures to dismiss the DMK government in the state.

Karunanidhi's view was that at the national level the DMK had to align with one of the two major national parties. An alignment with a secular party like the Congress would have been preferable. But after the Jain Commission charges blaming Karunanidhi for Rajiv Gandhi's assassination, Sonia Gandhi was maintaining a studied distance from the DMK. Besides, it was actually easier to deal with Vajpayee who had been Karunanidhi's friend from the days of the Emergency.

Karunanidhi always felt obliged to explain his actions in anticipation of criticism. But when the alliance between the DMK and the BJP was officially announced, the Dravidian scholars and academics were aghast. K. Veeramani, general secretary of the DK, said, 'Philosophically it is an unnatural alliance. The people of Tamil Nadu will reject it entirely.' The left parties and the TMC who were the DMK's allies called it sheer opportunism for which the DMK had sacrificed its secular policy. Professor P.V. Inderesan, political observer and commentator, however, said that it was 'a very welcome development in Indian politics. It would help parties like the BJP and the DMK, with different ideologies, understand each other better. The distance between them will decrease and there will be more tolerance.'[1] But DMK party members from the minority communities felt betrayed. As long as the alliance with the BJP lasted, the DMK lost its vote bank among the minorities, Muslims as well as Christians.

Karunanidhi's front looked formidable. Along with the BJP, Vaiko's MDMK (he had by now had a rapprochement with Karunanidhi) and S. Ramadoss's Pattali Makkal Katchi (PMK) had come together with the DMK. The Tamil Nadu Rajiv Congress (TRC) under the leadership of Vazhappadi Ramamurthy, who till recently had been with Jayalalithaa (and on whose behalf Jayalalithaa had seriously bargained for a plum ministerial post in the Vajpayee government), now also joined the DMK bandwagon.

Kicking off the election campaign from the Marina beach had become a ritual for the Dravidian rationalist parties, both the DMK and the AIADMK. On 23 July Ramamurthy organized a mega meeting at the Marina to proclaim the DMK front's strength. Though there were tensions between the cadres of the DMK and of the MDMK and PMK, on top of the embarrassing ideological differences with the BJP, one emotional appeal to the electorate was understood and appreciated by the audience: the unjust withdrawal of support to the BJP government by Jayalalithaa, and imposing the burden of a fresh election on the taxpayer.

While defeating Jayalalithaa was of paramount importance and a matter of honour for the BJP, a powerful alliance with a national party was an absolute necessity for the DMK to destroy her. The Muslims and the left parties had joined the AIADMK front as had a couple of Dalit outfits. Karunanidhi did not want to take any chances. He made a conscious effort to ease tensions between the cadres of his allies and kept reiterating in his meetings that the alliance was to 'save the country; save Tamil Nadu and save democracy'. It looked like he was trying his best to hide his embarrassment at having gone for an alliance with the BJP that shocked his supporters in the minority communities.

But Jayalalithaa seemed less concerned about keeping her partners, including the Congress, in good humour. She even missed meeting Sonia Gandhi with whom she was scheduled to jointly address an election rally at Vellore, on account of being held up by traffic. Sonia waited, then addressed the crowd without her glamorous ally and left for Delhi.

Jayalalithaa behaved as if the elections were about her alone – a referendum on her 'justifiable' actions. She went on a massive tour even before the Congress had finalized its list of candidates and therefore the leader of the AIADMK was not able to specifically speak in support of the Congress candidates. At times it looked like a campaign for the Assembly in which the main issue was one between her and Karunanidhi. She did not know that the crowds that thronged this time were also wary of her words. People were heard saying that she could not be trusted. 'She will betray the Congress as she did the BJP.' This was also a point that the DMK was harping upon. *The Hindu* quoted Karunanidhi as saying, 'If the Congress indeed came to power, Sonia Gandhi will run away to Italy, unable to bear Jayalalithaa's tantrums.'

~

In the midst of all the election theatrics Karunanidhi was also focused on hastening the hearing of Jayalalithaa's cases. He was assured that in at least four of the cases – Pleasant Stay Hotel, the TANSI land scam involving her illegal purchase of government land, the colour TV scam and the disproportionate assets case worth Rs 66.65 crore – the verdict would be against her. But he was not confident about the poll results. If the Congress came to power, Jayalalithaa would become stronger and resume her game of trying to pull down his government. The only way to prevent that was to speed up the case verdicts in the special courts before the election results were out. His officers, prosecution lawyers and the police worked overtime. Nevertheless, Karunanidhi protested to an inquisitive reporter, 'How can we hasten the cases? The law will take its course.' There was a setback when the special court judge V. Radhakrishnan acquitted Jayalalithaa in the coal import deal case, which had allegedly caused a loss of Rs 650 million to the government.[2]

The prosecution lawyer was at once replaced. But the government cleverly recommended that the special court judge Radhakrishnan be promoted to the high court, bypassing nine seniors above him.

The reason was clear: Karunanidhi did not want Radhakrishnan to hear the other cases against Jayalalithaa and pass judgements that would upset his plans. There was nothing that Jayalalithaa could do except wait.

~

The much-awaited 1999 general election results were announced. In an astonishing reversal of her fortune, Jayalalithaa who had stormed the citadel of national politics with eighteen MPs was now reduced to an ordinary regional leader with a paltry ten MPs. On the other hand, her arch-enemy Karunanidhi emerged as an important star in national politics with his front securing twenty-six seats, twelve of which were won by the DMK.

Karunanidhi at once expressed his satisfaction and assured the Central government that his party would not try to pull it down, since all the coalition partners were mature people. When Murasoli Maran was asked if the DMK would put conditions to the Vajpayee government, he retorted, 'We are not like the AIADMK.'

~

The DMK became part of the National Democratic Alliance (NDA) government under Vajpayee. Jayalalithaa being their common enemy strengthened the bond between Karunanidhi and Vajpayee. There was more bad news for Jayalalithaa. Murasoli Maran became the commerce and industries minister in the Central government; Ram Jethmalani, with whom Jayalalithaa had had a fight, was now the law minister. The DMK's T.R. Baalu and A. Raja were also in the Cabinet.

Cabinet posts were important to the DMK because they would grant the party some indirect control over Jayalalithaa. But the lure of Cabinet posts actually weakened the DMK. Karunanidhi failed to voice his dissent at crucial times like the Gujarat riots, when thousands of Muslims were killed and attacked under Narendra Modi's BJP government. The DMK chose to remain silent every time the issue of building the Ram temple in Ayodhya cropped up. It must have been extremely embarrassing indeed to the man who had expressed in very strong words his disapproval way back in 1992, when karsevaks began their march to Ayodhya, intent on demolishing the Babri Masjid. Chief Minister Jayalalithaa, however, supported the building of the Ram temple in Ayodhya in the disputed area. On 5 December Karunanidhi wrote in *Murasoli*: 'What does karseva mean? Service to god or service to sow seeds of unrest? They say Ram was born in the Treta Yuga. Dvapara Yuga arrived and has passed. When one says this is Kali Yuga it means twenty lakh years have gone by. They say Ram was born there twenty lakh years ago. Who saw that, I wonder. Who has written about it? Now by insisting that this is the exact place, how just is it to demolish Islamic history?

'If you say you want a temple for Ram in Ayodhya, we have no quarrel about that. But if you say to build the temple you will demolish Babri Masjid, we will not agree!'

The next day, to the shock of the nation, karsevaks demolished the Babri Masjid. Karunanidhi again came out with a statement to the press, strongly condemning their action and the Centre's failure to prevent it: 'For not taking steps to prevent such a dastardly deed, the Centre will have to take full responsibility for what is going to happen.'

For a regional leader, from a state so far away from the scene of the mosque's destruction, and to react so strongly to an issue with which the people of Tamil Nadu had no emotional connect, was a manifestation of Karunanidhi's deeply held belief in secularism. He predicted, rightly, that it would leave a deep scar on the soul of the nation.

According to A. Raja, Karunanidhi regretted the alliance. 'He told us many times that he should not have gone with the BJP, especially after the Godhra killings and riots. He said once that the BJP had converted Hindutva, which was a school of thought, into a religious anthem. But he had given his word that he would remain in the alliance for five years. It was a political pledge he had to keep.'[3]

Karunanidhi's break with the BJP was catalysed by a personal tragedy. Murasoli Maran, Karunanidhi's much-loved nephew and Cabinet minister in the BJP government, was undergoing treatment in a hospital in America. After Maran's death in November 2003 (the funeral in Chennai was attended by Prime Minister Vajpayee, Deputy Prime Minister L.K. Advani and several Cabinet ministers, including Defence Minister George Fernandes), Karunanidhi decided to pull out of the BJP government and also the alliance, with which he had been growing increasingly uncomfortable. Murasoli Maran had persuaded him into the alliance, and now that he was gone, he felt less obliged to continue with it.

There was another reason that precipitated his break with the BJP. In spite of the impressive presence of the BJP bigwigs at Maran's funeral, Karunanidhi suspected the BJP was getting closer to Jayalalithaa. And Jayalalithaa had clearly indicated she was tilting towards the BJP for the general elections due the following year (2004) by openly attacking Congress president Sonia Gandhi as a foreigner who should not be allowed to become the prime minister of India.

The DMK, which had always been uncomfortable being associated with the Hindutva party, breathed a collective sigh of relief. The enmity between Jayalalithaa and Karunanidhi played a decisive role in determining which national party at the Centre the DMK and the AIADMK would ally with. And since Jayalalithaa would in all likelihood go for an alliance with the BJP in the 2004 elections, it seemed a foregone conclusion that the DMK would ally with the Congress.

And so it came to pass. In 2004 Jayalalithaa's enemy Sonia Gandhi became a friend of the octogenarian Dravidian leader who was once accused by the Congress party of being instrumental in facilitating the assassination of Rajiv Gandhi. Sonia Gandhi, who was in desperate need of a strong ally in Tamil Nadu, graciously dismissed the accusation as baseless.

~

We must roll back now to 2000 and the pending court cases against Jayalalithaa. As mentioned earlier Karunanidhi, while being careful not to interfere in the functioning of the judiciary, had tried to hasten the court cases against Jayalalithaa before the 2001 state Assembly elections.

The start of the new millennium did not augur well for Jayalalithaa. In February the high court judge V. Radhakrishnan, who had acquitted her on the coal import scam, now indicted her, her former minister Selvaganapathy, along with IAS officer H.M. Pande, and Rakesh Mittal and P. Shanmugam, proprietors of Hotel Pleasant Stay, for having collectively conspired to violate environmental laws to build extra floors in the hotel situated in Kodaikanal, a hill station. He sentenced them all to one year's rigorous imprisonment and a fine of Rs 2000.

When this news reached the streets of Chennai, pandemonium broke out. At the AIADMK party head office, lower-rung workers resorted to violent protests. The riots spread like wildfire throughout the state. Ten buses were burnt and ninety damaged. The police seemed paralysed as the violence reached a savage height when some angry AIADMK enthusiasts set fire to a bus full of women students of the Tamil Nadu Agricultural University, Coimbatore. Three girls, Gayatri, Kokilavani and Hemalalithaa, were burnt to death and sixteen sustained burns.

Jayalalithaa blamed Karunanidhi for this horrific incident, calling it a part of his plan to sully the AIADMK's name before the three Assembly by-elections coming up. Even Karunanidhi's detractors were flabbergasted by this outrageous allegation. Indeed the AIADMK enthusiasts had no way of hiding their involvement in the bus burning. They had informed all the TV channels about their road blockade so that Amma would know how loyal and devoted they were to her. The incident was filmed not only by Sun TV but also Jaya TV and photographed and reported in graphic detail by local reporters. AIADMK men were seen pouring petrol over the bus and igniting it. Also seen were teachers and students crying for mercy.

A more sensational court verdict came on 9 October 2000. In the TANSI land case, Jayalalithaa and Sasikala were convicted in the lower court, which sentenced her to two years' rigorous imprisonment and a fine of Rs 50,000. The political implications were deadly. Jayalalithaa was disqualified from contesting the 2001 Tamil Nadu Assembly elections!

The DMK party members were jubilant. 'She is finished,' they said. Karunanidhi was careful not to express what he felt. He was in any case confident the DMK would be voted back to power, considering the good work his government had done. He could rest assured the people would reward him for it.

The court's indictment emboldened him further. Jayalalithaa could not contest elections for another six years. She could appeal in a higher court and come out on bail of course but the 2001 elections were not for her.

Karunanidhi's respite was short-lived. There was no dearth of twists and turns in the political theatre when Jayalalithaa was the prima donna.

15

The Wounded Tigress Fights Back

On 24 April 2001 Tamil Nadu was gearing up for Assembly elections and the four most closely watched constituencies were Krishnagiri, Andipatti, Bhuvanagiri and Pudukkottai. The star candidate in these constituencies was former chief minister Jayalalithaa. In spite of being barred from standing for elections for six years, she had filed her nomination papers in four places.

But the four returning officers rejected her petitions one after the other, saying that Jayalalithaa's election petition came under the Representation of the People Act, Section 3, which disqualifies a person 'convicted by a trial court for an offence (in the TANSI land corruption case) and been sentenced to more than two years' imprisonment, to stand for election'. Jayalalithaa was defying yet another rule: a candidate's nomination could be rejected if 'the candidate has been nominated from more than two constituencies . . .'

She expected her applications to be rejected, but consummate actor and political player that she was, she knew how to appeal to the sentiments of the electorate. She embarked on her election campaign like a wounded tigress.

'Karunanidhi has deliberately planned to destroy me. I shall fling away his mask and expose his true face!' she would begin, and then vehemently declare that he had heaped false cases on her, submitted concocted evidence and coerced election officials to reject all her four nomination papers. 'Do you know why he does all this? Because his son must be installed in power, he must continue to loot and plunder! You, only you, can bring to an end the evil deeds of Karunanidhi! For me, it is the verdict of the people that is more important than all other verdicts.'

Karunanidhi could see through her game plan. As her campaign became more and more aggressive, his campaign sounded more and more defensive. 'The law performed its duty. I do not have the authority to interfere in the decisions of the election officials. Did I advise anybody to buy the TANSI land? If she had asked me, wouldn't I have told her, speaking from experience as a former chief minister, "Amma, you can't buy government land, it's wrong!"' When his party workers laughed and cheered, he thought his words had hit home. When he described the welfare schemes introduced by his party, and asked them, 'Shouldn't good governance continue?' a loud chorus would break forth from the crowd: 'It must continue!' Karunanidhi became increasingly confident that the DMK would come back to power. How could Jayalalithaa, convicted for corruption and sentenced to imprisonment, even though she could appeal this verdict – ever dream of coming back? No sir, her story was over.

But the people of Tamil Nadu thought differently. As she stood before them like an ascetic, without a single gram of gold on her person, she would spread her sari pallu dramatically and ask for their 'alms'. Women wept and men looked visibly moved. They brought the AIADMK back even though its leader was not allowed to contest the elections. The AIADMK–Congress front won 196 of the 234 Assembly seats with AIADMK bagging 132, while the DMK–BJP front won just thirty-seven, out of which the DMK's share was a mere thirty-one. The voters were clearly dismissive of the court verdict against Jayalalithaa.

Karunanidhi was blindsided by the results. He said bitterly, 'I consider the verdict a gift from the people of Tamil Nadu for the successive achievements of our rule in the past five years.'

Jayalalithaa had cleverly roped in a number of parties in her alliance, while the DMK had got the BJP, which had no presence in Tamil Nadu. Moreover, all the minority votes went to Jayalalithaa.

Disregarding the law, she was elected leader of the legislative party in the Assembly. Article 164 of the Indian Constitution gives the Governor freedom to ask any person to become the chief minister and Fathima Beevi, the Tamil Nadu Governor, who had earlier made legal history as the first Indian woman to be appointed a Supreme Court judge, created history again by inviting Jayalalithaa to form the government. Jayalalithaa's brazen defiance of the rules was unprecedented and breathtaking at the same time. She doggedly held that the mandate given to the AIADMK was a mandate given to her: 'The people have given an overwhelming mandate for the AIADMK because they wanted *me* to be the chief minister. Any decision against swearing me in would have been an insult to the people's verdict,' she declared.

Her claim attracted widespread criticism. *The Hindu*, for example, in its editorial on 1 September 2001 commented:

> By staking her claim to become chief minister, Ms Jayalalithaa may have availed of certain ambiguities in the law over whether persons disqualified from contesting elections or convicted of corruption may occupy such office. But her hasty ascension . . . raised questions of disturbing moral and legal import . . . None of these ticklish matters would have arisen if Ms. Jayalalithaa had shown the maturity and wisdom to refrain from rushing to occupy the chief ministerial chair.[1]

Even as questions raised about the legality of her ascendance to chief ministership remained unanswered, she acted in her imperious way, sacking and shifting her ministers and officers at will and bullying journalists suspected of being pro-DMK.

In DMK circles there was an uneasy quiet. They expected the worst from the angry and bitter woman who had regained power against all predictions of her political doom and was now waiting for a chance to wreak vengeance on the villain in dark glasses who had thrown her in jail for twenty-eight days, who had harassed her with umpteen cases, hoping to break her will. She was waiting to pay back her foe in the same coin.

~

But no one, not even her bitterest foe Karunanidhi, could have imagined the nightmare that befell him on the dawn of 30 June 2001.

At about 2 a.m. Karunanidhi was dragged out of his bed from his residence in Chennai. The seventy-eight-year-old DMK leader was not even given time to change his clothes. The telephone lines were cut and the house filled with stiff, unfriendly policemen who were there to carry out Amma's orders – the same policemen who had stood respectfully to attention in front of the old man as long as he was the chief minister. Karunanidhi called up Murasoli Maran on his mobile phone. Maran, who was also a Union minister, happened to be in Chennai that day. Within minutes he reached the spot. The Sun TV crew arrived too and the police, perhaps drunk with the authority the uniform gave them, didn't stop them, perhaps hoping to appear as heroes.

The cameras captured it all – the damning evidence of the violation of human rights and the abuse of power. TV audiences across the state watched in disbelief as one terrified, frail old man screaming 'Aiyo' was dragged down the stairs by ten policemen; his rubber sandal falling off one wobbling foot before he was bundled into the van like a convicted criminal. They witnessed the rude exchange of words when Maran asked the police to produce the arrest warrant, and the physical scuffle with the Union minister, a heart patient. The police meted out similar treatment to T.R. Baalu, another Union minister from the DMK, who arrived on the scene. It was a shocking spectacle and Sun TV knew how potent the material was – and aired it all without a break.

Karunanidhi's arrest was followed by a spate of other arrests that included former municipal and administration minister Ko. Si. Mani, and former chief secretary K.A. Nambiar. Maran had to be admitted to the intensive care unit of Apollo Hospital as a result of the physical assault by the police. The excuse for the crackdown was charges of massive corruption. M.K. Stalin was the prime accused in this along with his father and others for amassing financial gains in the construction of flyovers in Chennai during the DMK regime. Stalin surrendered after a few hours. Twenty journalists were also taken into custody.

The incident created outrage not only in Tamil Nadu, but also in Delhi. A team from the ruling NDA led by Defence Minister George Fernandes came from Delhi, visited Karunanidhi in the Central Jail in Chennai and recommended President's rule in Tamil Nadu. But Prime Minister Vajpayee was reluctant to take a hasty step against a regime that had won a huge popular mandate. The immediate casualty was Tamil Nadu Governor Fathima Beevi, who had already been widely criticized for having sworn in Jayalalithaa as chief minister. The Centre now decided to recall her as 'she had failed to objectively reflect the situation in Tamil Nadu.' This sent a strong warning to Jayalalithaa, who soon thereafter ordered the release of Karunanidhi and the two Union ministers.

The release order was intimated to the media over the phone. It read, 'Taking into consideration the advanced age of Karunanidhi, the chief minister of Tamil Nadu, J. Jayalalithaa has ordered his release on humanitarian grounds. However, the cases against him will continue to proceed in the courts of law.'

Even hard-bitten journalists were moved when Karunanidhi held a press conference to relate his story. 'Mohamad Ali [DIG] pulled me down by my right hand which sprained my shoulder. I can't raise my hand. This is the hand I write with.' He told the journalists how his legs were swollen after he had been brutally manhandled by the police: 'I cannot stand for more than a couple of minutes as they dragged me down the steps, my legs banging against each stair.'

The case against Karunanidhi, his son and twelve others

pertained to alleged financial irregularities to the tune of Rs 12 crore in the construction of ten flyovers in Chennai.

The arrest was ordered on the basis of an FIR lodged by a municipal commissioner, a man who had faced charges of corruption earlier. The FIR was widely believed to be a concocted one, as Jayalalithaa was itching for retribution. She and her campaigners had thundered during her election campaigns that the corrupt Karunanidhi and his son would be taught a lesson and put behind bars. A woman campaigner from the AIADMK had used obscene words to describe how Karunanidhi would be thrown into prison, stripped even of his loincloth. An AIADMK member revealed: 'Madam is not as interested in the strength of the charges filed as she is to see them behind bars for at least one day.' After all, AIADMK supporters said, didn't Amma also languish in jail for twenty-eight days?

But Jayalalithaa forgot that there should be a method even in madness. You cannot knock at the door of anyone, let alone the former chief minister, in the dead of the night and say you were going to arrest him without an arrest warrant. And you can't drag him down like a criminal if he demands to see the arrest warrant.

Jayalalithaa's arrest in 1996 only happened after the high court had rejected all her anticipatory bail applications. And she was informed of her impending arrest well in advance, after daybreak. She had time to bathe, dress, do her puja, have her usual breakfast, pack and bid a proper goodbye to her partymen at the porch with a terse victory sign 'Nalai namathe!'

As Karunanidhi was whisked off to prison, he could hardly speak and hurriedly scribbled in a journalist's notepad 'aram vellum' (justice will prevail). After his release there was no mention of the cases against him. For Jayalalithaa it was the humiliation of

Panchali that had to be avenged; it was an all-consuming rage which ran beyond reason or logic. She was also in a hurry.

On 21 September 2001 the Supreme Court declared that 'the appointment of Jayalalithaa as chief minister of Tamil Nadu, which took place on May 14, was unconstitutional and void'.

~

An emergency meeting of the AIADMK ministers and district secretaries was held at Jayalalithaa's house in Poes Garden. Out of the blue she appointed a first-time MLA from Periyakulam, O. Panneerselvam, as the chief minister. Panneerselvam appeared dazed in the pictures published in the newspapers the next day. He and the ministers who were sworn in fell at Jayalalithaa's feet and sought her blessings. Amma herself looked amazingly calm and composed.

She claimed there would be no change in governance policies and schemes she had instituted. For all practical purposes, it was she who was still the chief minister. The bureaucrats stayed cautious and tight-lipped as they waited for Amma to come back.

That happened sooner than expected. By the middle of December, the Madras High Court acquitted her and the others accused in the TANSI case. Now free of that obstacle, she had to win an Assembly constituency to come back as chief minister of Tamil Nadu.

The sound of crackers at the AIADMK office rent the air, while the DMK took in this news with sombreness. Jayalalithaa stood for election from the R.K. Nagar constituency and won with a handsome mandate. Her brief absence from the helm of affairs was barely felt.

Back in the chief minister's seat, she was her imperious, whimsical self. And heady with her return to power, she went on to press the self-destruct button. In July 2003 she invoked the Essential Services Maintenance Act (ESMA) on one lakh government employees who had demanded a pay on par with Central government employees and advance bonus for festivals and had gone on strike when the government refused. The strikers' employment was terminated. The dismissed employees' defiance crumbled. They wept in front of the TV cameras, promising they would never again defy Amma's orders. When finally all except three thousand of the strikers were reinstated, they praised Amma's kind-hearted gesture. But many government employees vowed never again to vote for her.

Then Jayalalithaa suddenly announced that Chennai's nearly century-old Queen Mary's College for women would be demolished to set up a new secretariat. M.K. Stalin, who was president of the DMK's youth wing, won brownie points by rushing to Queen Mary's College to soothe the staff and students, but the principal was pulled up by Jayalalithaa for allowing him inside the campus. Then followed her ordinance against forced conversion and the ban on animal sacrifice (there were rumours that she followed the advice of the Kanchi Sankaracharya).

Jayalalithaa then filed cases against senior political leaders in the Opposition parties, the DMK in particular, for supporting the strikers. She turned even more hostile towards the press. The Speaker of the Assembly issued warrants of arrest against N. Ram, and his brother, N. Ravi, who obtained a stay for the arrests from the Supreme Court. All these acts reflected her autocratic and vindictive manner of functioning and alienated large sections of the population as well as the press.

She had already received another drubbing from the Supreme Court. K. Anbazhagan, general secretary of the DMK, petitioned the Supreme Court requesting that all the cases filed against Jayalalithaa in Tamil Nadu be moved to the courts of another state since people had lost trust in the Chennai courts when Jayalalithaa was in power and the apex court transferred the cases to the Karnataka special courts.

The Opposition parties were not allowed to speak in the Assembly. 'The lady is poking a honeycomb,' Karunanidhi warned. 'It will be difficult for her to take the sting.'

And so it turned out to be. Within two years she lost all the goodwill she had earned in 2001. '*Makkal theerpu mahesan theerpu.*' The people's verdict is God's verdict, she had said back in May 2001 when she took her oath as chief minister, violating the Constitution. This time around, when she had come back legitimately, the people turned against her.

~

In preparation for the 2004 Lok Sabha elections Karunanidhi planned his strategy with new vigour. Anticipating that Jayalalithaa would align with the BJP, he roped in a large group of secular parties – the MDMK, the PMK, the Dalit Viduthalai Chiruthaigal Katchi, the left – as well as the minorities to join him. The Congress too supported this front. Sonia Gandhi graciously set aside the Jain Commission report and came forward to join hands with him.

Not only Karunanidhi but also the people of Tamil Nadu seemed intent on bringing Jayalalithaa to her knees.

~

Jayalalithaa was shell-shocked at the results of the 2004 Lok Sabha elections. The AIADMK–BJP alliance received a severe pummelling at the hands of the DMK-led Democratic Progressive Alliance which bagged all the forty Lok Sabha seats, including one from Pondicherry.

Karunanidhi's thumping victory in the national elections revived the DMK's hopes of resurgence in Tamil Nadu. The Congress formed the government at the Centre, with Manmohan Singh as prime minister. The DMK's alliance partners, the PMK and the left, were happy because they now wielded influence at the Centre, having got Cabinet berths, thanks to the grand old patriarch's pre-election alliance with the Congress. They were only too willing to join hands with him for the 2006 Assembly elections. Most importantly, it was 'for a cause' as they put it – a fight against the 'anti-people rule' of their common enemy, Jayalalithaa, who had insulted and betrayed them all in varying degrees whenever they had had the misfortune to align with her.

Jayalalithaa still believed her popularity alone would see her through despite her rivals' strong coalition.

A third factor had emerged in the form of a new party called the Desiya Murpokku Dravida Kazhagam (DMDK) floated by the actor Vijayakanth. Vijayakanth projected himself as the harbinger of a clean rule after years of suffering caused at the hands of the corrupt DMK and AIADMK regimes. He had no ideology to offer nor was he clear about how he would tackle corruption, but his public speeches were drawing huge crowds.

More worrying for Karunanidhi were the poll surveys that showed Jayalalithaa's popularity soaring despite her being the head of an incumbent government. She was reaping the benefit of the good work some district collectors had done post the tsunami and the floods.

She adopted a new image – no longer the autocratic empress but the benevolent mother, the protector of the Tamils, a humble woman who toiled twenty-three hours in a day for their welfare. She had victory within her grasp.

If the DMK panicked, it was reflected in its manifesto presented on the eve of the elections. It promised great largesse and many freebies to the voters, such as rice at Rs 2 a kilo, free TV sets and free gas connections to those below the poverty line, and 2 acres of land to the landless poor. The left and other partners in the coalition were dumbfounded. How could these promises be fulfilled? However, they did not air their doubts publicly. Jayalalithaa hastily denounced the DMK manifesto as a cheap gimmick and a lie, but soon announced some freebies that *she* would offer.

It may have been an election gimmick but the DMK manifesto was a masterstroke. Karunanidhi had never been a favourite among women voters, unlike MGR. But now he appeared as a gentle patriarch who took care of their needs. He was even going to fulfil their dreams of owning a TV, a special lure for the TV-crazy women of Tamil Nadu. If you voted for him, you could get 2 acres of land too!

As if to defy all rumours about his failing health, Karunanidhi went about campaigning with astonishing tenacity. The image of the elderly Karunanidhi leaning on the shoulder of the youthful, cherubic Dayanidhi Maran, his grand-nephew who was Central minister for communication and information technology, coupled with the lure of freebies, charmed the voters. The DMK coalition came out victorious, though surprisingly the DMK failed to get an absolute majority.

Vijayakanth's DMDK won just one seat, but the party got a surprising 8 per cent vote share, more than the PMK or the MDMK, parties of more than fifteen years' standing. The AIADMK did not do too badly, winning sixty-seven seats, and thus emerging as the single largest party after the DMK. The Congress, which won thirty-five seats, hoped to get some ministerial posts but Karunanidhi, thanks to a private assurance from Sonia Gandhi that it would be the DMK alone that would rule in Tamil Nadu, managed to deflect them. And so in 2006 it was the DMK back in power – never mind if it was a minority government, supported from outside by coalition partners who could be relied on not to pull out midway.

Doubts about the DMK fulfilling its electoral promises were laid to rest when Karunanidhi dramatically signed the government order to sell ration rice at Rs 2 a kilo, minutes after the government was sworn in. Within a month, distribution of free TV sets and gas connections began in stages.

Power rejuvenated Karunanidhi. His wit and memory were as sharp as they had been four decades ago. His health too seemed more robust. He was now on a strict vegetarian diet and practised yoga for an hour every morning under the guidance of Deshikachari, a well-known yoga teacher. But he knew this would be his last tenure as chief minister and that he would have to prepare wisely for the future of the party and his family before it was too late. After years of careful grooming, his son, Stalin, he knew, would carry on his legacy.

Once the administrative reins were in his hands there were various ways to keep Jayalalithaa and Vijayakanth, potential rivals to the heir apparent, on their toes – filing corruption charges against them for illegal construction of buildings, illegal possession of land and so on. Even old cases against Jayalalithaa could be raked up, such as questioning the legality of her filing nomination papers from four places during the 2001 Assembly elections. Court cases could break the back of the fund-starved Vijaykanth, and cases against Jayalalithaa could debar her from standing for elections again.

~

Karunanidhi's fifth and last tenure as chief minister of Tamil Nadu was a particularly active one. Between 2006 and 2011 a large number of schemes were announced. Karunanidhi had a great desire to do everything on a grand scale, to build structures and introduce schemes that would speak not only of the glory of his regime but have a lasting impact on the lives of the people. The state spent heavily on building a grand new secretariat-cum-assembly building and one of Asia's largest libraries, the Anna Centenary Library, in Kotturpuram, Chennai.

Samacheer Kalvi, Tamil Nadu's unique school education policy that promised uniform and equitable education to all, was also introduced. Among other major schemes were Kalaignar Maruthuva Kaappeettu Thittam (Kalaignar health insurance scheme for the poor) and exclusive reservation within the backward caste quota for Muslims, as well as reservation for Arundathiyars within the scheduled caste quota. Karunanidhi was determined to give real substance to the concept of a 'welfare state'.

Samacheer Kalvi was an ambitious, carefully crafted scheme that would ensure everyone had access to the same quality of education.

There was a popular perception, rightly so, that private institutions were better than government schools. This disparity resulted in commercial exploitation by private schools and kept quality education out of the reach of the poor. Tamil Nadu had different systems of education, such as the state board, matriculation, Anglo-Indian, CBSE and ICSE, each with a different syllabus, different patterns of examination and evaluation. Karunanidhi's instruction to Thangam Thennarasu, the minister put in charge of this scheme, was, 'Education must be uniform for everyone, irrespective of whether they study in government schools or private schools.' While urban upper-middle-class families preferred CBSE and ICSE, the two most popular syllabi were the state board that covered the rural poor in government schools and the matriculation syllabus, which was taught in private schools. A team of experts was formed to conduct a detailed analysis of the different syllabi to bring them on par with the CBSE syllabus, which was, arguably, of a higher standard. This had to be done phase by phase or it would hurt students in the rural areas. Karunanidhi went through copies of old textbooks and observed how unattractive they must be for children. He advised Thennarasu to go to Singapore and study the model of education there. He told him, 'Go to Singapore, pick up the textbooks there and see how they have done it. The font size has to be large. Improve the quality of the textbooks.' He also wanted to introduce computer education.

Predictably, the AIADMK lambasted the new syllabus for being substandard and politically loaded, with chapters in textbooks singing Karunanidhi's praises and extolling the DMK's achievements. The private matriculation schools also vociferously opposed it. It turned into a court battle at the Madras High Court which gave its verdict on 30 April 2010, allowing the curriculum to be implemented but instructing that the objectionable political content be deleted. Justice Prabha Sridevan (retired), who was with Justice P.P.S. Janardana Raja, in the quorum that scrutinized the syllabus and gave the judgement, says that it was a sensible scheme. 'In no other state were there so many streams of education as Tamil Nadu had. All the states have only two boards – the State Board and the Central Board. The mere fact that historically this state had four streams of education does not mean that the state, with the avowed object of ensuring social justice and quality education, cannot bring in a uniform quality-based system of education.'

When the government changed in 2011, Jayalalithaa delayed the implementation of Samacheer Kalvi, declaring that the curriculum was poor. The schools were worried: Samacheer syllabi books had already been printed and classes had to be started. The matter went to the Supreme Court which categorically told the state government in its verdict on 9 August 2011 to 'implement the Samacheer Kalvi within ten days'.

~

There was another major project – the construction of the ambitious new secretariat-cum-assembly building at a cost of Rs 1200 crore. Karunanidhi laid the foundation stone for the new building at Omandur Estate in 2008 and Prime Minister Manmohan Singh inaugurated the premises in March 2010. There were delays in completing the construction that caused worry. Thennarasu, who was given charge of overseeing the construction, recalls, 'He [Karunanidhi] would come three times a day to check on the progress of the secretariat.' Though he was annoyed at the delays and had announced the date of opening, he never raised his voice in anger, but he would not visit the site for a couple of days. Thennarasu took this as a sign of disapproval and worked longer hours to supervise progress even on Sundays. Once Karunanidhi showed up at the construction site at midnight when Thennarasu was there alone. Worried that Karunanidhi had come to admonish him Thennarasu went up to his car to give him an update. Karunanidhi interrupted him. 'Forget about all that. We can speak about that tomorrow. They told me you were here alone. So I came to see you,' said the chief minister and sat with the young man on the steps. According to Sandhya Ravishankar in *Karunanidhi: A Life in Politics*, 'Thennarasu breaks down remembering the moment. "What a leader, what a great man, he was. Everyone used to tell me he was like a mother. I experienced it that day. He sat with me for about ten minutes and then left."'[2]

Karunanidhi was then in his eighties.

The inauguration was set for March 2010 and the prime minister had been invited. But the dome of the building was not yet ready. The film art director Thotta Tharani was roped in to create a temporary dome worth Rs 3 crore for the inauguration. The media, reflecting public opinion, went to town criticizing the extravaganza held for the inauguration of the building even before the construction was complete. This unsettled Karunanidhi.

~

The third big project that Thennarasu was entrusted with was the building of the Anna Centenary Library. It was a remarkable modern structure that is now the pride of Chennai. Built on 8 acres of land in Kotturpuram, the nine-floor library's plinth area is 3,33,140 square feet and has the capacity to accommodate 1.2 million books. There is an integrated library management system that includes automated issue and return of books, user smart cards to access controls, radio frequency identification technology and self-check counters. The library can accommodate 1250 persons. It includes other facilities like an auditorium with a seating capacity of 1280. Scholars, writers and students were thrilled.

~

Within a year of the completion of the library, Jayalalithaa was back as chief minister and hell-bent on undoing all of Karunanidhi's work. She changed the grand new secretariat into a multi-speciality hospital, spending Rs 7 crore more. If that hurt Karunanidhi's feelings, the news that she planned to convert the Anna Centenary Library into a children's hospital must have crushed his heart.

People began to express their disapproval of this plan. Perhaps the widespread public opposition made her drop the idea, but during her tenure from 2011 to 2016 the AIADMK government made it a point to neglect the library's maintenance.

~

The most laudable scheme, introduced by Karunanidhi in 2009, was the one that aimed at making healthcare more affordable for the poor. The Maruthuva Kaappeettu Thittam targeted one crore families, providing medical insurance cover to the tune of Rs 1 lakh to each. The scheme assured the cardholder complete cashless treatment for the amount insured. The government would pay the insurance premium of Rs 500 per year and about Rs 1500 crore was spent on the scheme. While all medical procedures were not covered under the insurance scheme, major surgeries such as heart bypass surgery were. When Jayalalithaa came back to power in 2011, she understood how successful the scheme was and therefore did not disband it, but changed the name to Chief Minister's Comprehensive Health Insurance Scheme.

During his chief ministership from 2006 to 2011, Karunanidhi was in his late eighties, but showed amazing energy and attention to detail in implementing the schemes, even monitoring and following Assembly proceedings from his hospital bed when he had to undergo surgery for a severe back problem.

~

Alas, for all his vision and skills in governance, and his vigour and ability in implementing his schemes, he was not able to control his own partymen. Many regional strongmen of the DMK allegedly indulged in large-scale land-grabbing and corruption. They had grown far too powerful within the party and Karunanidhi not only did nothing to rein them in, he stood by them. Perhaps he felt obliged to them for their contribution to the DMK's electoral victories and turned a blind eye to their questionable methods and tactics. This was a major weakness in Karunanidhi's later years.

Karunanidhi had an austere personal lifestyle and shunned extravagance and luxury. 'Kalaignar had no desire to acquire or own wealth. He led a simple life,' says senior DMK leader Durai Murugan. 'When Rahul Gandhi visited him at his Gopalapuram residence he expressed surprise that a person who was chief minister five times lived in such a modest house.'

But his last tenure was so riddled with controversies, scandals, internecine rivalry and the violent behaviour of his hot-tempered son, Alagiri, that all the good he had so painstakingly done for the welfare of the state got obliterated from public memory.

16

Family Matters

Karunanidhi believed in the old adage 'blood is thicker than water'. Cho Ramaswamy, his biggest critic, once said, 'Karunanidhi's weakness was his love for his family.' Karunanidhi was indeed a devoted family man, but his family was a large, extended one, fraught with competing ambitions, bitter rivalries, and emotional complexities.

There were two living wives, children from three wives, grandchildren, nephews, grand-nephews – many of them talented but ambitious. It is a wonder how he managed to juggle everyone and keep the flock together. He did not succeed entirely.

Muthu, his eldest son, born to his first wife Padma who died after childbirth, grew up in Gopalapuram with his father. More than his stepmother, Dayalu, it was Karunanidhi's elder sister who lived in the same street, who took care of Muthu. Karunanidhi was very attached to him and wanted him to get a good education. Muthu, however, was not too keen on studying, but showed interest in writing scripts for films and also acting. Muthu was quite a handsome youth, with a good physique. And so, at a time when Karunanidhi's rivalry with MGR became intense, he tried to promote Muthu as an actor, hoping he could wean away MGR's fans. To shore up Muthu's self-confidence, he installed him in a separate house (though in the same street in Gopalapuram), and fixed his marriage to the girl he had fallen in love with. Muthu acted in a few films but his acting career never took off. To Karunanidhi's sorrow, he then fell into bad company and became an alcoholic. Karunanidhi took charge of Muthu's two children – a son, Arivunidhi, and a daughter, Thenmozhi – and ensured they were well educated and well settled in life. But he could not reform his son. A drunk Muthu would often stand before Karunanidhi's house and abuse his father for not giving him money when he demanded it. When Muthu fell ill and was hospitalized, Karunanidhi went to see him and wept, lamenting that his eldest son had ruined his life. But what really broke Karunanidhi's heart was the news that Muthu had taken Rs 5 lakh from Jayalalithaa. Muthu eventually snapped ties with his father and his siblings, who were never close to him. Now, abandoned by his own children, he lives alone in Neelankarai, a suburb of Chennai. He was not seen even at his father's funeral.

Dayalu, Karunanidhi's second wife, who lived with him in the family home in Gopalapuram, bore him three sons, Alagiri, Stalin[1] and Thamilarasu, and a daughter, Selvi.

Rajathi, Karunanidhi's 'partner' but not his legal wife, lived with her daughter Kanimozhi in a house in CIT Colony, not far from Gopalapuram.

The late Murasoli Maran and Murasoli Selvam were the sons of Karunanidhi's elder sister Shanmugasundarathammaal.

Karunanidhi was very close to her. She was highly respected and consulted on all important family matters. Karunanidhi's daughter Selvi married her son Murasoli Selvam.

The Marans, from all accounts, appear to be the brightest in the family tree – not merely because of the political connections they established thanks to Karunanidhi but also due to their own business acumen and good education. Murasoli Maran, Karunanidhi's favourite nephew, was just ten years younger than him and 'closer to him than his own sons'. A postgraduate in the arts with another degree in law, he was intelligent and articulate, fluent in English, well read and like Karunanidhi had versatile talents as a journalist, writer, orator and film scriptwriter. He was an MP for thirty-six years and served in the Union Cabinet under three prime ministers – V.P. Singh, I.K. Gujral and Atal Bihari Vajpayee. Murasoli Maran was an effective voice for Karunanidhi and for the DMK in Delhi, and had an impeccable reputation for being able, disciplined and incorruptible. When he died in 2003, a bereaved Karunanidhi said that Maran had been like his own conscience.

Murasoli Maran's sons, Kalanidhi Maran and Dayanidhi Maran, are the famous 'Maran brothers' whose combined business and political clout were formidable at one point. Sun TV, the channel owned by Kalanidhi Maran, is said to have been started with Rs 1 crore that was gifted to him by Karunanidhi. The Sun network today is valued at $4 billion by *Forbes Magazine*. The Sun Group owns TV channels, radio stations, newspapers and a movie production house, among other things.

Dayanidhi Maran, an economics graduate who also did a management course at Harvard Business School, developed a special expertise in media, TV and cable technology as an associate of his brother Kalanidhi. He won three terms in the Lok Sabha in the 2004, 2009 and 2019 general elections. Dayanidhi proved adept at politics. After the death of his father he was inducted into electoral politics in 2004 by Karunanidhi who made him stand for the general elections as the DMK candidate from the Chennai Central constituency. He won with a huge margin of 1,34,000 votes. He was then appointed Union minister for communications and information technology in the Congress-led Manmohan Singh government. In his three-year stint as telecom minister, Dayanidhi Maran delivered tangible results. During his tenure the call rates of mobiles and landlines were reduced, which in turn fuelled the growth of subscriptions. He was also instrumental in garnering a large amount of foreign direct investments into the IT sector. Multinational telecom companies including Nokia, Motorola, Ericsson, and Dell set up units in the country, impressed by the laptop-wielding young minister. His ministry introduced the 'one rupee, one India' plan, enabling calls across the country at the rate of Re 1 per minute. By 2007 his ministry had achieved its target of 250 million phone connections – up from 75 million in 2004.

The growing popularity of Dayanidhi Maran and the advantage the Sun TV network gained because of his ministerial office became a cause of unease within Karunanidhi's extended family.

As the patriarch of such a huge clan, Karunanidhi had little time to delve into the simmering cauldron of aspirations, jealousies and frustrations within his family. Sometimes he felt like the blind Dhritarashtra, groping in the dark to assuage their conflicting demands and desires.

Apart from the resentment against the growing clout of the Maran brothers, he also had to contend with the bitter sibling rivalry between his sons, Stalin and Alagiri.

Karunanidhi tried hard to mediate between the two but never succeeded. Stalin's steady rise in the party since the Emergency days, when he had played an active role in opposing Indira Gandhi and suffered in jail for it, and Karunanidhi's clear preference for him over his elder brother, aroused deep envy and resentment in Alagiri. While Stalin was made head of the DMK's youth wing in 1982, Karunanidhi tried to ease Alagiri's resentment by sending him to Madurai and making him in charge of the DMK's south zone. Alagiri went on to build a fiefdom of his own in the southern districts. He rose to notoriety with what became known as the Thirumangalam formula – the large-scale distribution of money to voters during the by-polls in Thirumangalam near Madurai, in 2009. Alagiri used gangs, violence and crime to consolidate his power.

Stalin was the opposite, quiet and polished, never openly critical of his brother. He had earned his spurs in the DMK, joining the party as a student at fourteen, jailed during the Emergency and elected four times to the Assembly from 1989. He was the first directly elected mayor of Chennai in 1996 and was re-elected in 2001. At that time he was also an MLA. But Jayalalithaa, who had by then come to power, tried to clip Stalin's wings by bringing an amendment that prevented a person from holding two posts. The Madras High Court struck down the law but said that a person could not stand for the mayor's post twice.

As mayor, Stalin's work was widely appreciated. Among other civic improvements, he built several flyovers that considerably eased the flow of traffic in the city. He was, by all indications, the chosen son who would inherit his father's mantle one day, even though Karunanidhi never formally anointed him as his successor during his lifetime. He remained president of the party till his death. Stalin was, however, made deputy chief minister in 2009 and executive president of the DMK when Karunanidhi was seriously ill in 2017.

~

But in 2007 the main family problem that plagued Karunanidhi was not the sibling rivalry between his sons, but the strife between his sons and his grand-nephews, the Maran brothers.

It came out into the open after the Tamil daily *Dinakaran* (dated 8 May 2007) owned by Kalanidhi Maran's Sun TV network, carried an opinion poll on who should be Karunanidhi's successor in the DMK. The results showed that 70 per cent of the voters wanted Stalin as Karunanidhi's successor; only 2 per cent wanted Alagiri, while another 2 per cent voted for Karunanidhi's daughter Kanimozhi. Party sources said Karunanidhi was annoyed that such a survey was done when he was still alive and that he had asked the newspaper not to publish it, but the paper went ahead anyway, since it had already advertised it.

In Tamil Nadu, where even tabloid journalism is often taken as gospel truth, this was enough to ignite violence. The very next day supporters of the 'thenmaavatta muthalvar' (chief minister of southern districts), as Alagiri was referred to, burnt down the Madurai office of *Dinakaran* for publishing the opinion poll, which clearly underlined Alagiri's unacceptability to the people of Tamil Nadu. The office was ransacked, windows and doors broken and petrol bombs hurled inside. Shockingly, top police officers chose to wait for 'political clearance' from the chief minister's office before deciding to stop the attackers. By the time Karunanidhi gave the go-ahead to the police, the situation had spiralled out of control, leaving two employees and a security guard of the media group dead.

In its news bulletins, Sun TV directly accused Alagiri of unleashing his goons on the group's office in Madurai and called for his arrest. It also pointed out repeatedly that Alagiri was already involved in the pending murder case of T. Krishnan, a former DMK minister. It added that Alagiri had a poor track record – in 2000, when Karunanidhi disowned him politically, he had instigated violence.[2]

The people of Tamil Nadu, avid watchers of Sun TV, the most popular TV channel in the state, were appalled at visuals of the violence inflicted by Alagiri's men on the *Dinakaran* office, and the DMK quickly initiated a damagecontrol exercise to counter the adverse effect of Alagiri's behaviour. Arcot Veerasamy, the state minister for electricity and a confidant of Karunanidhi, let it be known that Kalanidhi's brother Dayanidhi Maran, Union minister for communications and information technology had allegedly threatened state home secretary S. Malathi to either 'arrest Alagiri or face the consequences'. The DMK then held a meeting and issued a resolution condemning the 'anti-party activities' of Dayanidhi Maran, and 'authorized' its leader Karunanidhi to take necessary action against him in whatever manner he deemed fit. The young Maran, who had won much praise within a short period for his performance as a Union minister, sent in his resignation from the Union Cabinet.

The DMK resolution was of course an attempt to portray the decision as one taken by the party and not by Karunanidhi himself, prompted by his sons Stalin and Alagiri. It could not appear that in a power struggle between his sons and his grand-nephews, he would protect his sons.

None of those present at the meeting raised the fact that the arson, looting and murder by hooligans owing allegiance to Alagiri also involved serious questions of law and order and of freedom of the press. Nor did they ask the chief minister, who also held the home portfolio, why the state police had watched in silence as thugs ransacked the *Dinakaran* offices, threw petrol bombs and beat up the employees. No one dared ask who was responsible for the loss of three innocent lives due to a family squabble with which the victims were not connected. The party seemed to project the view that it was all justified because the provocation for the attack was the publication of the findings of a survey in the daily that asked the blasphemous question 'Who should be Karunanidhi's political heir?'

The timing of the survey was undoubtedly bad. It was on the eve of the celebration of Karunanidhi's fifty years as a legislator. Also, since Karunanidhi's sons had reconciled to the fact that Stalin would in all likelihood succeed Karunanidhi as chief minister while Alagiri would be the chieftain of the southern region, the survey was seen as mischief-making on the part of the Maran brothers.

When Alagiri came to attend the grand Chennai golden jubilee function in honour of his father, he was received at the airport by senior ministers and officials and taken through the VVIP route. Karunanidhi made it clear that his son was above reproach, but he also silenced the media by announcing that the task of probing the tragic events at Madurai would be handed over to the CBI as his 'own son was blamed to have been behind it'.

The Hindu, which had strongly condemned the violence instigated by Alagiri's supporters in Madurai and had demanded a CBI enquiry, went absolutely quiet after the chief minister's assurance and also perhaps because Sun TV itself went silent on the whole issue. It was obvious that the leader was in total control of the party as well as his family. Dayanidhi held a press conference to declare he was innocent and that Karunanidhi would always be his leader and he would remain and die a DMK loyalist.

~

When Karunanidhi made Dayanidhi, a political greenhorn, stand for the Lok Sabha elections and then got him a Union Cabinet post as communications and IT minister, he had believed that just as Murasoli Maran, his trusted confidant and nephew, was a great help to him at the Centre, so would Dayanidhi be for Stalin.

Karunanidhi had failed to see the inevitable. The smart, ambitious and media-savvy Dayanidhi and Kalanidhi with his shrewd business mind were a formidable combination. They were extremely successful in whatever they did. Stalin and Alagiri, neither well educated nor fluent in English, may have watched their growth with increasing insecurity.

To an outsider it would indeed be inexplicable that the DMK was interested only in condemning Dayanidhi and expressed no outrage at the arson and murder committed by Alagiri's supporters. But the fact of the matter was that there were few sympathizers for the Maran brothers among the Tamil public. The huge media network they owned and the resources at their command made the Marans the target of much public ire.

Fissures between the Maran brothers and Karunanidhi's family had first surfaced when Kalanidhi started making moves to become the sole owner of the Sun network. He is said to have acquired shares held by Karunanidhi's wife Dayalu Ammal for less than 15 per cent of their actual worth. DMK sources considered the Marans truly heartless to have cheated Karunanidhi so, especially since they had started Sun TV with his money.

While money proved to be the point of friction at one end, there were political rivalries between the Marans and Karunanidhi's immediate family too. Party sources say that Dayanidhi had made the cardinal mistake of publicly criticizing Stalin's 'below average' performance as a party worker and also as a state minister. So when *Dinakaran* went ahead and published the poll survey findings, triggering savage protests from Alagiri's men, Karunanidhi was right, they said, in cutting this upstart Maran to size and showing him the door.

With Dayanidhi Maran's resignation from the Union Cabinet, Karunanidhi requested the prime minister to hand over the important communications and IT portfolio to the DMK MP A. Raja, a Dalit who was already then Cabinet minister for environment and forest. Dayanidhi's resignation left another slot for a ministerial birth at the Centre vacant, and Karunanidhi did not want to let go of it, having bargained for a specific number of berths for the DMK. He chose Radhika Selvi, widow of a powerful Nadar from Tuticorin, feared as a don, to fill the slot.[3] She was made minister of state for home affairs.

No tears were shed for the Maran brothers, either in the media or in political circles. The huge media network they owned and the resources at their command, strengthened by Dayanidhi's political clout, had made them brazen, arrogant and deeply unpopular. The virtual monopoly of their Sumangali Cable network, their enormous influence in thwarting the expansion projects of other channels like Jaya TV and Raj TV and their unethical ways of stifling the sales of other magazines and dailies to increase the circulation of their journals *Kungumam* and *Dinakaran* turned those running both the visual and the print media against them. The channels run by the AIADMK and the PMK and other private channels had suffered no end because of Sun TV's monopoly over cable operators who feared antagonizing them.

When Jayalalitha was in power, she tried to bring an ordinance to make cable operation a state-owned venture but at that time Karunanidhi went personally to request the Governor, Surjit Singh Barnala, who was his friend, not to give his assent to the bill.

After the violence in Madurai, Sun TV, which functioned from Anna Arivalayam, the DMK party headquarters, was asked to vacate the premises and move to another building. The space became the office of Kalaignar TV, and Dayalu Ammal and Kanimozhi were made nominal directors of the Kalaignar TV channel.

The general feeling among the DMK cadres at this time was that despite its negative fallout, the *Dinakaran* episode had brought Karunanidhi's children closer. 'There is no rivalry between Stalin and Alagiri,' declared T.K.S. Elangovan, the DMK's organizing secretary. 'Stalin will be our next leader and everyone including Alagiri has accepted him.' It also meant that Alagiri would have his say in controlling the party in the south and, when the party was in power, even in the selection of IAS officers and police officials – never mind if it meant wielding extra-constitutional authority. Karunanidhi must have deemed this the best arrangement to avoid friction between the brothers.

Soon after, Karunanidhi nominated his daughter Kanimozhi, a convent-educated postgraduate in economics, a poet and journalist, to the Rajya Sabha. Karunanidhi had earlier promoted Dayanidhi Maran at the Centre, hoping he would be of help to Stalin in his dealings with the Centre. And now the same could be expected of Kanimozhi. After all she too was fluent in English and what couldn't a woman do that a man could? Besides, the modest and unassuming Kanimozhi would never pose a threat to Stalin. So the plan was perfect – Kanimozhi at the Centre, Stalin the future chief minister and Alagiri the monarch of the southern region. He was aware of the rumblings in the party from male aspirants who felt they were more eligible to be nominated to the Rajya Sabha than his daughter. But age had made him more vulnerable, and some past experiences had taught him that he needed trustworthy people at the helm. And that meant family.

The dynastic tussles exposed how fragile the political system that Karunanidhi had nurtured had become. For this he could blame nobody but himself. It was his habit to say with great emotion that the party was his family. The members of the party were his 'udanpirappugal' (brethren). Now his own family seemed to have become the most significant symbol of the party. And as a result, the party looked weak, devoid of moral authority and credibility.

~

On the morning of 3 December 2008 all the newspapers in Tamil Nadu carried big colour pictures of Karunanidhi's united family, the Marans included, smiling as they clustered around the patriarch. Karunanidhi realized that a rift in the family would affect their political and financial fortunes and benefit none of them. The family feud had tarnished the party's image in the public's eyes. He was also aware that he and the DMK needed Kalanidhi Maran and Sun TV, especially with the 2009 Lok Sabha elections imminent. Pragmatism apart, there was also a deep emotional bond with the Maran brothers – their father, in Karunanidhi's own words, was 'dearer to me than my own sons'. The Maran brothers called Karunanidhi thaatha (grandpa). Moreover, Karunanidhi's daughter

Selvi was married to Murasoli Maran's brother Selvam. She was apparently extremely upset when the feud seemed impossible to mend and pleaded with Karunanidhi to relent. So, though the 'disloyalty' of the Marans after all he had done for them had upset him greatly, he found it in his heart to forgive and forget, and bring them back into the family fold.

~

For the 2009 Lok Sabha elections, the DMK continued its alliance with the Congress-led UPA. The Congress came to power in the Centre again and the DMK won an impressive eighteen Lok Sabha seats. Karunanidhi got a Cabinet post for Dayanidhi as minister for textiles, while A. Raja got the information technology portfolio again, even though Prime Minister Manmohan Singh was reportedly not in favour of reappointing Raja due to a controversy about the allocation of 2G spectrum during Raja's tenure in the previous UPA rule. But the biggest surprise for Karunanidhi's own party cadre was that he got a Cabinet post in Delhi for Alagiri, who had never crossed the borders of Tamil Nadu and did not speak either English or Hindi. Perhaps Karunanidhi thought keeping Alagiri busy in Delhi as minister for chemicals and fertilizers would temper his resentment towards his brother Stalin. But this blatant promotion of his undeserving son put Karunanidhi down in the eyes of his party members and his alliance partners.

Gopanna, a senior Congress leader in Tamil Nadu, echoes a commonly held view when he says, 'Karunanidhi should have been firm in letting Stalin alone remain in party politics. Stalin entered politics early and passed through every step like any other member. Karunanidhi never gave him positions just because he was his son.

It took forty years for Stalin to become deputy chief minister. Stalin's rise was democratic. If Karunanidhi had kept the others of the family out of politics, his stock as a political leader would have been very high, comparable to that of Jyoti Basu. Bringing Alagiri into politics was a very big mistake. It led to a lot of problems later that could have been avoided.'

Senior DMK member Durai Murugan, like others in the party, was also perplexed by this decision. 'We do not understand why thalaivar did that,' he says. In keeping with the DMK's code of discipline they remained quiet. But they also remembered that, in 2000, the DMK general secretary, K. Anbazhagan, had requested partymen at the behest of Karunanidhi not to have any truck with Alagiri since he had violated party discipline. And yet the same Alagiri was later given charge of the southern region.

There was a reason why Alagiri was given that charge, says DMK member K.P. Ramalingam. After Vaiko left the party, the DMK had become weak in the southern part of Tamil Nadu. Karunanidhi recognized Alagiri's organizational skills and considered him the person to revive it. He was proved right when, under the leadership of an aggressive Alagiri, the DMK won all the three by-elections in the region. It was also then that Alagiri's cash-for-vote Thirumangalam formula emerged.

As satrap of southern Tamil Nadu, Alagiri surrounded himself with men who did not care for the rule of law. There were constant clashes between his men and Stalin's supporters in and around Madurai. These hit their peak with the murder of Tha. Kiruttinan, a DMK loyalist and former minister who was highly influential in Sivaganga district. He was Stalin's friend and Alagiri did not get along with him. Alagiri wanted his own man in Sivaganga. Krishnan lived in Madurai. On 20 May 2003 Kiruttinan was brutally axed to death by four men in the middle of the road near his house, just as he left for his morning walk. His wife said she was certain the killers were Alagiri's henchmen. Alagiri was arrested the same day, even before the post-mortem, and put in prison. Jayalalithaa was in power then and Alagiri claimed innocence, saying he was a victim of political vendetta. The alleged killers were also arrested.

When the DMK came to power in 2006, the case was shifted to the Chittoor (Andhra) courts under a Supreme Court order. In May 2008 the courts acquitted Alagiri and his co-accused due to lack of evidence.

~

Alagiri could not find his feet in Delhi. He avoided attending Parliament, afraid that he would be required to speak. He found the atmosphere alien and intimidating and yearned to be back in Madurai where he had lived like a king. The man who was called 'anjaanenjan' (fearless heart) by his loyalists back in Madurai suffered from an inferiority complex in Delhi.

Karunanidhi could sense this move had not gone down well with his party workers. But what did they know about the difficulties of a man who had to keep the women in two houses content, deal with sibling rivalry and grapple with the expectations, anxieties, anger, jealousies and insecurities of all of them? He loved them all. He trusted them all. They would not desert him as some members of the party had done when he was in distress; or betray him like MGR and Vaiko whom he had trusted the most. With age his faith in his own blood grew stronger.

All his calculations proved wrong when it came to Alagiri's

Delhi appointment. Alagiri's hatred for his brother was too deep to dislodge. Karunanidhi found no parallel for this kind of fraternal enmity in any of the epics. He wondered how his son could have such venom in his heart for his younger brother, born of the same womb. Stalin urged his father to take action against Alagiri and his henchmen as the prestige of the party was at stake. Finally, in January 2014, in a move to curtail Alagiri, his supporters were expelled from the DMK for anti-party activities. Stalin had already started replacing the cadres in Alagiri's strongholds with his own loyalists. Many more aides of Alagiri were thrown out while he was away in Singapore.

On his return on 24 January a furious Alagiri went straight from the airport to his father's house in Gopalapuram. There he physically shook awake the sleeping ninety-year-old man and berated him. Later in the day he was suspended from the party and a few weeks later expelled.

An agonized Karunanidhi relayed to the press what had transpired that morning. 'Alagiri has nurtured an inexplicable hatred towards Stalin,' he began. 'On January 24 he entered my bedroom and told me that Stalin would die in three or four months. Do you think there could be words worse than those to break my heart? Will any party worker call on his leader, wake him up rudely from his sleep early in the morning to make a complaint about another party worker?'

This was a message to Alagiri's aides that no mercy would be shown to a violator of party norms even if he was the son of the leader.

But it was the pain of a father, rather than that of a political leader, that marked Karunanidhi's visage that day. The journalists present were moved at the plight of this old man, still the undisputed leader of a major Dravidian party, but broken in spirit, drained of all energy. And the 2014 general elections were just months away.

~

The decline had set in motion five years ago when he had sent Alagiri to Delhi as a Union minister. Well aware that this had disappointed his party, he wanted to remind them that he was still their tallest leader and beloved patriarch.

And so he organized the classical Tamil language conference at Coimbatore, where not the greatness of the Tamil language but that of Kalaignar Karunanidhi as the sole protector of Tamil was projected. Some of the papers selected for the literary sessions were on Karunanidhi's prose and his daughter Kanimozhi's poetry. Songs of praise were sung as the leader sat with his wives, sons, daughters, grandsons and granddaughters in the front rows, while the scholars sat behind them. Schools and government offices all over the state were closed for five days and thousands of cadres were brought to celebrate the leader in the name of Tamil Tai.

This was also the period when allegations of goondaism and large-scale land-grabbing by DMK workers and district heavyweights resurfaced. Unfortunately even when the complaints reached the chief minister, the guilty went unpunished. 'That was his weakness,' says Durai Murugan. 'He would call them and admonish them severely but when they wept and said they were sorry, and begged his forgiveness, he would let them go.' Karunanidhi naively trusted his deputies to behave, while his attention was on administrative and welfare schemes. He did not realize the permanent damage they did to the party, as well as to his reputation as the chief minister of the state and president of the DMK.

~

But 2006 to 2011 was not just a period when Karunanidhi faced family problems and a tragic decline in his stature; it was also a time when he shone as a visionary and enlightened chief minister, with his schemes to improve every aspect of the lives of the people, from education to healthcare to food security.

By 2011 the tide had turned against him, making way for Jayalalithaa's return. In the Assembly elections in May 2011, she won with a massive majority. And she would go on to win in the next Assembly elections in 2016, becoming the chief minister of Tamil Nadu for two consecutive terms. Would Karunanidhi ever be able to raise his head again?

17

The 'Mother of All Scams'

There was more pain and trauma in store for Karunanidhi in the year 2011.

'I hear that there is talk that something has seriously gone wrong in the distribution of 2G spectrum.' Karunanidhi's voice shook as he spoke on the telephone to A. Raja, Central minister for information technology. 'It seems questions are being asked why there was a change from the original plan of holding an auction. They say there is a big scandal as the allotment was fraudulently given to a select few. Is it true? *En peyarai keduthoodatheit*.' Don't ruin my reputation.[1]

Raja had great respect and affection for the DMK patriarch, and it saddened him to hear his revered leader sound so agitated. Raja tried to explain over the phone why they did not go for an auction.

Karunanidhi got to know about the brewing controversy from N. Ram, a good friend and reliable source, who would not create a scare if there were no substance to it. Karunanidhi now advised Raja to meet N. Ram and explain the whole thing, just as he had done to him. 'You may be a Central minister, but Ram is a big man and you must show respect to him.'[2]

Raja sat with N. Ram for more than two hours and presented his case, while the latter listened patiently. But the 2G spectrum genii had already grown so big, it could not be contained easily. It affected not only the destiny of Karunanidhi, but also that of his daughter Kanimozhi, and the future of the DMK.

What was the 2G spectrum story?

It was actually a leap to second-generation (2G) telephony. Spectrum or airwaves are a natural resource and a national asset. The government allocates frequencies of these electromagnetic waves after what remains of their use by the defence establishments, to telecom and communication companies to operate their voice and data services.

Raja was excited that he had been entrusted with the task of allocating 2G spectrum to various telecom companies. 2G had the potential of bringing about a communications revolution. It was meant to make phone calls cheaper, mobile networks more accessible to Indians and connect the country like never before – all of which it did.

Since 1994, allocation of spectrum had happened through auction or bidding. The only exception was in 2008 when A. Raja was the minister for information technology – the Telecom Regulatory Authority of India (TRAI) and the Department of Telecom (DoT) along with the minister opted for the first come, first served method. The idea was to make spectrum allocation more transparent instead of it being monopolized by the big gamesters alone. This was not to the liking of established companies, which preferred the auction method.

The call for allotment of 2G spectrum to various interested

companies was made in August 2007, with 1 October being the deadline. Over 575 applications arrived, out of which forty-six were old players.

A. Raja writes in his book *2G Saga Unfolds*, 'It was observed and recorded that in view of the large number of applications pending and to discourage speculative players, we may close receiving applications on 1 October . . .'

On the basis of the availability of spectrum and the quantum of spectrum that would become available soon, it was later decided to consider in the first phase all applications received until 25 September 2008. DoT found that several applications received by 25 September qualified to receive the allotment. And since the availability of spectrum was limited, they decided to stop further applications, thus bringing forward the deadline by a week. The way this decision was conveyed to the press created the impression that there was a sudden change in the date. There were loud protests from the corporate sector, questioning the change in date. They said that the procedure seemed dubious.

There was also news that the price was fixed at the market price that prevailed in 2001. That led to the charge that it caused an enormous loss to the government. It was pointed out that those who purchased spectrum at a lower price sold it on to IT companies at a high rate.

Meanwhile, the prime minister and the finance ministry raised concerns about the procedure adopted by Raja and his team, as per documents leaked to the media at that time.

Suddenly the 2G spectrum deal became the subject of a big controversy and the Opposition said it smelt a rat. The Janata Party president Subramanian Swamy (who merged his party with the BJP in 2013) sought Prime Minister Manmohan Singh's permission in November 2008 to prosecute Raja over allegations of corruption in the issue of 2G licences.

Raja and DoT and TRAI explained periodically to the media that they had gone by the rulebook and done nothing wrong. A belligerent Swamy took the case to the Supreme Court. In 2009 the Central Vigilance Commission (CVC) began a probe into the allegations. In September 2009 the Supreme Court declared it a Rs 70,000 crore scam.

By October 2009 the CBI entered the scene under direction from the Supreme Court, filing an FIR against unknown DoT officials and unknown private companies.

A month later the issue exploded.

The Comptroller and Auditor General's (CAG) report on the 2G spectrum allocation was leaked to the media before it was tabled in Parliament. CAG Vinod Rai, who was about to retire, had pinned a mind-boggling Rs 1,76,000 crore loss to the government!

Print and visual media went to town with the news, touting it as the greatest scam India had ever seen. They never once questioned the CAG's loss figures. Raja was chased by cameras everywhere he went, hounded by reporters in Delhi and Chennai. When Karunanidhi saw the visuals on TV he felt it was he who was being hounded and chased. He must have regretted not heeding Prime Minister Manmohan Singh's advice against reinstating Raja as IT minister.

Central government monitoring agencies such as the CVC, CAG, CBI and the Supreme Court each looked into the case almost independently. Each concluded Raja had had his own agenda. The truth became a blur and the trial a mockery.

The CAG's figures of loss to the government may have been inflated, but they could not be ignored. This turned into a powerful weapon in the hands of the Opposition – the BJP – who stalled proceedings in Parliament for several weeks and raised its verbal assault on the UPA government to a hysterical pitch.

So aggressively did the BJP fling the charge of unprecedented corruption in the UPA in the allocation of 2G spectrum that the public mood turned against the UPA. Even those who didn't know what the alleged scam was about or who Raja was believed that a minister in Manmohan Singh's Cabinet was hugely corrupt.

For Manmohan Singh there was no option but to have Raja resign, who agreed only after Karunanidhi too asked the same of him. However, he continued to support him and even said that Raja was accused because he was a Dalit. On 2 February 2011 Raja and two of his assistants were arrested. Karunanidhi could do nothing, though the DMK was an ally of the ruling UPA and also part of the government. It didn't help that the media in north India was not very sympathetic towards Karunanidhi, who had bargained plum ministerial berths for his partymen.

In May 2011 came the Assembly elections in Tamil Nadu. Jayalalithaa's campaign speeches in every district aggressively addressed the 2G scam: 'DMK plundered the nation!' she cried. The crowds at her rallies may not have understood what this scam was, but they were convinced that Jayalalithaa's corruption paled in comparison. They even began to believe that all the allegations against her were lies spread by the DMK. Jayalalithaa was back in power with a thumping majority.

During her victory celebrations, she announced to her partymen, 'The DMK story is over!' The roaring cheers from the AIADMK headquarters shook the walls of Karunanidhi's residence at Gopalapuram, which was a stone's throw away.

~

Just a week after the election results another thunderbolt struck Karunanidhi – an allegation that a Rs 200 crore loan was circuitously given to Kalaignar TV, the DMK mouthpiece, by some beneficiaries of the 2G spectrum. Kanimozhi was a director of Kalaignar TV at that time.

The CBI described the loan as kickbacks for getting spectrum. Raja had already been jailed. On 20 May 2011 a Delhi court ordered Kanimozhi's arrest.

Karunanidhi, eighty-seven, was shattered. Alagiri, Stalin and a few DMK senior members who were with him when the news arrived failed to be of any comfort to him. Karunanidhi eventually pulled himself together and left for the CIT Colony house where Kanimozhi's mother Rajathi Ammal lived. As he arrived at the gate reporters swarmed around him and asked the distraught man how he felt.

'How do I feel? If your daughter were arrested how would you feel? She was held for no fault of hers,' was his response.

He had no words to console Rajathi, who broke into uncontrollable sobs. For the first time in his life, he was so desperate he saw nothing but darkness ahead. He had never lost his nerve when his party suffered defeats in elections, he would quickly recover his fighting spirit, crack jokes and make everyone around him laugh. On the day he was arrested and dragged down the stairs into a police van he may have suffered physical pain but his spirit remained unbroken. When twenty-three-year-old Stalin was arrested during the Emergency, he stayed calm. But now, fear gripped his heart. The future seemed so uncertain and completely beyond his control, beyond the control even of the Central government since the 2G probes were under the Supreme Court's watch. To whom could he appeal? 'It's a matter between the court, the accused person and the probing authority,' said Congress spokesperson Abhishek Singhvi while Kanimozhi headed for jail on being denied bail.

Kanimozhi was taken to Tihar Jail and lodged in sub-jail number six in a single occupancy cell, 15 x 10 foot in size. She showed amazing composure and dignity as she followed the cops silently to her new abode.

When Karunanidhi watched Kanimozhi being taken by the police to Tihar Jail on TV he broke down. 'They are taking our daughter like a sacrificial goat,' he wept.

Karunanidhi could notionally upset the UPA apple cart by withdrawing from the alliance with the Congress, but expediency demanded that he keep his share of power in Delhi. Once again he came to the painful realization that he had no one but himself to blame for the turmoil he was in.

As Vinod Sharma, political editor, *Hindustan Times*, commented, 'The story would have been different had Karunanidhi acceded to the prime minister's wish to drop [A. Raja as] telecom minister in June–July, 2010 in the wake of the CBI probe. Then came the damning CAG report, the UPA–Opposition face-off over setting up a joint parliamentary committee (JPC) and the Supreme Court's decision to oversee CBI investigations.'

Raja was in jail for more than a year and Kanimozhi for 190 days before they could come out on bail.

Meanwhile, Enforcement Directorate officials landed up at Karunanidhi's Gopalapuram home to question Dayalu Ammal, who was named as one of the directors in Kalaignar TV. This despite Karunanidhi asking for reprieve for his aged wife, who was reportedly afflicted with Alzheimer's.

Peter Alphonse describes the atmosphere of those days, saying: 'We Congress members were actually terrified at that time by the way the BJP went about putting pressure on the Congress government, accusing it of the mother of all scams . . . Vinod Rai's mindboggling figure quoted as loss to the government frightened us all. It made us think there may be some truth in it. We could do nothing about it. We could not defend ourselves. It was even said nothing could have happened without the knowledge of Manmohan Singh.'

Kanimozhi revealed later in an interview, 'When my father spoke to me about Kalaignar TV I did not want to be in it. I said I am not interested in associating with television media, and that I will not be able to accept a lot of things there. Finally he convinced me because he wanted it to be a family-run thing.' She said that her father felt great remorse when she was caught in an alleged fraud connected to Kalaignar TV. 'He knew I wasn't making any decisions at Kalaignar TV. I was completely clueless as to what was going on. I think that made him feel very bad. He came regularly to see me in jail [Karunanidhi was by then wheelchair-bound], and became emotional. I told him it is an experience and I was learning a lot and reading a lot.'[3]

Kanimozhi was especially close to Karunanidhi, widely believed to be his favourite. She shared his passion for reading and writing poetry and he believed she brought him luck, for it was after her birth that he rose to prominence in the DMK. For the favourite daughter who had led a comfortable life away from the glare of public scrutiny, the stint in jail like an ordinary criminal must have been traumatic.

'Kalaignar was devastated,' says Durai Murugan. 'I had never seen him like that. The fear that the allegations of the 2G scam may be true was what affected him most, I think . . . The day he went to Tihar Jail and saw Kanimozhi there, he came back and wept. "It is entirely my fault," he moaned. "She was only interested in poetry and literature and I forced her into something she did not want."'

After seven long years of hearings, the CBI court in Patiala House in Delhi pronounced the verdict on 21 December 2017. Judge O.P. Saini acquitted every one of the accused, stating in court, 'I have no hesitation in holding that the prosecution has failed to prove the charges beyond reasonable doubt. So all are acquitted.'

Raja, a lawyer by profession, had argued the case himself with confidence and conviction.

His book, *The 2G Saga Unfolds*, came out in January 2018. In it he attacks Vinod Rai, former CAG, for being driven by political motives; he attacks Sunil Mittal, chairman, Bharti Enterprises, and also then Solicitor General, G. Vahanvati, for placing him at the centre of the so-called scam. But he has words of respect for Manmohan Singh and Karunanidhi, who had his back through it all even if they couldn't do much under the circumstances.

When news of the acquittal came, Karunanidhi had a tracheostomy tube down his throat and was unable to speak. But he still managed to get out the word 'magizchi' (happy).

18

Player on the National Stage

In or out of power, Karunanidhi stood tall on the national stage.

'I do not know to speak English,' Karunanidhi would say if a journalist went to interview him in English. His political life had started with the anti-Hindi agitation in Tamil Nadu, so he made it a point never to learn Hindi either. Yet, the man who spoke only Tamil established a rapport with political leaders from all over India, most of whom knew not a word of Tamil. Karunanidhi didn't allow language to be a barrier when he wanted to communicate with people.

How did this politician who spoke only Tamil become accepted and respected by Hindi/English-speaking non-Tamils, especially those of north India who habitually looked down upon 'Madrasis'? The English language media in north India largely treated him with condescension, as a rather crass local leader, and had criticized his strident demands for state autonomy in the 1970s and 1980s as secessionist. His opposition to Brahmins and the Hindu religious structure and his anti-Hindi stance further alienated them. But Jayalalithaa – fair and beautiful, polished and glamorous – could always count on sympathetic coverage and attention in the English language media. She spoke English with a convent accent and knew Hindi too.

Yet it was Karunanidhi who was largely instrumental in making Tamil Nadu one of the best-performing states in terms of all social and economic indicators. And in stark contrast to Jayalalithaa, Karunanidhi had cordial relations with leaders of other states and was considered a reliable ally at the Centre.

M.G. Rajamanickam, a retired IAS officer who worked closely with him for several years, says, 'Karunanidhi knew enough English to communicate in simple sentences but if there were some intricate and technical issues being discussed he would tell me to take over. If he did not agree with the other person's point of view, he would say that straight, without hesitation. He certainly did not have any aspirations to go to Delhi. But he wanted Tamil Nadu to get its due, and its interests to be recognized by the Central government.'

His goal was Tamil Nadu's development and he realized early on how important it was to have a constant dialogue with the Centre. His autobiography contains vivid details of his trips to Delhi and his interactions with prime ministers, Cabinet ministers and Opposition leaders.

When Karunanidhi took over as chief minister for the first time in March 1969, he accompanied Law Minister S. Madhavan to Delhi to meet Prime Minister Indira Gandhi and her Cabinet ministers. He had 'a pleasant forty-minute meeting with Indira Gandhi'. He also met External Affairs Minister Dinesh Singh and Home Minister Yashwantrao Chavan. Karunanidhi writes how the minister for food and agriculture, Jagjivan Ram, embraced him warmly and sanctioned 10,000 tonnes of rice as a first instalment of food aid for Tamil Nadu and approved the plan to set up three sugar mills in the state.

But the warmth was conspicuously missing when Karunanidhi met Deputy Prime Minister and Finance Minister Morarji Desai. Karunanidhi was stuck in traffic and arrived five minutes late for the appointment. Morarji Desai was in a foul mood and snapped, 'How long do I wait for you? Do you think I have no other work?'

When Desai asked Karunanidhi and his team to take a seat, Karunanidhi felt like he was sitting on 'a chair of thorns'. The young chief minister asked the Union finance minister to grant Rs 5 crore for the state. Desai's face 'reddened'.

He said, 'I do not have a tree in my garden that grows money.'

Karunanidhi was taken aback at Desai's harshness.

The Tamil Nadu team left Morarji Desai's office in a huff, but Karunanidhi could gauge that there were problems between the prime minister and her deputy.

Bhupesh Gupta, leader of the CPI, and Congress member Chandra Shekhar questioned the finance minister's budget sops in Parliament for allegedly favouring the Birla group. It was pointed out that Desai's daughter-in-law and her two minor children were shareholders of a company in the group. Desai was furious that a junior member from his own party had the audacity to point a finger at him. He wanted Indira Gandhi to take action against Chandra Shekhar, which she did not. The rift became public. Desai, K. Kamaraj and other members of the Congress's old guard closed ranks, while the younger Congress members supported Indira.

Karunanidhi saw promise in the younger group led by Indira and decided to back them when the need arose. That time came soon enough. When President Zakir Hussain died on 3 May 1969, Vice President V.V. Giri took charge as acting president. Karunanidhi writes in his autobiography, 'The senior Congress leaders were working hard to select a president who would be someone who would not cooperate with Indira Gandhi.'

The contenders were V.V. Giri (who stood as an independent candidate), Neelam Sanjiva Reddy (the choice of the old guard, including Congress president S. Nijalingappa and Morarji Desai) and Jagjivan Ram (suggested by Indira Gandhi). Sanjiva Reddy was declared the Congress's presidential candidate.

Karunanidhi was touring Thanjavur when reporters asked him to comment on the presidential candidate. This was Karunanidhi's opportunity to make his stand clear. 'I feel this decision is disappointing. This is Mahatma Gandhi's birth centenary year. They should have made a Dalit the candidate, a wish that Gandhi always had. They should have made Babu Jagjivan Ram the president.'

Indira Gandhi and her allies got the hint that Karunanidhi would not support Sanjiva Reddy's candidature. Bhupesh Gupta and Karunanidhi met in July 1969. The DMK, CPI and CPI(M) decided to back Giri for president. Karunanidhi then invited the leaders of all Opposition parties to meet either in Chennai or Delhi, and Delhi was ultimately chosen as the venue.

On 16 July 1969 Indira Gandhi suddenly removed Desai as finance minister, though he would continue as deputy prime minister. On 19 July an ordinance was passed by the Union Cabinet to nationalize banks in the country, which Acting President V.V. Giri signed.

Karunanidhi reached Delhi on 21 July for his meeting with the Opposition leaders. Over the next two days he held talks with Bhupesh Gupta, Atal Bihari Vajpayee, George Fernandes, West Bengal chief minister, Ajoy Mukherjee, and deputy chief minister, Jyoti Basu, Punjab chief minister, Gurnam Singh, the

Indian Muslim League's Qaid-e-Millath Muhammad Ismail and V.K. Krishna Menon, among others.

They knew the Congress seniors had forced Indira Gandhi's hand to submit Reddy's nomination. However, she put her foot down when asked to send letters requesting all the Congress MPs to vote for Reddy. She hoped the Opposition's support would swing the vote in Giri's favour. That is what happened – Giri won by 14,500 votes.

Karunanidhi writes in his autobiography, 'If V.V. Giri had lost the election, senior leaders in the Congress would have become more powerful and she would have had to resign as prime minister. If you compare the votes, it is clear that if Giri had not got Tamil Nadu's votes Sanjiva Reddy would have become president.'

Karunanidhi supported Indira's nationalization of banks and he also supported Indira when she abolished the privy purses for former princely states through a constitutional amendment. DMK leader K.S. Radhakrishnan points out, 'It was Kalaignar's stand that helped Indira Gandhi to continue in power' during that time. Radhakrishnan adds, 'Till now in most of the Parliamentary elections, it is the alliance with the DMK that has helped form the government at the Centre. It happened during Indira Gandhi's time, then when Morarji headed the Janata Party after the end of the Emergency, then again in 1980 when Indira came again to power. When V.P. Singh became prime minister in 1989, then when Deve Gowda and later Gujral came to head the government; when Vajpayee became the head of the NDA government in 1999 and from 2004 for the next ten years when the Congress under Manmohan Singh headed the UPA government – all were possible because of Karunanidhi's shrewd alliance strategy.'

~

Apart from playing an important role in the formation of governments at the Centre, Karunanidhi prioritized obtaining greater autonomy for states. As a result of his dogged pursuance a committee headed by a retired high court judge, P.V. Rajamannar, was constituted, as mentioned earlier, to look into the matter in detail. After much deliberation over the report submitted by the committee in April 1974, the Tamil Nadu Assembly passed a resolution accepting its recommendations.

Tamil Nadu was the first state in the country to pass such a resolution. It would take eight years for other states to catch up. In 1983 Karnataka chief minister Ramakrishna Hegde picked up the Rajamannar committee report and organized a meeting of chief ministers of the southern states to discuss state autonomy. In the same year, Jammu and Kashmir Chief Minister Farooq Abdullah held a meeting with chief ministers of many states including N.T. Rama Rao of Andhra Pradesh and Jyoti Basu of West Bengal, at which they hailed the DMK government's resolution on state autonomy and adopted it.

The DMK's reputation was growing in other states, so much so that the powers-that-be at the Centre were eager for an alliance with it. Indira Gandhi got into trouble with the judiciary when her move to nationalize banks and abolish the privy purse were both challenged and struck down, which brought the general elections forward to 1971. The Congress had already split. Indira Gandhi needed a dependable ally. She called Karunanidhi to Delhi and they met for an hour. After returning to Chennai, Karunanidhi held a meeting with the party's executive council in which they decided to dissolve the Assembly and go in for elections along with the Centre. Karunanidhi explained, 'We have taken this decision in the public interest . . . It is true that our government can continue in power for another year. But if there are elections every year and leaders keep changing, it will affect governance and ultimately the people.'

The alliance for the state was decided. The DMK would have as its electoral allies the Congress(R), both the left parties, the Praja Socialist Party, the Tamilarasu Kazhagam, the Muslim League and the All India Forward Bloc. On 8 January 1970 they met to decide upon seat allocations. On 19 January Indira Gandhi arrived in Chennai and had an hour-long discussion. But the talks broke down. The DMK said it would give five to seven parliamentary seats to the Congress and ten to fifteen Assembly seats. The Congress wanted more.

Karunanidhi knew very well that the Congress needed the DMK. Senior Congress leaders like M. Bhaktavatsalam, former chief minister of Madras State, C. Subramaniam and Mohan Kumaramangalam met Karunanidhi to persuade him to allot at least eighty Assembly seats and more than twenty Lok Sabha seats to the Congress. Karunanidhi flatly refused and stuck to his original offer. Bhaktavatsalam was furious and said there would be no more. Karunanidhi writes that a fuming C. Subramaniam said, 'This is a matter of our self-respect.' Karunanidhi laughed and replied, '*Our movement* is all about self-respect.'

As the Tamil Nadu Congress(R) went ahead and released its list of candidates for the state, Karunanidhi announced the DMK candidate list on 24 July 1970. That day around midnight a desperate call came from Indira Gandhi and her senior adviser G. Parthasarathy. 'How did this happen?' they asked. Karunanidhi replied, 'It is not our mistake. Your Tamil Nadu wing released their list of candidates. It is only after that that the DMK released its list.'

They asked Karunanidhi to consider giving at least twenty Assembly seats and ten Lok Sabha seats to the Congress.

Karunanidhi replied, 'It is not possible to give you any Assembly seats any longer but I will think about whether I can give some parliamentary seats.'

Karunanidhi cleverly kept the Congress(R) out of the state Assembly but gave them ten Lok Sabha seats in Tamil Nadu. Indira Gandhi had no choice but to accept. She was almost down on her knees, gloats Karunanidhi in his autobiography.

In March 1971 the country went to the polls. Indira Gandhi returned as prime minister and Karunanidhi as chief minister of Tamil Nadu. The DMK won 180 out of the 234-member Assembly, while of the thirty-nine Lok Sabha seats contested the DMK won twenty-three, the Congress(R) just nine and others six, thus vindicating Karunanidhi's decision to not give the Congress(R) the number of seats it wanted.

But Indira didn't forget the humiliation that Karunanidhi had subjected her to over the seat sharing. She hit back by exploiting his rift with MGR and helping engineer the split in the DMK, with MGR breaking away to form his own party, the ADMK. And she supported MGR in his corruption charges against Karunanidhi's government in the state, which led to its dismissal. As a result, Karunanidhi would be out of power for more than a decade, from 1976 to 1989.

~

In 1975, when Indira Gandhi imposed the Emergency the DMK was one of the first and strongest voices to condemn it, even though it was in alliance with the Congress(R).

On 12 June 1975, when the Allahabad High Court ruled that Indira Gandhi's disputed election from Rae Bareli in Uttar Pradesh was null and void because she had resorted to illegal methods to win the seat, her opponents demanded her resignation.

The Opposition led by Morarji Desai decided to start a countrywide protest, but days before that, at the behest of Indira Gandhi, President Fakhruddin Ali Ahmed declared the Emergency under Article 352 of the Indian Constitution.

Relations between Karunanidhi and Indira Gandhi worsened, with the former's open and relentless condemnation of the Emergency and its excesses. Indira Gandhi thus found it opportune to befriend MGR who had become critical of Karunanidhi. Hundreds of DMK men, including Karunanidhi's son Stalin, were arrested. But Tamil Nadu became a safe haven for many others oppressed by the draconian regime that the Centre imposed during the Emergency. Karunanidhi made it possible for magazines, pamphlets and other material condemning the Emergency to be printed there and then circulated in other states. Indira Gandhi, citing corruption allegations on the basis of MGR's letters to the President, subsequently dismissed his government in 1976. She allied with MGR in the 1977 elections and the DMK allied with the Janata Party headed by Morarji Desai.

Desai became the prime minister in 1977. Indira Gandhi was defeated decisively in the general elections but in Tamil Nadu the Congress was unscathed because of MGR's popularity. The DMK lost the election to MGR's AIADMK, and as mentioned earlier, pushed Karunanidhi and the DMK out of power until 1989.

Within a year the Janata Party members began quarrelling among themselves and the government's existence became increasingly precarious, with Home Minister Charan Singh, Defence Minister Jagjivan Ram and Prime Minister Morarji Desai at loggerheads. Before the planned no-confidence motion could make any headway, Desai resigned and Charan Singh was sworn in as prime minister on 28 July 1979. MGR found it expedient to support the Centre, no matter who came to power. Charan Singh inducted two AIADMK MPs as ministers in his Cabinet. But his government did not last long and mid-term polls were declared in 1980.

~

In the third volume of his autobiography Karunanidhi writes in detail about Biju Patnaik, with whom he had a close connection – a fact that few people in Odisha and Tamil Nadu are aware of. The politics of Tamil Nadu may have been vastly different if Biju Patnaik's master plan of September 1979 had succeeded. He had attempted and nearly succeeded in the merger of the DMK and the AIADMK. Karunanidhi writes, 'Biju came on 12 September 1979 and discussed the merger issue with me in detail. After the discussion, I had put a few conditions for the merger. We accepted that MGR would continue as chief minister. MGR had okayed the merger formula wherein the unified party would take the name of the DMK and the flag of the AIADMK.' Biju was very happy and hugged MGR after he gave his consent. His main intention was to block Indira Gandhi's political manoeuvres and the rise of Congress. But MGR then backed out and the merger never happened.

Indira Gandhi found out about these developments and Biju's role. She sent her confidant C.M. Stephen to Tamil Nadu. He contacted Murasoli Maran, urged him to forget the past and conveyed Indira's desire for an alliance with the DMK again.

Karunanidhi then met Indira Gandhi in Delhi, and once again formed an alliance with the Congress(R), ignoring the fact that he had been the most virulent critic of the Emergency, that his government had been dismissed by her and that her government had put hundreds of DMK members including his son Stalin in prison and tortured them. Just a few months earlier, when Indira visited Madurai, the DMK cadres had expressed their anger, blocking her way with black flags and shouting 'Go away Indira!' The DMK cadres were shocked that their leader had now gone to Delhi to shake hands with the same Indira Gandhi.

Karunanidhi, after his return from Delhi, explained to his partymen that Indira Gandhi had apologized to the nation for the excesses committed during the Emergency. Indira came back to power with a stunning majority in the 1980 general elections, but Karunanidhi again lost to MGR in the Assembly elections. Indira now had her revenge on MGR, who had supported her opponents when she was out of power between 1977 and 1980. The AIADMK government was dismissed and fresh Assembly elections announced.

Karunanidhi decided to ally with the Congress(R) for the state elections. But before the alliance could be finalized, local Congress members spread a rumour that once the elections were held there would be a Congress chief minister in the state. Karunanidhi acted immediately and stopped talks with the Congress(R) midway. Indira Gandhi then stepped in and assured him that the chief minister's post would go to the DMK. But in May 1980 MGR once again beat Karunanidhi to become the chief minister.

~

As mentioned earlier, following MGR's death in 1987, Tamil Nadu descended into chaos. A succession war broke out between MGR's wife, Janaki, and Jayalalithaa, the propaganda secretary of the AIADMK. Nedunchezhiyan, who was the acting chief minister, gave way for Janaki, who was sworn in as chief minister. But her government lasted just twenty-three days from 7 to 30 January 1988. In the wake of violence in the Assembly during the confidence motion president's rule was imposed, due to a complete breakdown of law and order in the state.

President's rule was extended for six months so the Assembly elections could coincide with the general elections that came on 21 January 1989. Karunanidhi had sensed the way the wind was blowing and joined the National Front alliance with N.T. Rama Rao, V.P. Singh, Chandra Shekhar, Biju Patnaik, I.K. Gujral, Surjit Singh Barnala and others. The first public rally of the National Front took place in Chennai on 17 September 1988. The AIADMK, which had allied with the Rajiv Gandhi Congress in 1984, continued with that alliance. But in the 1989 elections, the Congress lost, and the DMK came back to power in Tamil Nadu, along with the National Front at the Centre. Karunanidhi was back in the chief minister's seat after ten long years. V.P. Singh took over as prime minister on 2 December 1989. And once again Karunanidhi emerged as a major player on the national stage.

Karunanidhi writes in his autobiography: 'My biggest contribution to national politics was in helping to form the National Front in 1989. Though the government under V.P. Singh did not last long, it implemented the recommendations of the Mandal Commission to grant reservation to the most backward communities.'

Karunanidhi had made a fervent appeal to the Centre for such a reform way back in October 1973 at a meeting of backward and oppressed classes held in Allahabad.

As the Mandal Commission recommendations were being passed by Parliament, protests broke out in north India as the forward castes took to the streets. The DMK and Karunanidhi were the solid support on which the Mandal reforms were pushed and defended. A close friendship developed between Karunanidhi and V.P. Singh, and when there was a crisis in his government it was Karunanidhi's help that Singh sought.

The coalition government stood on a fragile wicket, with the BJP giving support from outside. In July 1990 Devi Lal, deputy prime minister in V.P. Singh's government, charged a number of Union ministers with corruption in an interview with *Illustrated Weekly of India*. V.P. Singh demanded that his deputy furnish their names. Devi Lal kept silent. V.P. Singh then removed him from the post of deputy prime minister in August.

Karunanidhi received an urgent phone call from N.T. Rama Rao, chief minister of Andhra Pradesh, that day, asking him to take the first flight to Hyderabad the next day and come with him to Delhi to hold talks to resolve the crisis. Both the leaders reached Delhi and met the prime minister. The talks went on past midnight. It was decided that no one would replace Devi Lal as deputy prime minister. Karunanidhi and Rama Rao convened a meeting of the National Front, where the partners expressed their faith in V.P. Singh's prime ministership.

~

A new and serious problem cropped up when L.K. Advani, a senior leader of the BJP, decided to start a rath yatra (roadshow) across several states to garner support for building a Ram temple at the disputed site in Ayodhya. The BJP was an ally that gave support from outside to the V.P. Singh government.

Advani refused to heed the National Front's protests or the concerns expressed by the prime minister that the rath yatra would provoke communal riots. Advani threatened that if the rath yatra was stopped the BJP would withdraw its support to the government. On 22 October 1990, as Advani's rath yatra reached Samastipur in Bihar, he was intercepted and arrested. The BJP withdrew its support immediately and the National Front government lost its majority in Parliament. Chandra Shekhar, who had been a harsh critic of V.P. Singh, split the Janata Dal. There were sixty-eight MPs with him while V.P. Singh was left with eighty-three. Chandra Shekhar then struck a deal with Rajiv Gandhi's Congress and assumed charge as prime minister.

But Karunanidhi had voted in favour of V.P. Singh during the confidence motion in Parliament, which V.P. Singh lost. Chandra Shekhar made a note of it. Rajiv Gandhi's Congress was in alliance with the AIADMK and they too waited for an opportunity to strike.

Says M.G. Rajamanickam, 'Though Kalaignar had a good relationship with all the prime ministers that were in power in Delhi, it was with V.P. Singh that he had an emotional closeness and understanding. Though V.P. Singh hailed from a royal family the concern he showed for social justice and implementing reservation for the socially downtrodden touched his heart.'

It was a time of conspiracies and betrayals, writes Karunanidhi in his autobiography. There was news that Jayalalithaa was making frequent trips to Delhi to meet with Rajiv Gandhi. A rumour went around that Karunanidhi's government would be dismissed any moment. Karunanidhi recounts that he got a call from External

Affairs Minister V.C. Shukla, asking to meet him in Chennai on 28 January 1991. Shukla wanted Karunanidhi's opinion on the Sri Lankan issue before heading to Colombo. The two held a long discussion on the crisis. Karunanidhi felt that since the meeting was very cordial the rumour of the impending dismissal of his government was false.

The next day Tamil Nadu Governor Surjit Singh Barnala, a good friend of Karunanidhi, was summoned to Delhi and asked to dismiss the DMK government. Barnala declined to do so. V.P. Singh along with his supporters rushed to the President to halt the dismissal, but to no avail. Since the Governor had refused, the President himself imposed president's rule, dismissing the DMK government and the Assembly on 30 January 1991. The dismissal was based on allegations that the DMK government was encouraging the LTTE and other militant groups and providing them shelter and freedom to carry out their activities in the state.

Chandra Shekhar's government too did not last long. The Congress, on whose support the government stood, learned that two policemen had been ordered to spy on Rajiv Gandhi's residence. On 5 March 1991 the Congress walked out of Parliament, shouting against the ruling party. Murasoli Maran of the DMK, a Lok Sabha MP then, criticized Prime Minister Chandra Shekhar's inability to answer the Congress whose puppet he was, since it was their support that kept him in power. Chandra Shekhar retorted that he was nobody's puppet, but resigned from his post.

The next elections were slated for May 1991. As Rajiv Gandhi toured Tamil Nadu, he was assassinated by an LTTE suicide bomber at Sriperumbudur, less than fifty kilometres from Chennai. The whole of Tamil Nadu was shocked, upset and ashamed that such a heinous crime had taken place on its soil. Public opinion turned against Karunanidhi, holding him and the DMK responsible – even though at the time of the assassination Karunanidhi was not in power. In the elections that followed, the DMK was routed and Jayalalithaa, who was in alliance with the Congress, came to power. It was a huge setback for the DMK.

~

The following year, 1992, as karsevaks began their march to Ayodhya intent on demolishing the Babri Masjid, the DMK began conducting protests and public meetings. Jayalalithaa, however, supported the building of the Ram temple in Ayodhya in the disputed area. On 5 December Karunanidhi wrote in *Murasoli* that they would not agree with the demolition of the mosque to build the temple.

When the Babri Masjid was demolished the next day, Karunanidhi condemned the act and the Centre for failing to prevent it.

His reaction to an issue that was far removed from his own state reflected Karunanidhi's belief in secularism. He predicted, rightly, that it would leave a deep scar on the soul of the nation.

~

The DMK came back to power in 1996. But the Lok Sabha elections that year resulted in a hung Parliament, and Karunanidhi would play a leading role in the formation of the new government at the Centre. Chandra Babu Naidu, leader of the Telugu Desam Party and at that time chief minister of Andhra Pradesh, invited Karunanidhi for an urgent meeting at Delhi. Held at Tamil Nadu

House, the meeting was attended by almost all the important regional leaders such as the West Bengal chief minister, Jyoti Basu; CPI(M) general secretary, Harkishen Singh Surjit; CPI general secretary, Indrajit Gupta; Bihar chief minister, Lalu Prasad Yadav; former Union minister, Madhav Rao Scindia; Karnataka chief minister, Deve Gowda; and P. Chidambaram and G.K. Moopanar of the TMC. It was an impressive gathering. The regional parties would have to form a credible coalition and select a leader. They agreed that V.P. Singh should be requested to accept the prime minister's post, but when they met him, Singh declined. They came back to Tamil Nadu House to discuss the matter further. Karunanidhi's name was proposed but he too declined and proposed Deve Gowda's name, which was generally accepted. That would be the first non-Congress, non-BJP coalition of just the regional parties, called the United Front. The idea was exciting. But since the BJP was the single largest party, President Shankar Dayal Sharma invited Atal Bihari Vajpayee, leader of the BJP, to form the government with the rider that it should prove its majority within a fortnight. Vajpayee's government fell within thirteen days.

And so Deve Gowda was sworn in on 1 June 1996 as the eleventh prime minister of India.

Murasoli Maran and T.G. Venkatraman of the DMK were labour minister and minister for surface transport respectively; and the TMC's P. Chidambaram became finance minister. The Congress agreed to support the United Front government from outside.

Deve Gowda recalls how deftly Karunanidhi handled those critical days. V.P. Singh was the unanimous choice of the United Front. 'But he flatly refused. The next choice was Karunanidhi. He refused saying, "I know my height. I am not fit for that office." But he was very firm that someone from the south should get the post. It was he, along with Murasoli Maran and Moopanar, who worked hard to push my name. It is not easy to form a government at the Centre that is dominated by Hindi- speaking leaders. There were taunts and snide comments about the non-Hindi-speaking south Indian leaders whose knowledge of English was also poor, even within the members of the United Front and among the north Indian Hindi and English journalists. But Karunanidhi somehow with great presence of mind and statesmanship managed the situation. At one point of time the north Indian media commented, "India's capital is Madras, not Delhi."'

Gowda continues, 'During the ten months that I was the prime minister, Karunanidhi's oft said words were, "You have gone from the south. Do something more for the south."'

The friendship between Chandra Babu Naidu and Karunanidhi during this period helped him sign a pact with Andhra Pradesh for the Telugu Ganga project and the allocation of Krishna waters for Chennai and the dry northern part of Tamil Nadu.

But the United Front government, a fragile coalition, was short-lived. In April 1997 the Congress withdrew its support because of some differences with Deve Gowda, but agreed to continue its support if a candidate of its choice was installed as prime minister. Its choice was I.K. Gujral and the government survived, only to fall again after parts of the Jain Commission report were leaked, indicting the DMK for having facilitated an atmosphere in Tamil Nadu for the LTTE to carry out the assassination of Rajiv Gandhi.

~

General elections were announced yet again and the BJP came to power in a coalition. Jayalalithaa's AIADMK was an important ally, with its eighteen members in the Lok Sabha. Vajpayee became the prime minister. His government lasted just thirteen months, before Jayalalithaa pulled the rug from under his feet, after Vajpayee refused to dismiss the duly elected DMK government, which was in power in Tamil Nadu.

In September–October 1999, the country went to polls once again.

The DMK joined the NDA headed by the BJP. The NDA came to power with Vajpayee as the prime minister and the DMK got three ministerial berths, with Murasoli Maran, T.R. Baalu and A. Raja joining the Cabinet.

Karunanidhi remained a faithful ally, though he suffered from guilt all those five years because his party had deviated from its secular ideology to join hands with the BJP, with its belief in Hindutva.

DMK insiders say that Karunanidhi's feelings of guilt tormented him even more after the Godhra killings and riots.

But he felt morally compelled to abide by the political promise he gave to Vajpayee to support his government. Moreover, he had great respect and admiration for Vajpayee. He was able to establish a warm relationship with the prime minister who was, like him, also a poet, even though he realized that as a member of the BJP, Vajpayee's politics was conditioned by the dictates of the RSS.

~

Although Karunanidhi could not connect with Sonia Gandhi in the same direct way that he did with Vajpayee and V.P. Singh, his opinion of her would come across clearly during his private conversations and public statements. Once he described her as thyaga thiruvilakku (lamp of sacrifice) at a public forum. His own partymen thought that this was a bit of an exaggeration. He then elaborated: 'A woman born in a foreign country became a widow at the age of forty. She could have gone back to her home country. But there was a party that needed her. She stayed back in the country to which her dead husband belonged, decided to revive the party of her husband and mother-in-law who were brutally assassinated by terrorists. She could have dressed any way she wished. But she adopted our culture, wore our clothes, worked for our country and speaks of secularism like a true Indian.'

Karunanidhi explained further: 'Annie Besant came from Ireland. She embraced Hinduism and taught caste-based politics and wanted to maintain untouchability as "ordained by god". The country accepted her and called her a martyr. But when a woman born in a foreign land says I have no religion or caste, my earth is not just the one I was born in but also that of my husband's, a woman who proudly maintains that her nationality is Indian – why do people who hail Annie Besant hesitate to hail Sonia Gandhi? That is the reason why I call her thyaga thiruvilakku.'

Karunanidhi's defence of Sonia Gandhi was probably also in response to the harsh words with which Jayalalithaa attacked Sonia Gandhi. He was even prepared to support Sonia for prime ministership during UPA-1, when the Congress won in the 2004 general elections.

Sonia Gandhi, on her part, demonstrated great respect for Karunanidhi. Though the Jain Commission had directly charged Karunanidhi with 'facilitating conditions that were conducive' to the LTTE's assassination of her husband, she magnanimously extended a hand of friendship to Karunanidhi.

As the leader of the DMK, Karunanidhi played his cards tactically, choosing to ally with the resurgent Congress under the leadership of Sonia Gandhi in 2004 and 2009, the UPA-1 and UPA-2, when both the governments needed the DMK's help. The DMK in return got the Cabinet posts it demanded.

In 2010 the relationship came under strain because of the 2G scandal, in which the DMK's A. Raja and Karunanidhi's daughter Kanimozhi were charged and later imprisoned. But he realized that the Congress could not help them, and so relations remained unbroken.

In the 2014 general elections the DMK decided not to ally with any national party. The results came as a blow to Karunanidhi – the DMK was out of power in the state as well as the Centre. The country was swept by the Modi wave. By 2016 Karunanidhi's body and spirit were battered. His health deteriorated, he lost his ability to speak and M.K. Stalin took charge of the party.

19

Autumn of the Patriarch

You stopped speaking – did you think there was nothing to gain by
Speaking to us?
Or, did you think you have spoken all that had to be said?
Don't you know that we are the keepers of your words?
Our world will cease to exist without you . . .
You sit like the Buddha under the Bodhi tree
We wait – even those who hated you, abused you,
Who said you were the reason for all the ills that afflict the Tamils,
all wait with us for a few words
That will lead us through the stormy way . . .

These were the anguished words that Kanimozhi penned in Tamil when Karunanidhi could no longer speak after the tracheostomy tube had been inserted in his windpipe to help him breathe. It was a cruel fate for a man known for his eloquence and outstanding oratorical skills. His muse, the Tamil language, seemed to have deserted him. Was he being punished for having been overindulgent in the past, producing millions of words day after day as if there was no tomorrow? Did the muse now say to him, 'Enough, now it is time for you to rest'? How could he express the thoughts that kept crowding his brain, which was still razor-sharp? He could not even use his fingers to write any more.

He had fought many battles – won some and lost many. At times he acknowledged the folly was his alone. Like Shakespeare's Cassius, he believed in the idea that 'the fault is not in our stars, but in ourselves'. He fell countless times but picked himself back up. He was quick with a joke to dispel the gloom when he saw forlorn faces around him. 'We stood in the battlefield and lost, but the war will go on,' he would say and restore his men's hope in trying times.

He would often reminisce about his childhood and never forgot the humiliation his parents faced, the memories burned deep in his subconscious. Why did his father, so talented and learned, have to stand at a respectful distance with his head bent and shoulders bare before much lesser men who sat on their teak wood swings chewing paan, just because of his caste?

As a boy he wondered if he could some day stand before the sons of those men and sing a song of victory, head and shoulders high, fully clothed.

He did not know then that he was at the threshold of a new world, that he would fight against the fallacies of those times and claim the richness of his linguistic and cultural heritage as a Tamil.

He had marched into that new world with mentors like Periyar and Anna. Periyar's words 'religion is the root cause of evil, the Brahmin who perpetuates the caste system as ordained by religion is the villain' lit the fire within his young mind and shaped his sense of justice. Driven by a crusading zeal for doing away with caste-based discrimination, pledging himself to improve the lives of the most marginalized and vulnerable people of Tamil Nadu, he became chief minister for the first time at forty-five.

Though he deviated from the paths of his mentors, Anna always remained his idol. When the tracheostomy tube was removed and he was undergoing speech therapy in 2017, the therapist asked him, 'Who do you like?' Karunanidhi answered, 'Arignar Anna.' When Anna passed away in 1969 he wrote a moving elegy, ending it with 'How will I live without you, Anna? My heart is too weak to bear your absence. Lend me your heart, Anna, I shall keep it safe and return it to you when I meet you.'

When Karunanidhi lifted prohibition, he was criticized for going against Anna's ideals. But he defended his action with his usual reasoned logic: 'Anna himself agreed that prohibition had failed. Prohibition is a question that must be dealt with on an all-India basis. Tamil Nadu cannot work in isolation. We asked the Centre for compensation so that we could maintain Prohibition. But the Centre refused.'

Even MGR who created a big hue and cry over the issue had to concede that continuing with prohibition was ultimately impractical.

~

Karunanidhi never sat idle, even when he was out of power. In the years when he was not chief minister he had more time to spend on reading and writing, his passions. He wrote his last script at the age of ninety for a TV serial based on the life of the eleventh-century Vaishnavite saint Ramanuja, who strove for an egalitarian society. Karunanidhi the atheist was fascinated by Ramanuja, head of an orthodox religious mutt who wanted to improve the lot of the oppressed and backward classes.

Words flew from his pen with astonishing ease. Karunanidhi has over a hundred titles to his credit, mostly historical fiction, which was his forte, but also poems and novels. His notable novels include *Romapuri Pandian, Thenpandi Singam* and *Ponnar Shankar*. Other works include his paraphrasing of *Tolkappiyam,* a treatise on Tamil grammar; volumes of fictional stories woven round the *Thirukkural,* the second-century ethical text; poems of love and valour from Sangam poetry which had no place for class and caste division; and dramatization of the Jain epic *Silappatikaram* which valorized the chaste wife and the gifted courtesan in equal measure.

His six-volume-long autobiography *Nenjukku Needhi* is more than an expansive documentation of the political and social history of his time. From Sangam literature to the Russian revolution to American history, there is not a subject he does not touch. His racy style and vivid descriptions of events and personalities bear testimony to his incredible memory – and to think he wrote this in a time before Google or the internet! His Tamil expressions may at times be archaic and theatrical but his wit, humour and empathy cannot be missed, nor his candid introspection. And there is never a bitter or abusive word even when recounting moments of betrayal and hurt. He emerges from his autobiography as a man with a genuine zeal for social reform, and a personality which is commanding as well as vulnerable.

Karunanidhi's film scripts remain memorable. He wrote seventy-three of them, in addition to nine plays and two TV dramas. He was one of the first scriptwriters to demand credit and recognition for his work, and set the ball rolling for the rest. People went to see films like *Parasakthi, Rajakumari, Manthiri Kumari, Marudhanaattu Ilavarasi* multiple times just to hear his dialogues. Not only did his scripts make films hits at the box office, actors became famous because of his lines. Kamal Haasan once said that when he was four he had memorized a speech delivered by Sivaji Ganesan in *Parasakthi*, which was written by Karunanidhi.

His motto 'udal mannukku uyir thamizukku' – this body unto dust; this life unto Tamil – was immortalized by director Mani Ratnam in *Iruvar*, which was based on Karunanidhi's life.

He especially cherished the title Kalaignar. And as an orator, he effortlessly mesmerized a whole generation. Alliteration and rhyme were a hallmark of DMK leaders' speeches, but Kalaignar's words were so heartfelt that they bowled audiences over.

The DMK cadres' title for him – Thalaivar – was also truly earned. He would lovingly address them, '*En yurinum melaana udanpirappugale*!' My brethren, dearer than my life!

His writing and his politics, his persona as Kalaignar and Thalaivar complemented each other. As V. Geetha, writer and feminist activist, observes, 'Karunanidhi's writing was not incidental to his politics. His writerly personality defined his political selfhood – his ability to draw on the Sangam corpus of poems and to quote verbatim from them in the middle of a political or social speech established him as a worthy inheritor of a past that was not sullied by caste and Brahminical Hinduism.'[1]

~

However, the thalaivar was not above human faults. And his fall from grace was as monumental as his rise to power. His mistakes were scrutinized under a magnifying glass, and he was so severely judged that his remarkable achievements as an administrator and social reformer were obliterated. Even though none of the corruption charges against him were proved, the allegations in the Sarkaria Commission and the Jain Commission are still raked up by his detractors.

One of the predominant thoughts in Karunanidhi's mind in his final days was what turned MGR into his foe.

He wondered why people never criticized MGR the same way, questioning his motives and all his attempts to improve governance.

Karunanidhi believed it was the stigma he carried from birth as a Sudra. Print media during his early political years was mostly owned by Brahmins. His open criticism of Brahmins, of the caste system and of religion could have turned them against him.

Karunanidhi was very keen on the Sethusamudram Shipping Canal Project that would create a shipping route in the shallow straits between India and Sri Lanka.

He believed it would bring economic ease and prosperity to the southern districts of Tamil Nadu. But the Hindu Munnani and other fanatical groups raised a hue and cry, demanding an alternative route because the proposed one would destroy the Adam's Bridge or Ramar Sethu – the mythical bridge built by Lord Ram's vanar sena in his war with Lanka to bring home his abducted wife, Sita. The UPA government at the Centre supported Karunanidhi's proposal. The Janata Party's Subramanian Swamy, the Hindu Munnani's Ramagopalan and several others took the matter to court after considerable money had already been spent on the project. They said it would hurt the sentiments of Hindus.

Karunanidhi found this ridiculous and irrational. He burst out angrily in front of the TV cameras: 'Ram is a lie.' There is no historical truth in an epic that depicted Ravan, a Dravidian, as a villain, he stated. He ridiculed mythology and Hindu sentiments. He became belligerent, pressurizing the Centre to implement the project. He called for a bandh in Tamil Nadu in late September 2007 to demand implementation of the project. But the Supreme Court termed the bandh illegal.

He could not defy the highest court of law. He decided to go on a fast instead. Why did people seem to think an atheist had to be an immoral man? Ah, they do not know what turned him into an atheist. He would still cringe at the memory of his father standing bare-chested before the Brahmin mirasdar. There was an untold sabaltern narrative that his community – Isai Vellalar – suffered in silent anger.

It is indeed ironical, he would tell his close associates, that people seem to have forgotten or forgiven 'the god-fearing, temple visiting' Jayalalithaa who had been convicted by the courts for corruption and jailed twice. Her cadres said that *he* had falsely foisted those charges against her. She ruled as an authoritarian, secretive dictator, gagged the press and created an atmosphere of fear among her partymen and the bureaucracy. Yet people venerated her, deified her; she was loved and adored by the masses as Amma the giver, the benevolent universal mother.

After her 2011 victory Jayalalithaa had declared the DMK a finished story. Karunanidhi wondered if the DMK would ever establish its hold on Tamil Nadu again. Just before the May 2014 parliamentary elections, every street had billboards proclaiming her as the next prime minister of the country. She was out on bail from the Parappana Agrahara Jail in Bangalore on medical grounds, serving a four-year sentence for the disproportionate assets case. It is *her* story that is over, he thought. But then, by May 2015, the

Karnataka High Court had absolved her and her cronies of all the charges. How was that possible?

There were murmurs in his party that the prayers offered by the AIADMK men and women for her release – they circumambulated the corridors of the temples, ate rice spread on their mud floors, bathed the gods with milk and honey and sandal paste – had worked this miracle. He did not know whether to blame the gods or the people who held such beliefs. In the 2014 Lok Sabha elections, Jayalalithaa swept the polls, the AIADMK winning thirty-seven of the thirty-nine seats, while Karunanidhi's DMK drew a blank. It lost face at the Centre. It was the so-called 2G scam, for which the DMK and the UPA government were blamed, that brought about this debilitating defeat.

The BJP masterfully played up the issue with promises of a corruption-free future, projecting Modi as the redeemer of India from the tainted Congress government. The Modi avalanche swept all the others away. But at least Karunanidhi could take some comfort from the fact that with Modi's overwhelming victory, Jayalalithaa could not be the kingmaker or the queen at the Centre.

~

In 2016, when it was time for the Assembly elections, Karunanidhi was wheelchair-bound while Stalin had been working hard to galvanize the party cadres with his namakku name dhittam (self-help projects). He was touring every district in the state and there were reports of a very positive response. Stalin and his men were confident of a return to power but Karunanidhi wanted to secure their position with more support.

The DMK projected Karunanidhi as the chief ministerial candidate, hoping his frail form would evoke sympathy. People felt sorry for the old man being paraded in his wheelchair, whose incoherent speech they could not decipher.

He tried to rope in smaller parties like Vijayakanth's DMDK but grew anxious as the talks failed. The only ally left was the Congress that had also fallen in public esteem because of the 2G scam and its lack of action in the ethnic war in Sri Lanka in 2009.

The PMK, under Anbumani Ramadoss, decided to contest alone. The VCK, DMDK, TMC banded together as the Makkal Nala Koottani (People's Welfare Front), with Vijayakanth as their candidate. Karunanidhi was flabbergasted. Rumour had it that the front had been formed to dilute the DMK's votes, in exchange for huge sums of money. Later investigative reports revealed the AIADMK as the source of that money.

The strategy worked: the DMK lost just by 1.5 per cent votes, and Jayalalithaa came back to power for a consecutive five-year term with an absolute majority of 134 seats. The DMK–Congress alliance, however, got ninety-three seats, the largest number ever for an Opposition.

Karunanidhi, then ninety-two, won the Thiruvarur constituency, just as he had won every election since 1957. And the old and ailing leader who campaigned sitting in a wheelchair bagged 1,21,473 votes, defeating the AIADMK's R. Panneerselvam by a margin of 68,366 votes, the highest margin by which he had ever won.

But the fact remained that the DMK had lost and the AIADMK was back in power.

Stalin kept saying, '*Idhu jananayaka vetri illai. Pana nayaka vetri.*' This is not a victory of democracy. It is a victory for moneycracy.

It was widely reported that the ruling AIADMK had also paid the voters liberally.

Karunanidhi had seen jealousy, pettiness and even a few betrayals but never such large-scale crossovers of friends and parties for money. Politicians had stooped to becoming mercenaries.

During the sleepless nights that now became frequent, he must have worried about the party's future and the problems his son would have to face. Stalin had worked hard to enthuse the cadres and had taken the party to the verge of victory. Karunanidhi had said proudly, 'Stalin means work, work, work.' Stalin had earned the reputation of being a good administrator, and an upright man. But he was no Machiavelli. That was a shortcoming in today's politics. But Karunanidhi was sure Stalin would never deviate from the party's secular principles and that, he believed, was most important for Tamil Nadu and for India's future.

~

In September 2016, Karunanidhi's health took a turn for the worse. He was admitted to Kauvery Hospital. In a strange coincidence, Jayalalithaa was admitted to Apollo Hospital at the same time, just four months after assuming power. The news that she was in the ICU sent tremors of anxiety across the state.

It was a revealing moment for the DMK patriarch. He had of late turned philosophical in his thinking and writing. That is why in 2014 he had begun writing the TV serial on Ramanuja, wanting to delve deeper into the secular, inclusive religion that the rebellious saint had propagated. He said that though he was an atheist, Tamil bhakti hymns moved him because of the beauty of the Tamil words. Now he felt it was something more. For him, it was not just about telling the story of an extraordinary life; it was also about understanding an extraordinary philosophy of life that taught love and compassion for all.

As he and Jayalalithaa both lay in hospital, his mind must have gone back to the epic battles the two of them had fought, battles that had played such a big role in shaping the modern history of Tamil Nadu. They stood on unequal ground – she a Brahmin woman, much younger than him, a sophisticated, convent-educated and vulnerable woman pushed into politics by circumstances, much against her will; he belonging to a backward community, drawn to politics as a teenager, of his own will and his passion for an ideology. He was clever, wily and earthy, lacking her polish and fluency in English and Hindi. He had ridiculed her, dragged her to court, arrested her, put her in jail – but look, she rose every time like the phoenix, dared to challenge him and beat him hollow, to gloat, 'The DMK is a finished story!' What an amazing woman. A lone warrior who ran her party with an iron hand.

And here she was in the ICU, an orphan with no kith or kin. How lonely she must feel, the lady who had lived and ruled like a queen!

He, on the other hand, had a whole battalion to call his own, not just his immediate family but the entire DMK. When he claimed in his public speeches that everyone in the DMK 'is born of the same womb' and they are all 'blood of its blood' it meant that when he suffered setbacks and defeats and illness, they would all rally round him. When he cried he did not cry alone. He had spun a web of love around himself.

Durai Murugan's eyes tear up when he recalls the time he had to undergo heart surgery. Karunanidhi called him the night before, and sensing how nervous Durai Murugan was, offered to sleep in his room that night to keep his spirits up. There are many more such anecdotes, not just from partymen, but others too whom he had reached out to spontaneously in their hour of need.

Karunanidhi was still in the ICU when Jayalalithaa passed away on 5 December 2016. It was hard to believe that such a ferocious fighter in life had lost her battle against illness. He sent a message of condolence from his bed expressing his sadness at her death, adding, 'Though she died young her fame will remain forever.'

~

From then on Karunanidhi started counting his days. He had given up on life when words deserted him for good. He did not face death with fear. Actually he was eager to welcome it. But he recovered and was brought back home to the tumultuous cheering of the cadres who had lined up along the lanes leading to his Gopalapuram residence. When they saw him wheeled out of the vehicle they cried in unison, '*Thalaivar vaazhga! Kalaignar vaazhga!*' Long live the leader! Long live Kalaignar! The patriarch's eyes were moist as he smiled but could not speak.

Struggling with his speech he managed to convey to Stalin and other senior members of the party that a crisis in the AIADMK after their leader Jayalalithaa's demise could not be ruled out. But the party had come to power with a majority. Therefore the DMK should not, under any circumstances, try to capture power through the back door. The DMK, he told them firmly, should only come to power properly, elected by the people.

When Panneerselvam was called upon to don Jayalalithaa's mantle, it looked like a smooth succession. As the new leader of

Tamil Nadu, he performed his duties with diligence, oblivious to the conspiracy hatching behind his back.

Panneerselvam was surveying the ravages of an oil spill along the coast at Ennore when he was called to Poes Garden, the residence of Jayalalithaa, which her companion Sasikala had made hers, and was told that Chinnamma (mother's younger sister) was going to be elected in his place by the legislators of the AIADMK, and he must step down. Panneerselvam had never been a rebel but found this humiliation hard to bear. He sat in meditation at Amma's memorial for an hour and emerged from it with a clear and firm mind. 'I wish to reveal,' he told the waiting press, 'that my resignation from the chief minister's post in favour of Sasikala was forced.' He added, wiping his tears, 'I am revealing the truth now, motivated by the command I received from Amma's soul.'

But Amma's spirit did nothing further to help him deal with the power-hungry Sasikala's Machiavellian moves. Her ascent to the throne was not easy. Tamil Nadu Governor C. Vidyasagar Rao went missing to avoid swearing her in on 7 December, as she had planned. Her ambitions were audacious, given the several swords that hung over her head, including allegations of foul play in Jayalalithaa's death, the possibility of conviction in the disproportionate assets case that was pending judgement, and the widespread discontent in the state against her rapid rise in politics.

But surprisingly, AIADMK MLAs and ministers who were once jealous of Sasikala's closeness to their thalaivi, who had blamed her for the party's humiliating defeat in the 1996 Assembly elections, and who believed the corruption charges against Jayalalithaa were because of her association with Sasikala, now chose her unanimously as Jayalalithaa's successor.

On 8 February 2017, when Panneerselvam was preparing

to prove his strength in the Assembly, Sasikala, aware that the legislators would not want to let go of the power they had earned just six months earlier, in a bold move transported all the MLAs to the Golden Bay Resort at Kovathoor, beyond Chennai, to prevent them from walking into Panneerselvam's camp.

With the party having a mandate to rule for four and a half years more, she knew exactly what the concerns of the 134 AIADMK legislators were. Most of them had been handpicked by her and given tickets for the May 2016 Assembly elections and they were beholden to her. They had already started falling at her feet.

The anticlimax came on 14 February, with the long-awaited verdict of the Supreme Court: it convicted Sasikala, endorsing the special court's verdict earlier in which Jayalalithaa was convicted as the main accused. Sasikala had to leave almost immediately for Bengaluru and surrender. But before that she ensured her own man, Edappadi Palaniswamy, became chief minister in place of O. Panneerselvam. The Supreme Court verdict also made it clear that Jayalalithaa stood convicted, but the sentence was abated because of her demise.

By this time Karunanidhi may or may not have been abreast of all these developments. But the DMK would abide by his instructions and not pull down the AIADMK government even when there was a fair chance that they could do so. The warring groups in the AIADMK finally made a compromise: Edappadi Palaniswamy would continue as chief minister with Panneerselvam as the deputy chief minister. Together they went to the Election Commission to retrieve the party's two-leaves symbol so that it would not fall into the hands of yet another AIADMK faction that had cropped up – that of Sasikala's nephew Dhinakaran.

Jayalalithaa's death necessitated a by-poll in her constituency,

R.K. Nagar, in December 2017, when Dhinakaran stood as an independent. The results sent shockwaves in several directions. Dhinakaran won the seat by an incredible margin. The ruling AIADMK lost. Worse, the DMK that was expected to win lost its deposit.

It was a huge loss of face for the DMK, now led by Stalin. The party had never before looked so weak.

20

End of an Epoch

It is the first week of August 2018.

The police stand helpless, unable to control the swelling, surging crowds crying out, '*Thalaiva ezunthu vaa*!' Leader, get up and come!

The DMK cadres as well as ordinary people, young and old, and those without any party affiliation, thousands in number, have been camping on the roads leading to Kauvery Hospital in Alwarpet, Chennai, for nearly eleven days. They have travelled from all over Tamil Nadu for a glimpse of Kalaignar Karunanidhi who lies critically ill in the ICU, being treated for a urinary tract infection. He is ninety-four and, having lost his voice a couple of years earlier, has long stopped giving those soul-stirring speeches in lilting, poetic Tamil prose. Yet, they still expect him to come out and address them as before: '*En uyirinum melaana udanpirappukale.*' My brethren who are dearer to me than my life itself. He was always such a fighter, wasn't he? He would win this battle with the messenger of death too, they hope. Some of them have even pledged their lives to save their beloved patriarch. The deep emotional bond between Karunanidhi and his admirers is something that outsiders can't fathom.

Leaders of various political parties from all over India have been visiting the hospital. Family members keep going in and out, wiping their tears. And outside the hospital, the chant of the crowds continues: '*Thalaiva ezunthu vaa*!' Leader, get up and come!

Some followers have immolated themselves, unable to bear the thought of a world without Kalaignar. Stalin sends a quick appeal to party men not to succumb to emotions and commit such drastic acts. The leader would not like it, he says.

~

Unlike Jayalalithaa, who maintained a distance distance between herself and her partymen as well as the masses who adored her, there was no visible chasm between the DMK leader and his party cadres and the people. He remained accessible to all. It was regarded as one of the great strengths of the DMK that democratic procedure was scrupulously followed in party elections, even if each time Karunanidhi emerged the undisputed leader.

And now, as the end neared, DMK members wondered why he hadn't formally anointed anyone as his successor, even though he had clearly been grooming his son M.K. Stalin as his political heir. Was it because he was reluctant to give up his post even when he was no longer able to play any active role? No, most likely, it was to avert another ugly and possibly violent eruption of sibling rivalry between Stalin and Alagiri if he were to explicitly name Stalin. Now, it was not just his body that had become weak, it was his mind too. He no longer had the emotional strength for a family discord.

Karunanidhi had struck an emotional chord with voters in the last election he fought because they saw before them a nonagenarian, who had five times been chief minister, who was now clearly very frail, yet who pushed himself to travel through the state to campaign, to speak directly to them. In May 2016, a wheelchair-bound Karunanidhi was still waiting to write a fresh script – a dramatic finale that would bring down the curtain with the word '*shubham*'. All is well. But that was not to be.

The DMK lost those Assembly elections. But Karunanidhi himself won, and won with a record margin over his AIADMK opponent at Thiruvarur. He had been in politics for more than seventy years, and 2016 marked his fifty-ninth year as the DMK's star campaigner. In all those years he had never lost a single Assembly seat he contested.

~

Seasoned journalists who had witnessed Jayalalithaa's last days looked at the sea of humanity now surging outside Kauvery hospital and observed a difference. They had always thought Karunanidhi lacked the charisma of Jayalalithaa when it came to attracting crowds, but the spontaneous grief that emanated from the people now had not been seen when Jayalalithaa breathed her last. It looked like they had come to witness the last act, the grand finale of an epic – sad, poetic and grand.

On the evening of 7 August came the official announcement from the hospital: 'With deep anguish, we announce the demise of our beloved Kalaignar Dr M. Karunanidhi on 07.08.2018. Despite the best possible efforts by our team of doctors to resuscitate him, he failed to respond,' the statement said, adding, 'We profoundly mourn the loss of one of the tallest leaders of India and we share the grief of family members and fellow Tamilians worldwide.'

~

The street leading to Kalaignar Karunanidhi's residence in Gopalapuram is narrow and the house modest. Journalists climbing the narrow steps to the first-floor visitors' room could not fail to notice on the way up the saying written on the wall in bold letters: '*Kaalam pon ponradhu, kadamai kanponradhu.*' Time is like gold, duty is like one's eye. Karunanidhi would be sitting ready for the interview in his starched white veshti with a yellow shawl over his full-sleeved shirt and greet them with a warm smile as they entered. He was that rare chief minister who never refused an interview (he had started his career as a journalist, after all), who was unfailingly friendly and cooperative with the press. What a contrast to Jayalalithaa! His visitors could always look forward to a scintillating hour with him as they savoured his repartee, his frank answers, his shrewd political analyses and even his eagerness to discuss books and literature, for which he had a passion.

And what a fighter he was too! Even after his death his spirit seemed to be fighting – fighting for the right to be buried next to his beloved mentor, C.N. Annadurai.

Soon after his death M.K. Stalin along with his siblings and senior DMK members personally met E. Palaniswamy, requesting him to allot space behind Annadurai's memorial on the historic Marina Beach for his father. Formal letters of request had also been sent. To their dismay, the chief minister gave a non-committal reply.

That evening, the AIADMK government triggered a political crisis in Tamil Nadu when chief secretary Girija Vaidyanathan issued a statement expressing the government's inability to allot land near Marina Beach. She cited pending court cases to deny the DMK's request, and instead offered two acres of land on Sardar Patel Road near Anna University for Karunanidhi's memorial.

Stalin and the others felt the government was simply being mean and petty. Though coastal regulation zone rules prohibit any new construction on Marina Beach, the same government had made a special concession to allow Jayalalithaa's burial and memorial there in 2016. The DMK expected the same courtesy would be extended to its leader who had also been chief minister of the state five times.

When the news of the government's denial spread, angry DMK cadres protested on the streets. Stalin pleaded with them with folded hands to stay calm and not make the situation more difficult. He told them the DMK had appealed for justice in the judicial courts, challenging the chief secretary's statement.

On 8 August, the tension was palpable throughout Tamil Nadu as the state awaited the court's verdict. Meanwhile, to pay homage to Karunanidhi, both the houses of Parliament were adjourned and the Indian flag flew at half-mast. Leaders from all over the country, across the political spectrum, poured in to pay their respects to the departed leader whose body lay in state at Rajaji Hall – Prime Minister Narendra Modi, Defence Minister Nirmala Sitaraman, Congress president, Rahul Gandhi, Gulam Nabi Azad of the Congress, Akhilesh Yadav of the Samajwadi Party, Mamata Banerjee of the Trinamul Congress, Sharad Pawar, Farooq Abdullah and Omar Abdullah, actors Rajinikanth and Kamal Haasan, as well as Tamil Nadu Chief Minister Edappadi Palaniswamy and Deputy Chief Minister O. Panneerselvam. The crowds too thronged Rajaji Hall in enormous numbers, a turnout even bigger than when Jayalalithaa passed away. They had come not just for a final glimpse of a titan but to witness a historic moment, the end of an epoch with the passing away of the last of the giants who had ruled Tamil Nadu and captured the imagination of its people for half a century.

In the midst of the mourning, the air hung heavy with apprehension. And Karunanidhi seemed to be enjoying it all. His face seen through the glass cover of the casket looked surprisingly fresh and cheerful, as if he was watching the dramatic climax of a script he had written himself. When the verdict from the court came on the morning of 8 August, it spread like a massive wave through the crowds, shared in an instant through thousands of WhatsApp messages.

The Madras High Court directed the state government to allot land on Marina Beach for Karunanidhi's memorial.

Stalin broke down and so did his siblings and senior DMK leaders. The Tamil Nadu government declared a public holiday on the day. The state observed a seven-day mourning.

Karunanidhi was laid to rest with full state honours and his last wish – to lie next to his mentor 'Anna' – was fulfilled. The casket had an epitaph, which the leader had written for himself thirty-three years earlier. It read, 'The one who toiled without rest takes eternal rest here.'

Notes

Introduction

1. Scholars have since argued convincingly that both Sanskrit and Tamil scripts were born of the same mother – Brahmi – and have both had strong literary connections. The Tamil Brahmi script, according to I. Mahadevan, author of *Early Tamil Epigraphy*, was an innovative adaptation of the original Mauryan Brahmi script, in order to conform to the distinctive phonological character of the Tamil language.
2. N. Ram's speech during The Hindu Lit for Life Festival, January 2018, Chennai.
3. Ibid.

1. Born to Rebel

1. Interview with the author, 2004.

2. Love, Marriage and the Lure of Politics

1. Interview with the author, 2004.
2. Paraiyar is the name of a scheduled caste in Tamil Nadu. There

are three major sub-castes among the Dalits – Paraiyar, Pallar and Arunthathiyar. Paraiyars are spread across the northern and central belt of the state. The Pallars are in the southern region while the western region is home to the Arunthathiyars.

3. Even today, caste feelings are very strong and there are constant clashes among the backward classes and the Dalits, as well as honour killings – an evil that the Dravidian movement has not been able to address or redress.

3. Periyar vs Annadurai

1. RMV first joined the Dravida Kazhagam, then left it and joined Annadurai when he started the DMK. A great admirer of MGR, he followed him when the DMK split and joined the AIADMK started by MGR and was a minister in the AIADMK government under MGR and later Jayalalithaa.
2. Interview with the author, Chennai, 2004.
3. Interview with author, Chennai, 2004.
4. It had earlier been reported that he was in close contact with Mohammad Ali Jinnah of the Muslim League, who had demanded and got a separate nation for Muslims.
5. Gandhi, R. *Modern South India: A History from the 17th Century to Our Times.* New Delhi: Aleph Book Company, 2019.
6. Interview with the author, 2004.
7. Ibid.
8. Ibid.

4. The Rising Sun

1. From *Nenjukku Needhi*, Karunanidhi's six-volume autobiography. This and all subsequent quotes from the autobiography have been translated from the original Tamil by the author.

2. Gandhi, R. *Modern South India: A History from the 17th Century to Our Times.* New Delhi: Aleph Book Company, 2019.
3. Ibid.

5. The Anti-Hindi Conflagration

1. Kannan, R. *Anna: The Life and Times of C.N. Annadurai.* Penguin Books: New Delhi, 2010.
2. Narrated to the author in 2018 by a DMK member requesting anonymity.
3. Ravishankar, S. *Karunanidhi: A Life in Politics.* HarperCollins: New Delhi, 2018.
4. Interview with the author, March 2018.

6. Inheriting Annadurai's Mantle

1. Kannan, R. *MGR: A Life.* Penguin Random House: New Delhi, 2017.
2. Interview with the author, 2004.
3. Ibid.
4. Ibid.
5. Interview with the author, January 2019.
6. Kannan, R. *MGR: A Life.* Penguin Random House: New Delhi, 2017.
7. Interview with the author, January 2019.
8. Ibid.
9. Interview with the author, 2004.

7. MGR vs Karunanidhi

1. Pandian, M.S.S. *The Image Trap: M.G. Ramachandran in Film and Politics.* Sage India: New Delhi, 2015.
2. Ibid.
3. Interview with the author, 2004.

4. Dickey, S. 'The Politics of Adulation: Cinema and the Production of Politicians in South India.' In *The Journal of Asian Studies* 52 (2): 340–72. Association for Asian Studies: May 1993.
5. Interview with the author, March 2018.

8. The Emergency and the Rise of MGR

1. Interview with the author, March 2018.
2. N. Ram's speech at the Hindu Lit for Life Festival, January 2019.
3. Ibid.
4. Interview with the author.
5. Ibid.
6. Ibid.
7. Ibid.

9. The Long Shadow of Sri Lanka

1. Interview with the author in the late 1990s.
2. The full extent of MGR's illness was kept under wraps – he had in fact suffered a stroke that paralysed his right side and impaired his speech, he had diabetes and also suffered renal failure. On 5 October 1984 he was flown to New York where he stayed for three months. Lying in hospital, when he could neither speak nor sign his name, he filed his nomination for the Tamil Nadu Assembly–Lok Sabha elections being held in December 1984. His party won 132 of the 234 Assembly seats. He returned to India and was sworn in as the chief minister once again. The AIADMK was in alliance with the Congress, which came to power at the Centre with Rajiv Gandhi as the prime minister.

   Though MGR seemed to have recovered, doctors said his days were numbered.
3. Interview with the author, 2004.

4. Gandhi, G. 'End of an Epoch: On M. Karunanidhi's Death.' *The Hindu*. 8 August 2018.
5. Ibid.
6. Interview with the author, August 2018.

10. A Woman Scorned

1. Interview with the author, August 2018.
2. Ibid.

11. The Vaiko Affair

1. Interview with the author, 1993.

12. The Prima Donna

1. It was during this time that Subramanian Swamy slapped a disproportionate assets case on Jayalalithaa, Sasikala, Sasikala's sister-in-law Ilavarasi and nephew V.N. Sudhakaran. This case would go on for close to twenty years, finally ending in a 'guilty' verdict after Jayalalithaa's death in 2016, putting Sasikala and the others behind bars for four years.

13. Administrator Par Excellence

1. Balaji, R. 'A Patron of the Knowledge Industry.' *Hindu Business Line*, 7 August 2018.
2. N. Ram's speech at the Hindu Lit for Life Festival, January 2019.
3. Ibid.
4. Ironically, it was Jayalalithaa who would later destabilize the BJP-led government at the Centre, paving the way for yet another unexpected alliance in the history of Dravidian politics.

14. Strange Bedfellows

1. Interview with the author.
2. It was alleged that Jayalalithaa, on receiving a letter from N. Haribhaskar, the then Tamil Nadu electricity board chairman, had written in September 1992 to the prime minister seeking concurrence to import one million tonnes of steaming coal. After obtaining the clearance Haribhaskar took action, calling for global tenders in February 1993. The prosecution said the accused had entered into a criminal conspiracy by causing a loss of Rs 650 million to the government by signing a deal to buy coal at $40 per tonne to facilitate certain foreign firms when actually the initial price offer made by Prime Comexindo was $35.24 per tonne. The deal was done inspite of the objections raised by then public works secretary, K. Sundaram. The pages containing Sundaram's objections had disappeared from the file.

   The judge said that there was no evidence that Jayalalithaa was directly involved in the scam. On the other hand he framed charges against Haribhaskar and eight others under section 120 B (criminal conspiracy). He said the court 'could not presume or assume that the entire file, including the missing pages were placed before Jayalalithaa when she had affixed her signature'.
3. Ravishankar, S. *Karunanidhi: A Life in Politics*. HarperCollins: New Delhi, 2018.

15. The Wounded Tigress Fights Back

1. From an editorial in *The Hindu*, 1 September 2001.
2. Ravishankar, S. *Karunanidhi: A Life in Politics*. HarperCollins: New Delhi, 2018.

16. Family Matters

1. Stalin was born in 1953 when Joseph Stalin died. Karunanidhi, after addressing a condolence meeting for the Soviet leader, decided to name his newborn son Stalin.
2. In 2000, when the DMK's annual celebrations to commemorate the birth anniversaries of Anna, Periyar and the DMK were organized in Chennai, it was imperative for the party secretaries from all districts to participate. However, three secretaries from Madurai district did not attend because Alagiri stopped them, for reasons best known to him. Furious and embarrassed, Karunanidhi then asked K. Anbazhagan, DMK general secretary and education minister, to issue a statement which said, 'Since Alagiri has violated party's discipline he has caused extreme displeasure to thalaivar Kalaignar. All members of the party have been asked not to have any truck with Alagiri.' But Karunanidhi stopped short of expelling Alagiri from the DMK.
3. Radhika Selvi was the widow of Venkatesha Pannaiyar of Tuticorin, a rich and powerful man who was killed by the police in an encounter during Jayalalithaa's rule. He became a martyr among the influential Nadar community in the area. Radhika stood for the 2004 Lok Sabha election on a DMK ticket and won from Tiruchendur constituency.

17. The 'Mother of All Scams'

1. Ravishankar, S. *Karunanidhi: A Life in Politics*. HarperCollins: New Delhi, 2018.
2. Ibid.
3. Ibid.

19. Autumn of the Patriarch

1. Geetha, V. 'Karunanidhi and "Tamilness": Kalaignar's Literary, Cultural Legacy Cannot be Separated From His Politics.' *Firstpost*, 15 August 2018.

Acknowledgements

My most special thanks go to my friend K.S. Radhakrishnan, whose generous hospitality enabled me to stay at his house during my month-long visits to Chennai, where I used his huge personal library that houses Karunanidhi's six-volume autobiography, *Nenjukku Needhi*, his literary works and film scripts, his public speeches as well as the millions of words he wrote in the form of daily letters to the DMK cadres in *Murasoli*, the party organ. His library also contains an incredible archive of newspaper clippings and journals spreading over fifty years, filed with meticulous care. As a member of the DMK, Radhakrishnan also provided me valuable information and guidance, and helped arrange interviews with many political leaders. This book would not have been possible without his help.

Heartfelt thanks to Durai Murugan, K.P. Ramalingam, Peter Alphonse, Goppanna, Ravi Kumar, Thamizaruvi Manian, Shanmuganathan, Justice K. Chandru and R. Nallakkannu who graciously gave me time in the midst of their busy schedules and provided immensely helpful insights into my subject. I also thank senior journalist Maalan, Priyan and D.I. Aravindan who shared their views about Karunanidhi, each showing me a different perspective.

I am most grateful to N. Ram, R.M. Veerappan and the late Cho Ramaswamy, with whom I had long discourses while working on an earlier book and who I have quoted freely in this book. My gratitude also to Kanimozhi, V. Geetha, K.M. Vijayan, Sadanand Menon and scores of DMK and AIADMK leaders and journalists who have over the years deepened my understanding of Tamil politics.

My editor Nandini Mehta persuaded me to write this book on the amazing life of Muthuvel Karunanidhi who rose from humble beginnings to become the tallest leader in Tamil Nadu politics. Thank you, Nandini, for giving such meticulous attention to my work. You demanded clarity, made many beneficial suggestions and pushed me to make Tamil politics and culture as comprehensible as possible to non-Tamil readers.

Index

Aandipatti constituency, 160
- Abdullah, Farooq, 212

Advani, L.K., 76, 143, 146, 156, 219–20

Ahmed, Fakhruddin Ali, 79, 215

Al Umma, 145

Alagiri, M.K., son, 181, 190, 203
- cash-for-vote formula, 193, 244
- violent behaviour, 179, 185–89
- envy and resentment towards brother Stalin, 184, 192–96
- minister for chemical and fertilizer at Centre, 192–93, 195, 196
- and murder of Tha. Kiruttinan, 186, 193–94

All India Anna Dravida Munnetra Kazhagam (AIADMK), xvii, xxii, 68–69, 71, 75–76, 82–83, 91, 96, 103, 110, 117–18, 127, 152, 154, 158, 174, 203, 215–18, 220, 247
- 2011–2016, 177
- BJP alliance, 148–51, 170, 225
- Congress alliance, 162
- corruption charges, 94, 124, 128, 129–33, 147–48, 157–59, 160–61, 163, 166–67, 170, 173, 202, 234, 240
- crisis after Jayalalithaa's death, 239–41
- factional fighting after MGR's death, 110–15
- general election, 2014, 235
- Janaki group, 140
- split, 112
- Tamil Nadu Assembly election, 1977, 87
- Tamil Nadu Assembly election, 1991, 105

Tamil Nadu Assembly election, 1996, 129, 240
Tamil Nadu Assembly election, 2006, 170–71
Tamil Nadu Assembly election, 2016, 236–37, 239, 245
All India Forward Bloc, 129, 213
Alphonse, Peter, 139–40, 205
Anbazhagan, K., 54–55, 169, 193
Anna Centenary Library, Kotturpuram, Chennai, 173, 176–77
Anna Dravida Munnetra Kazhagam (ADMK). *See* All India Anna Dravida Munnetra Kazhagam (AIADMK)
Annadurai, C.N. (Anna), xxiv, xxvi, 7, 9, 11–13, 16, 18, 20, 33–35, 38–41, 47–48, 50–53, 78, 82, 108, 123, 135, 229, 246, 248
death, 95, 230
Karunanidhi, inherited mantle, 54–69
Periyar versus, 22–32
anti-Hindi agitation, 33–34, 41, 42–53, 57, 207. *See also* Self-Respect Movement; language issue
Arasar, Panagal, 5, 8
Arasu, A.P., 40
Arivunidhi, grandson, 181
Arumugam, Veerapandi, 116
Azad, Gulam Nabi, 247

Baalu, T.R., 154, 164, 225
Babri Masjid demolition, 1992, 145, 155–56, 222. *See also* Ram Temple issue
Backward Classes Commission, First (A.N. Sattanathan Commission), 59, 60
Backward Classes, reservation for, 60, 138
Bahuguna, H.M., 97
Banerjee, Mamata, 247
Barnala, Surjit Singh, 190, 218, 221
Basu, Jyoti, 193, 210, 212, 223
Besant, Annie, xxii, 226
Bhagwat, Admiral Vishnu, 149
Bhaktavatsalam, M., 44, 213
Bharathidasan, 16
Bharatiya Janata Party (BJP), 200, 202, 205, 219–20, 223, 235
AIADMK alliance, 147–50, 169, 225
DMK, alliance, 150–53
in Tamil Nadu politics, 143
Bharti Enterprises, 206

Bhuvanagiri constituency, 160

Central Bureau of Investigation (CBI), 85, 201, 203, 204, 206
Central Vigilance Commission (CVC), 201
Chandra Shekhar, 209, 218, 220, 221
Chandru, Justice K., 52, 59, 74, 83, 89
Chavan, Yashvantrao, 208
Chidambaram, P., 129, 133, 223
Chidambaram, S.P., 11
Chief Minister's Comprehensive Health Insurance Scheme, 178
China and India war, 1962, 30, 42
Chitti Babu, 82
coal import scam against Jayalalithaa, 153, 157
colour TV scam, 131, 133–34, 153
Communist Party of India (CPI), 10–11, 42, 65, 77, 84, 129, 139, 147, 209, 210
Communist Party of India-Marxist (CPI[M]), 52, 65, 77, 84, 210
Comptroller and Auditor General (CAG), 201, 202, 204
Congress, xxiii, xxv–xxvi, 6, 8, 10, 11, 16–17, 22, 24, 29, 157, 216, 220, 221, 224, 227, 235
    AIADMK, alliance, 218, 222
    conspiracy to split DMK, 64–68
    dismissed Karunanidhi's government, 80–83
    and DMK, relations/alliance, 48–50, 61–62, 143–44, 172, 183, 192, 204, 205, 227, 236
    general election, 1977, 92
    general election, 1991, 105
    general election, 2004, 226–27
    general election, 2009, 192
    and the language issue, 42–47
    Presidential candidate issue after Zakir Hussain's death, 209–211
    split, 61, 64–69, 212
    Sri Lankan issue, 96, 100–07
    and Tamil Nadu politics, 33–34, 36–37, 39, 43–46, 48–50, 59, 64–68, 129, 152–53, 169–70, 172, 217
    DMK, alliance, 93, 213–14, 217
Congress-O (Organizational), 61, 78, 87
Congress-R (Requisitionists), 61
Cuddalore Veeranam Drinking Water Project, 85

Dalit Viduthalai Chiruthaigal Katchi, 169

Dalmia, Ramkrishna, 37
Das, Mohan, 66, 99
Dayalu Ammal (second wife), 23, 50, 180, 181, 188, 190, 205
Democratic Progressive Alliance, 170
Department of Telecom (DoT), 199, 200
Depressed and Backward Classes Conference, Allahabad, 1973, 76
Desai, Kanti, 92
Desai, Morarji, 61, 92, 209–11, 215–16
Desiya Murpokku Dravida Kazhgam (DMDK), 236
Devi Lal, 219
Dharmalingam, Anbil, 85
Dharmambal. *See* Rajathi
Dhinakaran, 241–42
Dinakaran, 185–87, 189, 190
Dravida Actors Company, 14, 15, 16
Dravida Nadu, 12
Dravida Nadu, demand for, 96
Dravida Kazhagam (DK), 13, 15, 16, 18, 20, 23, 24, 26, 27–29, 34, 37, 96, 151
  split, 29, 31
Dravida Munnetra Kazhagam (DMK), xvii, xviii, xx–xxii, xxvii, 5, 29, 31–32, 54–58, 61–64, 65–66, 73, 170, 210, 244–45
  and BJP alliance, 151–55, 162
  Congress alliance/relations, 48–50, 61–62, 80–82, 192
  Congress (R) alliance, 93, 213–14, 217
  corruption charges, xxix, 65, 67, 74–76, 77, 81, 84–88, 104, 124, 164–65, 170, 178, 196, 202
  general election, 1991, 105
  general election, 1998, 146
  general election, 2014, 227, 235
  goondaism and land-grabbing, 196–97
  internal factions and rivalry, 34–35, 40–41
  and the language issue, 42–48, 50–51
  MGR's expulsion, 67–69
  after MGR's death, 112
  R.K. Nagar constituency by-poll, 241–42
  and RSS, 150
  split, 65–69, 119, 120–24, 214
  state autonomy, demand for, xxii, 32, 59, 61, 66, 81, 97, 141, 207, 212

succession issue after Annadurai's death, 54–58
Tamil Nadu Assembly election, 1967, 47–48
Tamil Nadu Assembly election, 1991, 105, 126–27
Tamil Nadu Assembly election, 1996, 129–30
Tamil Nadu Assembly election, 2006, 170–72
Tamil Nadu Assembly election, 2016, 236–37, 245
Dravidian identity, xxii, 5–6
Dravidian Movement, xxi, xxiii–xxiv, xxvii, 13, 26, 61, 119, 140
Durai, P., 115

Education streams in Tamil Nadu, 173–75
Eelam People's Revolutionary Liberation Front (EPRLF), 103, 104, 126
Elangovan, T.K.S., 190
Election Commission, 124, 241
electoral politics, 15, 24, 25, 35, 39, 172, 183
Emergency, 78, 184, 204, 211, 214–17
and dismissal of Karunanidhi's government, 79, 80–84, 87, 94, 103–04, 119, 126, 214, 215
and the rise of MGR, 80–94
Enforcement Directorate, 84, 205
Essential Services Maintenance Act (ESMA), 168
ethnic war in Sri Lanka in 2009, 236

farm labour system, 53
farmers' markets in Tamil Nadu, 136
Fathima Beevi, 162, 165
Fernandes, George, 149, 156, 165, 210
food shortages, 42–43

Gandhi, Indira, 57, 60–61, 66–67, 76, 77, 78, 80–81, 83, 86–87, 92–93, 96, 184, 208–17
disputed election from Rae Bareli, 214–15
imposed Emergency (1975–77), 78, 80–94, 184, 204, 211, 214–17
Gandhi, M.K., xxv, 16, 18, 22, 210
Gandhi, Rahul, 179, 247
Gandhi, Rajiv, 99, 101, 112, 119, 157, 218, 220, 221
assassination, 104, 105, 122,

126, 143, 150, 221–22, 224, 227
Gandhi, Sonia, 150, 152–53, 156–57, 169, 172, 225–27
Ganesan, Shivaji, 128, 137, 232
general election (Lok Sabha)
1952, 36
1957, 39
1967, 56
1971, 212–14
1977, 86, 87, 92, 215
1980, 92–93, 211, 216, 217
1989, 101, 112, 143–44, 218
1991, 105, 221
1996, 222
1998, 106, 146, 225
1999, 150, 154, 225
2004, 156–57,169–70, 183, 226
2009, 191, 192, 183
2014, 196, 227, 235
2019, 183
Giri, V.V., 61, 209–11
Godse, Nathuram, 22
Gopal, 13, 14
Gopalaswamy, V. (Vaiko), 120–25, 151, 193, 195
Gowda, H.D. Deve, 211, 223–24
Gujarat riots, 2002, 155, 156, 225
Gujral, I.K., 105–06, 143, 182, 211, 218, 224
Gupta, Bhupesh, 209, 210
Gupta, Indrajit, 223

Hegde, Ramakrishna, 212
Hindi. *See* language issue
Hindu, The, xx–xxi, xxvi, xxviii, 11, 76, 153, 162, 187
Hinduism, xxiii–xxiv, xxvi, 226
root of caste system, 6
Home Rule Movement, xxii-xxiii
Hussain, Zakir, 61, 209

Independence, 1947, 20
Inderesan, P.V., 151
Indian Peace Keeping Force (IPKF), 100–02
Indo-Sri Lankan Peace Accord, 1987, 76, 100, 101
Intelligence Bureau (IB), 120, 122, 123
and the Research and Analysis Wing, ego battles, 102
Iruvar, 232
Isai Vellalar community, 3
Ismail, Qaid-e-Millath Muhammad, 211
Iyengar, Kasturi, 4–5

Jagjivan Ram, 208–09, 210, 215
Jain Commission Report, 104,

105–06, 143, 148, 150, 169, 224, 226, 233
Jain, Justice M.C., 106
Jana Sangh, 76, 92
Janata Dal, 101
  split, 220
Janata Party, 87, 92, 94, 128, 200, 211, 233
  DMK, alliance, 1977, 215
Jaya TV, 158, 189
Jayakanthan, 142
Jayalalithaa, Jayaram, xvii, xx, xxi, 69, 86, 88–90, 105, 106, 110–19, 124–25, 126–34, 141–43, 145–47, 149, 150–59, 160–63, 165, 244, 246
  arrests, 130–34, 166
  authoritarian/autocratic and dictatorial, 127, 131–32, 168, 234
  corruption, allegations of/ convicted by courts and jailed, 124, 128, 129–33, 134, 147–48, 157–59, 160–61, 163, 166–67, 173, 202, 234, 240
  death, 239, 245, 248
  disproportionate assets case against, 128, 153, 234, 240
  hell-bent on undoing Karunanidhi's work, 177
  hospitalized, 237–39
  and Janaki Ramachandran, succession war, 111–13, 115, 117, 140, 218
Jayaraman, Chidambaram, 14
Jayewardene, J.R., 99
Jeppiar, 91–92
Jethmalani, Ram, 149, 154
Jeyaraman, J., 135
Justice Party (South Indian Liberation Front), xxii–xxiii, xxv–xxvi, 5–6, 8, 15

Kalaignar Maruthuva Kaappeettu Thittam, 173
Kalaignar TV, 190
Kallakkudy, protest over change of name, 37–38
Kamaraj, K., 37, 61, 62, 78–79, 88, 209
Kanimozhi (daughter), 49–51, 84, 128, 181, 185, 190–91, 196, 199, 203–04, 205–06, 227, 228
Kannadasan, 33, 40–41
  Vanavasam, 40
Kargil war, 1999, 150
Karunanandan, 17
Karunanidhi, Muthuvel
  accident, 38–39, 41

administrative skills, 89–90, 135–44
alliance strategy, 211–12
Brahmins and Hindu religious structure, opposition to, 207
birth, xxvii, 3–4
chief minister, five times, xxi, 140, 179, 245, 247
1969–1971, 57, 95, 135, 208, 230
1996–2001, 135, 136, 142–43
2006–2011, 135, 173–78
childhood and education, 1–4
Thiruvarur High School, 4, 5
corruption charges, 77, 81, 84–88, 104, 124, 130, 164–66, 173, 215, 233
death, 243–48
decline in stature, 196–97
failures in judgement, xxviii–xxix
family matters, 180–97
health, 228–29, 237–38
leader of Opposition, xvii, 88, 90
love, marriage and the lure of politics, 10–21
second marriage, 22–23
on the national stage, 207–27
Nenjukku Needhi (autobiography), xxvii, 5, 9, 12, 17, 19, 21, 22, 23, 26, 38, 56, 57, 63–65, 80, 89, 214, 216, 218, 220, 231
out of power, 80–90, 214, 215, 222, 230
and Periyar, xxvi, 6–7
scriptwriter, 18, 35–36, 41, 49, 133, 137–38, 182, 230, 231–32
Sri Lankan Tamils issue, xxviii, 94, 95–109, 119, 122, 221
weaknesses and shortcomings, xix–xx, xxviii, 125, 180
writer, poet and scholar, xxi, xxvii–xxviii, 11–14, 140, 182, 231–32, 243
Katchatheevu, was ceded to Sri Lanka, 76–77
Keezhvenmani, Thanjavur, 51–53
Khurana, Sundar Lal, 112
Kottaimedu, illegal activities, 145–46
Krishna River waters, 224
Krishnagiri constituency, 160
Krishnan, N.S., 36, 39
Krishnan, T., 186, 193–94
Kudi Arasu, 17, 18
kulakkalvi thittam, elementary education scheme, 36–37

Kuliththalai, 39
Kumaramangalam, Mohan, 65, 213
Kumaramangalam, Rangarajan, 123
Kungumam, 189
Kuththoosi, Chinna, xix

land reforms in Tamil Nadu, 59–60
language issue: anti-Hindi resentment among Tamils, 8–9, 11, 23, 32
  language riots of 1965, 43
  linguistic and regional identity, 29
  linguistic chauvinism, xxiii
Liberation Tigers for Tamil Eelam (LTTE), 96–102, 104, 106–09, 119–24, 126, 143, 221, 224, 226. *See also* Prabhakaran, Velupillai; Sri Lanka

Madhavan, S., 52, 208
Madras Legislative Assembly election, 1937, 8
Madras Municipal Corporation election, 1959, 40
Madras Presidency, under British Raj, xxii, xxiii, 8, 27
Maintenance of Internal Security Act (MISA), 82
Makkal Nala Koottani, 236
Malathi, S., 186
Manava Nesan, 10–11
Mandal Commission, 218–19
Mani, Ko. Si., 164
Maniyammai, 28–29
Manthiri Kumari, 19, 36, 232
Manu needhi thittam – justice for petitions, 59
Maran, Dayanidhi (grandnephew), 171, 182–89, 191–92
Maran, Kalanidhi (grandnephew), 182–89, 191–92
Maran, Murasoli (nephew), 58, 82, 86, 149, 154, 156, 164, 181–82, 188, 192, 216, 221, 223, 224, 225
Marudhanaattu Ilavarasi, 232
Marumalarchi Dravida Munnetra Kazhagam (MDMK), 124–25, 151–52, 169, 172
Maruthuva Kaappeettu Thittam scheme, 177–78
Menon, Gopala, 71
Menon, Madhava, 33
Menon, V.K. Krishna, 211
mid-day meal scheme, 88, 89
Mittal, Rakesh, 157
Mittal, Sunil, 206

Modern Theatres, 35
Modi, Narendra, 155, 227, 235, 247
Moopanar, G. K., 115, 129, 223, 224
Mukherjee, Ajoy, 210
Mukherjee, Pranab, 108
Mullivaikkal massacre, Sri Lanka, 18 May 2009, 108
Murasoli, xviii, xix, xxvii, 11, 19–20, 41, 82, 84, 90–91, 121, 155, 222
Murasoli, Selvam (nephew), 80, 181–82, 192
Murugan, Durai, 91, 115, 178–79, 193, 197, 206, 238–39
Muslim, Muslims, 145, 152
  fundamentalists, infiltration at Kottaimedu, xxviii–xxix
  reservation for, 173
  vote bank in Tamil Nadu, 147
Muslim League, 213
Muthu, M.K. (son), 21, 23, 64–65, 180–81
Muthuvelar (father), 1–4

Naidu, Chandra Babu, 222, 224
Nallakkannu, R., 139
Nambiar, K.A., 134, 164
Narayan, Jayaprakash (JP), 76, 77
Natarajan, Sasikala, 113, 127, 132, 133, 158–59, 240–41
Nathan Publications, 85
National Democratic Alliance (NDA), 147, 154, 165, 211
  and DMK, coalition, 225
national freedom movement, xxvi
National Front, 218, 219–20
nationalization of banks by Indira Gandhi, 60, 211, 212
Nedunchezhiyan (Navalar), 55–58, 67–68, 78, 85, 218
Nehru, Jawaharlal, 37, 93
Nijalingappa, S., 61, 210

Official Languages Act, 1963, 46

Padmanabha, 103, 104, 126
Padmavathi Ammal (first wife), 14, 17, 18–21
  died, 21, 22, 180
Palaniappan, 13, 14–15
Palaniswamy, Edappadi, 241, 246, 247–48
Pande, H.M., 157
Pandian, P.H., 115, 140
Panneerselvam, O., 167
Panneerselvam, R., 236, 239–41, 248
Parasakthi, (1952), 137–38, 232
Parthasarathy, G., 213
Patnaik, Biju, 216, 218
Pattali Makkal Katchi (PMK),

151, 152, 169, 170, 172, 236
Pawar, Sharad, 247
Periyar, E.V. Ramasamy Naicker, xxii, 11, 15, 17–18, 42, 57–59, 78, 220
  and Annadurai, differences, 20, 22–32
  authoritarian, autocratic, 25, 31
  anti-Brahminism, xxiv, xxv–xxvi, xxvii, 24, 27
  supported continuance of British rule, xxvi, 6
  demand for separate Dravida state, 26, 30, 32
  dubbed Independence Day as a day of mourning, 20, 24, 31
  Self-Respect Movement (Suyamariyathai Iyakkam), xxvi, 6–9, 14
Pillai, Ganapathiya, 52
Pillai, M. Kandasamy, 72
Pillai, Narayana, 30
Pillai, Sundaram, 95
Pleasant Stay Hotel, case, 153, 158
politics in Tamil Nadu, xvii, xxii, 10–21, 22, 26, 30, 35, 47, 58, 61, 69, 107, 111–13, 116. 118, 123, 126, 143, 148–51, 154, 183, 193, 216–18, 225–26, 232, 237–40, 245
Prabhakaran, Velupillai, 98–105, 107–09, 124. *See also* Sri Lanka
Praja Socialist Party, 213
Premadas, Ranasinghe, 102, 103
President's rule in Tamil Nadu:
  1988–89, 112, 218
  1991, 103–04, 112, 119, 221
  2001, 165
privy purses, abolition by Indira Gandhi, 60, 211, 212
Progressive Alliance, 63
prohibition, xxv, 89, 230
Public Distribution System (PDS), 135
Public Men's Conduct Enquiry Act, 1973, 75–76, 77
Pudukkottai constituency, 160

Radhakrishnan, K.S., 211
Radhakrishnan, V., 153–54, 157
Rahman, Mujibur, 81
Rai, Vinod, 201, 205, 206
Raja, A., 154, 156, 189, 192, 198–202, 204, 207, 225, 227
  2G Saga Unfolds, 200, 206
Raja, Justice P.P.S. Janardhan, 175
Rajagoplachari, C., xxv, 8, 9, 12, 27–28, 36–37, 57, 60
Rajakumari, 18, 232
Rajamanickam, M.G., 208, 220

Rajamannar Committee on Centre–State Relations, 59, 81, 212
Rajammanr, Justice P.V., 59, 212
Rajapakse, 108–09
Rajathi (Dharmambal), 49–50, 84, 181, 203
Rajathi Ammal (wife) (Dharmambal), 49–50, 84, 181, 203
Rajinikanth, 7, 129, 247
Ram Temple issue, 155
Ramachandran, Janaki, 111–13, 115, 117, 140, 218
Ramachandran, M.G. (MGR), 7, 18, 39, 55–56, 58, 65, 141, 171, 181, 195, 214–18, 230
  corruption charges, 89
  death, 87, 91, 100, 110–12, 116–18
  Emergency and rise of, 80–94, 214–15
  and Indira Gandhi, relations, 66–67, 94, 214–15
  and Jayalalithaa, 110–19, 127, 128, 130, 133
  versus Karunanidhi, 62–64, 67–69, 70–79, 82–92, 125, 148, 181, 195, 214, 217, 233
  political success, 71–74
  Sri Lankan issue, 96–100, 109
Ramachandran, S., 83
Ramadoss, Ambumani, 236
Ramadoss, S., 151
Ramagopalan, 233
Ramalingam, K.P., 117–18, 193
Ramamurthy, P., 52
Ramamurthy, Vazhappadi, 149, 151
Ramanuja, xxvii, 230–31, 237
Ramar Sethu, 233
Ramaswamy, Cho, 69, 93, 132, 134, 142, 146, 180
Ramjanmabhoomi issue, 147
Ranganathan, V., 43–44
Rao, N.T. Rama, 97, 212, 218, 219
Rao, P.V. Narasimha, 123, 129
Rao. C. Vidyasagar, 240
Rashtriya Swayamsevak Sangh (RSS), 83, 150, 225
Ravi Kumar, 108
Ravi, N., 168
Reddy, Neelam Sanjiva, 61, 210–11
regional assertiveness, 81
regional chauvinism, 46
religion, xxvi, 7, 139, 226, 229, 233, 237
Representation of the People's Act, 160
Research and Analysis Wing, 102
reservation:

for Arundathiyars, 173
for backward castes/ communities, 173, 218–19, 220

Saamy, A.S.A., 18
Sabaratnam, Sri, 99
Saini, Justice O.P., 206
Salem Steel Plant, Tamil Nadu, 60
Samacheer Kalvi, school education policy, 173–75
Samathuvapurams (Equality Villages), 139
Samayanallur Thermal Power Plant, 85
Sampath, E.V.K., 29, 40, 41
Samy, Pattukkottai Azhagiri, 9, 16, 26–27
Sangam poetry, xxiv, xxvii, 11, 231, 232. See also *Thirukkural*
Sangh Parivar, 149
Sarkaria Commission of Enquiry, 84, 86–87, 88, 93, 104, 130, 233
Sarkaria, Ranjit Singh, 84
Sathyanarayana brothers, 86
Sattanathan Commission. *See* Tamil Nadu Backward Classes Commission (1970)
Sattanathan, A.N., 59, 60
Scindia, Madhav Rao, 223
Self-Respect marriages' for non-Brahmins, xxvi, 6, 23, 48
Self-Respect Movement (Suyamariyathai Iyakkam), xxvi, 6–9, 14
language issue, 8–9, 42
Selvaganapathy, T.M., 143, 157
Selvam, Murasoli, nephew, 80, 181, 182, 192
Selvi, daughter, 181, 182, 192
Selvi, Radhika, 189
Sethusamudram Shipping Canal Project, 233–34
Shah, K.K., 81
Shankaracharya, of Kanchi, 145, 168
Shanmuganathan, personal assistant, xviii, 64, 67–68, 90, 109
Shanmugasundaraththammaal (elder sister) 82, 181–82
Shanmugam, P., 157–58
Sharma, Shankar Dayal, 223
Shastri, Lal Bahadur, 45
Shivappa, Justice C., 131
Shukla, V.C., 221
Singh, Chaudhary Charan, 92, 215–16
Singh, Dinesh, 208
Singh, Gurnam, 210

Singh, Manmohan, 170, 175, 183, 192, 201, 202, 205, 206, 211
Singh, V.P., 101, 182, 211, 218–21, 223, 225
Singhvi, Abhishek, 204
Sitaraman, Nirmala, 247
Sivalingam, T.M., 44
slum clearance boards, Tamil Nadu, 139
South Indian Liberation Front. *See* Justice Party
Sri Lanka
ethnic issue, Sri Lankan Tamils , 94, 95–109, 221
Tamil militants, 96, 98, 103, 119, 126
Sri Lankan refugees in Tamil Nadu, 97
Sridevan, Justice Prabha, 175
Sriperumbudur, Rajiv Gandhi's assassination, 104, 119, 126, 221
Stalin, M.K. (son), 51, 78, 82, 83, 121, 129, 164–65, 168, 172, 181, 184–85, 186–88, 190–95, 203–04, 215, 217, 227, 235–37, 239, 242, 244–48
Stephen, C.M., 216
Subagunarajan, V.M.S., 137
Subramaniam, C., 65, 213
Subramaniam, Baby, 99
Subramanian, Nirupama, xviii–xix
Sudhakaran, V.N., 128
Sumangali Cable network, 189
Sun TV, 128–29, 131, 158, 164, 182–83, 185–87, 189–90, 191
Sundaram, T.R., 36
Surjit, Harkishen Singh, 223
Swaminathan, M.S., 136
Swamy, Subramanian, 128, 200–01, 233

Tamil Eelam Liberation Organization, 99
Tamil Eelam Supporters Organization (TESO), 97, 99
Tamil identity, xxii
Tamil language conference, Coimbatore, 2014, 196
Tamil: language and culture, linguistic and cultural heritage, xxvii, 5–6, 11–12, 25–26, 30, 45–46
Tamil Manila Congress (TMC), 129, 147, 151, 223, 236
Tamil Nadu Agricultural Fair Wages Act (1969),
Tamil Nadu Agricultural University, Coimbatore, 158
Tamil Nadu Assembly election: 1967, 47–48

1971, 62–63, 213–14
1980, 94, 217
1989, 218
1991, 105, 119, 126, 222
1996, 129
2001, 157–59, 160–63, 169, 173
2006, 170–72, 194
2011, 86, 197, 202–03, 234
2016, 197, 235–37, 239, 241, 245
Tamil Nadu Backward Classes Commission, First (Sattanathan Commission), (1970), 59, 60
Tamil Nadu Biotechnology Board, 137
Tamil Nadu Congress (R), 213
Tamil Nadu Farmworkers' Fair Wages Act, 1969, 52–53
Tamil Nadu and Karnataka, Kaveri water dispute, 150
Tamil Nadu Land Reform Act, 1961, 59
Amendment, 1970, 59–60
Tamil Nadu Rajiv Congress (TRC), 149, 151
Tamil Nadu Secretariat-cum-Assembly building project, 175–76
Tamil Nadu State Marketing Corporation (TASMAC), 89
Tamil nationalism, 8, 42, 46, 101, 103, 107
Tamil Students Association, 11
Tamilarasu Kazhagam, 213
Tamils of India and Tamils of Sri Lanka, cultural differences, 97
Tamizhar Pathukaappu Peravai, 70
TANSI land scam, 153, 158, 160, 161, 167
Telecom Regulatory Authority of India (TRAI), 199, 201
Telugu Desam Party (TDP), 222
Telugu Ganga project, 224
Thambidurai, M., 149
Thamilarasu, M.K., son, 181
Tharani, Thotta, 176
Thenmozhi, granddaughter, 181
Thennarasu, Thangam, 174, 175–76
Thennavan, 13, 14
Thirunavukkarasar, 115
Thookkuththooki, 23
Thozilalar Mithran, 16
three-language formula, 48
2G spectrum, 192, 198–206, 227, 235, 236

United Front, 105–06, 143, 146–48, 223–24

United Progressive Alliance (UPA), 107, 192, 204, 211, 233, 235
  corruption charges, 202
  DMK alliance, 2004 and 2009, 227

Vahanvati, G., 206
Vaidyanathan, Girija, 247
Vaiko. *See* Gopalaswamy, V.
Vajpayee, Atal Bihari, 97, 148–51, 154, 156, 165, 182, 210–11, 223, 225
Veeramani, K., 29, 151
Veerappan, R.M. (RMV), 7, 24, 30–31, 62–63, 73–74, 111
Veerasamy, Arcot, 82, 186
Venkatraman, T.G., 223
Viduthalai Chiruthaigal Katchi (VCK), 108, 236
Viduthalai, 28, 57
Vijaykanth, 170, 172, 173, 236

Yadav, Akhilesh, 247
Yadav, Lalu Prasad, 223

CRAFTED FOR MOBILE READING

Thought you would never read a book on mobile? Let us prove you wrong.

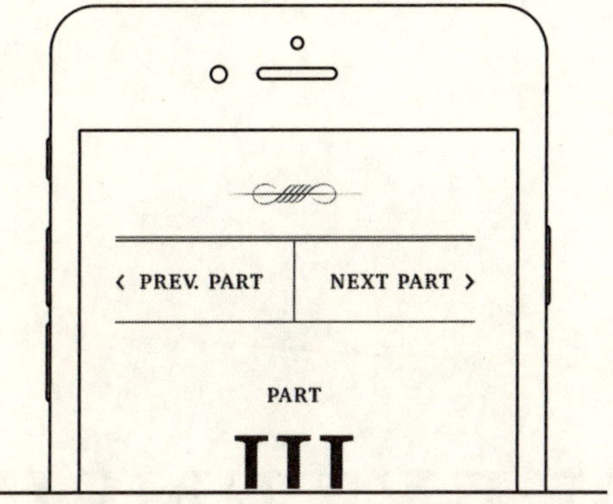

Beautiful Typography

The quality of print transferred to your mobile. Forget ugly PDFs.

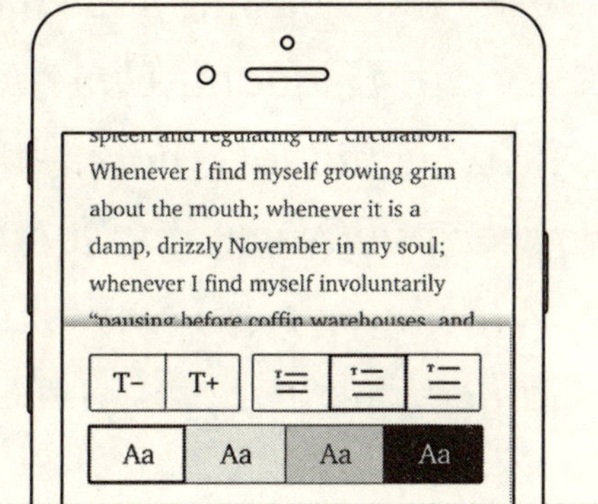

Customizable Reading

Read in the font size, spacing and background of your liking.

AN EXTENSIVE LIBRARY

Including fresh, new, original Juggernaut books from the likes of Sunny Leone, Praveen Swami, Husain Haqqani, Umera Ahmed, Rujuta Diwekar and lots more. Plus, books from partner publishers and loads of free classics. Whichever genre you like, there's a book waiting for you.

CRUCIBLES OF SIN
HITESHA
Can a Geek ever find Love?
Finding Juliet
Toffee
Mary Shelley
Frankenstein
A FAROOQ BESHI INVESTIGATION
COLD FLAKE
PRAVEEN SWAMI
How to Heal Your Broken Heart
A Psychiatrist's Guide To Heartbreak
DR SHYAM BHAT
MOIN and THE MONSTER
ANUSHKA RAVISHANKAR
Mafia Queens
stories of women from the ganglands
S. Hussain Zaidi
with Jane Borges
Foreword by Vishal Bharadwaj
Pakistan's Queen of Romance
UMERA AHMED
Nowhere Girl
A Story of Love & Forgiveness
THE BEHEADING
This Is How He Will Bless Her
ABHEEK BARUA
THE Peshwa
The Lion and the Stallion
THE INVISIBLE WOMAN
SAURBH KATYAL
ANGRY BIRDS FAN? READ THE BOOK!
ANGRY BIRDS TOONS
TOONS TALES
ARCHANA SABOO
ADIKOOL
in #AfricanAdventures
i am not a bimbette
Tarana Khan
She hates me. He loves me not but . . .
DON'T FALL IN LOVE
Vandana Shankar
KHUSHWANT SINGH
WE INDIANS

DON'T JUST READ; INTERACT

We're changing the reading experience from passive to active.

juggernaut.in

Ask authors questions

Get all your answers from the horse's mouth. Juggernaut authors actually reply to every question they can.

Rate and review

Let everyone know of your favourite reads or critique the finer points of a book – you will be heard in a community of like-minded readers.

Gift books to friends

For a book-lover, there's no nicer gift than a book personally picked. You can even do it anonymously if you like.

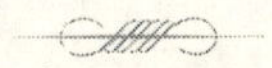

Enjoy new book formats

Discover serials released in parts over time, picture books including comics, and story-bundles at discounted rates. And coming soon, audiobooks.

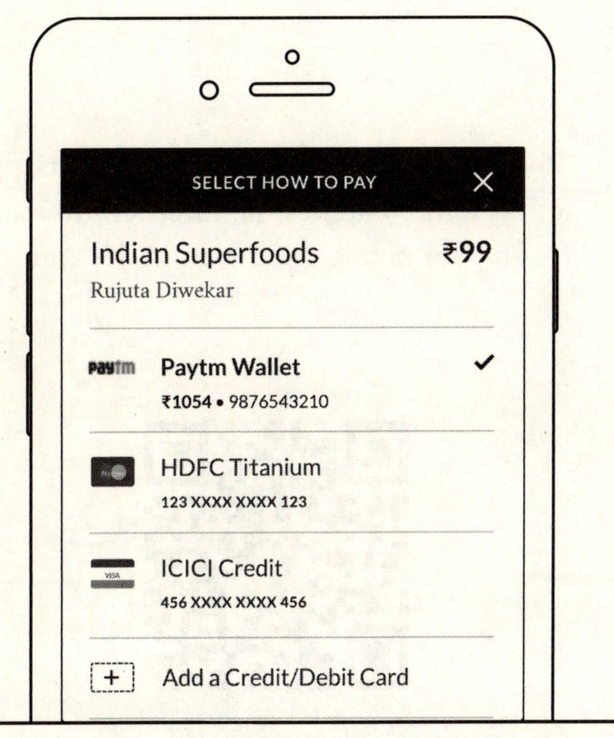

Paytm Wallet, Cards & Apple Payments

On Android, just add a Paytm Wallet once and buy any book with one tap. On iOS, pay with one tap with your iTunes-linked debit/credit card.

Click the QR Code with a QR scanner app
or type the link into the Internet browser
on your phone to download the app.

For our complete catalogue, visit www.juggernaut.in
To submit your book, send a synopsis and two
sample chapters to books@juggernaut.in
For all other queries, write to contact@juggernaut.in